FIRST RIVAL
OF THE
METROPOLITAN
OPERA

FIRST RIVAL OF THE METROPOLITAN OPERA

John Frederick Cone

Columbia University Press
NEW YORK   1983

The publisher gratefully acknowledges the assistance of the
Miriam and Ira D. Wallach Foundation
in the publication of this book.

Library of Congress Cataloging in Publication Data

Cone, John Frederick.
First rival of the Metropolitan Opera.

Bibliography: p.
Includes index.
1. Academy of Music (New York, N.Y.)—History.
2. Mapleson, James Henry, 1830–1901. 3. Metropolitan
Opera (New York, N.Y.) 4. Opera—New York (N.Y.)—History
and criticism. I. Title.
ML1711.8.N32A22 1983   782.1'09747'1   83-7427
ISBN 0-231-05748-2

Clothbound editions of Columbia University Press books are Smyth-
sewn and printed on permanent and durable acid-free paper.

Columbia University Press
New York   Guildford, Surrey

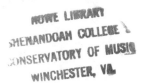

TO THESE FRIENDS AND THEIR CHILDREN—

Ruth and Bernard Brandt
Betty and Walter Hofmeister
Jean and Jesse Reese
Myra and Jan Rhebergen
Miriam and Ira Wallach

Contents

∽

Foreword

〜

*I*T HARDLY seems possible that one hundred years have passed since the opening of the Metropolitan Opera, an organization that came into being the same year as the Brooklyn Bridge but unlike the bridge was given birth for all the wrong reasons. That it now stands as a beacon of quality and standards in the opera world is part of an artistic miracle. All the "wrong reasons" were, of course, the social snobbisms of New York leveled against the new rich who came out of the Civil War with pockets bulging and a burning desire for a place in established society. Nothing represented the old guard so much as the Academy of Music on Fourteenth Street and Irving Place and the seasons of grand opera presented there, beginning in 1878, by the charming and clever "Colonel" James H. Mapleson, American manager of London's Royal Italian Opera Company, Covent Garden. "Colonel" Mapleson—few seemed to know where his honorary title came from—had, at least at first, the confidence and support of his principal stockholders and patrons, who included the social arbiters of the city. They had long made the Academy their special preserve, and for these nabobs, as well as the general musical public who helped fill his seats, the Colonel presented performance after performance of great artists in the basic Italian repertoire. In 1878 he had the field to himself, but five years later, in 1883, he faced his first competitive challenge with the opening of the new upstart company. How he dealt with this threat, and failed to win, is the essence of John Cone's fascinating book, and its publication this year during the Metropolitan centenary celebrations is another chapter in the ongoing relationship between Americans and the world of the opera.

For those of us who have spent a large part of our lives dealing with this elusive, maddening, frustrating, slippery, and glorious art form the one consistent message that emerges from the book is best described in the French expression that itself is almost a cliché—"plus ça change, plus c'est la même chose"—the more things change, the more they stay the same.

Opera is really impossible: by all odds it should not work. The elements that must be tamed to bring it off—trustees, star singers, comprimarios, musicians, choruses, dancers, choreographers, designers, directors, and conductors, to say nothing of the basic personnel needed to run a theater itself—have not changed since the French composer Lully started the whole glorious procedure. In connection with the Metropolitan in this century alone you can pick up the memoirs or biographies of Giulio Gatti-Casazza, Edward Johnson, Sir Rudolf Bing, and my own to find the same agonies and ecstasies: all that is needed is to change the dates and the names of the players.

But our friend John Cone, who is obviously a serious opera fanatic and historian, has specialized in the competitive problems of the Metropolitan. An earlier book concerned the powerful and determined Oscar Hammerstein the First, an opponent even more formidable than the good Colonel.

The nature of opera is explosive, the tendency of modern business management is to govern by committee, and these two tracks are on a constant collision course. The reason an opera house is a success has traditionally been—and in my view must continue to be—the shadow and passion of the impresario. Mapleson was one: so was Oscar Hammerstein I and Gatti-Casazza and Johnson and Bing and, I hope, myself. By its very nature an opera company is adrift without the strong hand of a leader, someone with the skills to seduce, cajole, balance different visions and priorities, and in the end triumph perhaps because of impossibilities.

By writing this book, Dr. Cone has done the opera world a great service: he has shown us our ancestry, the grafting on, if you will, of an art form polished and perfected in Europe to the crudities and roughness of our society, and how one organization has managed to weather all odds and emerge victorious.

As you read this book you will be enthralled by the legend of Adelina Patti, surely the first "prima donna assoluta," who dominated the Mapleson company much as Geraldine Farrar, Kirsten Flagstad, and Maria Callas were to do at the Metropolitan, each in their day. Hammerstein started out with the incomparable Edouard de Reszke and tried to engage his nonpareil tenor brother Jean, and the legends of opera companies and their stars have continued unbroken ever since.

Sometimes, as it happens, an operatic legend can be built in one's own family. My paternal grandfather, a fierce and devoted francophile, was a great friend of Jean de Reszke, and when he was dying my grandmother asked the tenor to come to their New York house, stand at the foot of the stairs, and sing a last time to her husband upstairs, confined to his bed. The story is that she held the bedroom door open while de Reszke sang from *Faust*, and my grandfather died when the aria was finished.

Of such stuff grand operas are made!

Schuyler G. Chapin
General Manager, Metropolitan Opera, 1972–1975
Dean, School of the Arts, Columbia University, 1976–

Acknowledgments

WITHOUT THE assistance, encouragement, unflagging interest of many this book would have remained unrealized. To all the author is deeply indebted and profoundly grateful.

I wish to acknowledge, first of all, the gracious permission of Her Majesty Queen Elizabeth II to quote from the diaries of her paternal grandparents: King George V and Queen Mary.

I wish also to acknowledge the following individuals, services, institutions: Marjorie R. Adkins, Chicago Public Library; Donald Anderle; Archives Nationales, Paris; Austrian Information Service, New York; Marcel Bally; Rose Bampton; William H. Barton, Wyoming State Archives and Historical Department, Cheyenne; the late Mrs. August Belmont, Jr.; August Belmont Sr. Papers, Rare Books and Manuscripts Division, the New York Public Library, Astor, Lenox, and Tilden Foundations; the Gordon Bergs; Dan Bertagna; Biblioteca de Palacio, Madrid; Bibliothèque de la Ville de Montréal; British Broadcasting Corporation, Llandaff Cardiff, Wales; British Information Service, New York; British Museum Library; Dolores Bryant, the Society of California Pioneers, San Francisco; Hilary K. Bulmer, the Brecknock Museum, Brecon, Wales; Mary Kay Burns, New Orleans Public Library; California Historical Society, San Francisco; the Dennis Campbells; Schuyler Chapin; Chicago Historical Society; Christie, Manson & Woods Ltd., London; the Alfred Clapps; Christy Clemons, St. Joseph Public Library; Dr. Michael Collins, Georgetown University; Columbia University Theater Library; Denver Public Library; Deutsche Bibliothek, Frankfurt am Main; the later Mme Pauline Donalda; Mark Drattel; Owen Edwards, BBC Wales; Frits van Eeden; Walter Ernst; the late Geraldine Farrar; Jean Favier, Directeur General des Archives de France; H. J. Fawcus, Blenheim Palace Archives; Marna Feldt, Swedish Information Service, New York; Free Library of Philadelphia Music Division; Free Library of Philadelphia Newspaper Division; Alys H. Freeze, Denver Public Library; Sr. Justa Moreno Garbayo, Royal Palace Archives, Madrid; Eleanor M. Gehres; General Research Division, the New York Public Library, Astor, Lenox, and Tilden Foundations; Denver Public Library; German Information Service, New York; the late Dr. Victorio Giannini; Robert Gingrich, Topeka Public Library; William Goff, research assistant in Kansas City, Missouri; Keith Hall; Collin B. Hamer, Jr., New Orleans Public Library; Gladys Hansen, city archivist, San Francisco Public Library; Christina M. Hanson, Beinecke Rare Book and Manuscript Library, Yale University; Harvard University Library; Eckart Henning, Geheimes Staatsarchiv Preussischer Kulturbesitz, Berlin; David Hinchliffe, research assistant; Historical Society of Pennsylvania, Philadelphia; Christian Howard; the late Mary W. Howard; the late Mme Maria Jeritza; Ghislaine Jouen, Archives de la Région de Haute-Normandie; Kansas State Historical Society, Topeka; Anna Keeler, Library of Congress; Constance Keene; Marjorie Kinney, Kansas City Public Library; G. A. Knight, Rothschild Archives, London; Irving Kolodin; Jane Langton, Registrar, Royal Archives, Windsor Castle; James A. Lea, Director, Adelina Patti Hospital, Wales; Mary L. LeBlanc, Tulane University Library; Robert Leidner; Walter Lippincott, Cambridge University Press; Ronald S. Lyons; Sir Robin Mackworth-Young; the Robert K. Massies; Renee Maxwell; Rosanne McCaffrey, Historic New Orleans Collection, New Orleans; Patrick McCormack; Dr. and Mrs. Alvin Melser; Metropolitan Opera Archives; Metropolitan Opera Guild; Mme Zinka Milanov; Monmouth College Library; Monmouth County Library, New Jersey; W. R. Moran; Michael Morton-Smith, Sotheby Parke Bernet & Co., London; Archie Motley, Chicago Historical Society; Jean-Marie Moulin, Conservateur en chef, Musée National du Château de Compiègne; John Mullane, History and Literature Department, Public Library of Cincinnati and Hamilton County; Museum of the City of New York; Musikhistoriska Museet, Stockholm; New-York Historical Society; New York Public Library Music Division; New York Public Library Newspaper Division; New York Public Library Special Collections Division; New York Public Library Theater Division; Dr. Robert M. Nogueira; Nordica Memorial Association, Farmington, Maine; Stan Oliner, Cheyenne Laramie Public Library; Edith Olsen; James Palumbo; Alberta Pantle, Kansas State Historical Society; Paris Opéra Archives; Erma Patrick, St. Joseph Public Library; Hofrat Mag. Dr. Franz Patzer, Magistrat der Stadt Wien, Wiener Stadt und Landesbibliothek; the late Mrs. John DeWitt Peltz; Pic Photographe, Paris; Pierpont Morgan Library; Dr. Richard Pipes; the late Rosa Ponselle; Peggy Poole; Princeton University Library; Elsie Pritchard; Eric Proudfoot; Richard V. Rafael, San Francisco Public Library Music Division; Eddie Roberts; Richard Robinson; H.R.H. Prince Vladimir Alexeivitch Romanoff; Arthur Rosenthal, Editor, Harvard University Press; Harold Rosenthal, Editor, *Opera*, London; Royal Opera House Archives, Covent Garden, London; Rutgers University Library; San Francisco Public Library Music Division; San Francisco Public Library Newspaper Division; San Francisco Public Library Special Collections Division; San Francisco Public Library Theater Division; Bidú Sayão; Norman Shaffer, Library of Congress; Wayne D. Shirley, Library of Congress; Betty Shouse, Kansas City Public Library; Elizabeth Sloan, Burlington, Iowa, Free Public Library; Ben Stinchfield, Publicity Director and Acting Archivist, Nordica Memorial Association; Gertrud Strobel, Archivist at Wahnfried, Bayreuth; Lord Swansea; Swedish Information Service, New York; Gethin Stoodley Thomas, BBC Wales; Elizabeth Tindall, St. Louis Public Library; Gerry Trimble; Edwin R. Turnley, Library of Congress; Utah Historical Society; Victoria and Albert Museum, London; Friedelind Wagner; Wake Forest University Library; Birgitta

Walin, Drottningholms Teatermuseum, Stockholm; Dr. Donald D. Warner; the late Herbert Weinstock; Roberta Wentzel; White Plains Public Library, New York; Nicole Wild, Réunion des Bibliothèques Nationales, Paris; Wojciech Wojtasiewicz.

Several individuals were especially helpful in research on Adelina Patti: W. Hofrat Dr. Anna Coreth, Direktor des Haus- Hof- und Österreichisches Staatsarchiv, Vienna, and the great prima donna's last husband Baron Rolf Cederström's daughter and niece: Brita Elmes and Carin Ekelöf, respectively. Others assisted in like research concerning Marcella Sembrich: Rose Bampton; Winifred Cecil; Mrs. W. Molyneau, the soprano's stepgranddaughter; John Skilton, Jr., who permitted me to research material in the Sembrich archives. As for the impresario James H. Mapleson, his great-nephew Alfred J. Mapleson shared with me some information concerning his illustrious ancestor. To these individuals I am deeply indebted.

Then, too, I should like to thank those who aided in the last phases of publication. Robert Y. Lock assisted with the photographs while Robert Tuggle, Metropolitan Opera archivist, graciously lent pictures from his collection. Of the ones at Columbia University Press who gave much assistance, I remember with gratitude William F. Bernhardt, Karen Mitchell, and Kenneth Venezio.

I also recall with gratitude Gerry Trimble and that delightful couple Mary and Bill Todt, all three reading proofs to the *n*th degree.

Finally, I am grateful to the dedicatees, their children, and a colleague, Mary Johnson, for the loyalty and understanding shown over the years.

Prologue

∾

MUSIC LOVERS have myriad reasons to rejoice in the centennial celebration of New York's Metropolitan Opera in the 1983–1984 season. Decade after decade this cultural institution has presented memorable performers and performances to worldwide acclaim, often affording pleasure and vivid recollections.

Even so, to some the Metropolitan in the beginning seemed destined for a short life, and an operatic rival actually tried to achieve just that: New York's patrician Academy of Music, with the veteran impresario James H. Mapleson there as the formidable adversary. This gentleman seemed obsessed with a fell purpose: total defeat of the new enterprise. Assisting him was one of the most celebrated operatic artists of the time, the legendary Adelina Patti, sole inheritor of the title *diva*.

The following pages tell primarily of Mapleson's siege and the Metropolitan's counteroffenses and victory, a triumph that served as a guide for surviving the abundant challenges of the years ahead.

New York's "world of fashion was still content to reassemble every winter in the shabby red and gold boxes of the sociable old Academy. Conservatives cherished it for being small and inconvenient, and thus keeping out the 'new people' whom New York was beginning to dread and yet be drawn to."

—*Edith Wharton,* The Age of Innocence

The "uproar was still going on. On the stage Adelina Patti, her diamonds and bare shoulders glittering, bowing low and smiling, with the help of the tenor who was holding her by the hand, was collecting the bouquets that came clumsily flying across the footlights."

—*Leo Tolstoy,* Anna Karenina

"Mr. Browne could go back farther still, to the old Italian companies that used to come to Dublin—Tietjens, Ilma de Murzka, Campanini, the great Trebelli, Giuglini, Ravelli, Aramburo. Those were the days, he said, when there was something like singing to be heard in Dublin. He told too of how . . . the gallery boys would sometimes in their enthusiasm unyoke the horses from the carriage of some great prima donna *and pull her themselves through the streets to her hotel. 'Why did they never play the grand old operas now,' he asked, 'Dinorah, Lucrezia Borgia? Because they could not get the voices to sing them: that was why.' "*

—*James Joyce, in* Dubliners, *recalling stars of Mapleson's troupe*

CHAPTER I

Alarums and Excursions

OPERA NEWS in the United States on December 30, 1882, alarmed, stunned, perhaps momentarily floored the fiery Englishman "Colonel" James H. Mapleson, who since 1878 had regularly presented opera at New York's patrician Academy of Music on Irving Place at Fourteenth Street, and who was currently presiding there as the American manager of London's Royal Italian Opera Company (Limited), Covent Garden. Directors of New York's newly erected Metropolitan Opera House had just announced their intention of retaining the highly successful American theatrical entrepreneur Henry E. Abbey as manager of the inchoate enterprise due to open ten months hence. A veteran impresario, Mapleson forthwith grasped the import of this startling development—opera war!

Hitherto Mapleson had contemplated only harmony between the two houses and thought he would have an ally at the younger place. For some time he had felt confident that the Metropolitan directors would appoint Herbert F. Gye, brother of Ernest Gye, Royal Italian Opera's General Manager. He based his confidence on the fact that for the past eighteen months the Gyes had been negotiating for the Metropolitan at the solicitation of its stockholders. The house secured, Mapleson had envisioned a future merger of Academy and Metropolitan forces, a venture in which he planned to play a major part when his contract with the Academy concluded in two years' time.

Related to this anticipated amalgamation had been Mapleson's recent agreement to join ranks with the Gyes in the formation of the Royal Italian Opera Company. Formerly the three had competed in London, with Mapleson at Her Majesty's Theatre and the Gyes at Covent Garden; in the United States the impresario had conducted his tours until the present season with his own company and without the Gyes' competition. United, they hoped to ensure for themselves a virtual monopoly of opera in England and the United States, as well as possession of the Metropolitan.

The day's casus belli made abundantly clear, however, the three men's best laid scheme for success in the new venture had evanesced into thin air. The gods heralding 1883 had riven New York's operatic heavens with violent thunderclaps.

Resolutely seizing the gauntlet, Mapleson snapped at his rival and the new house, calling the former a shadow and the latter a new Broadway brewery, mellifluously insisting he would not be intimidated by the nascent enterprise, grandiloquently asserting that the Royal Italian Opera and its American manager need neither fear nor tremble. Stone walls did not an opera house make.

Of course, much of what the impresario said reeked of fanfaronades intended solely for the public. In private Mapleson must have known he would need all his resourcefulness to combat Abbey; the onerous task was his alone. According to the agreement with the Gyes, he had sole control of and responsibility for the company while in the United States. Above all, Mapleson anticipated that the ensuing war would be nothing less than *guerre à outrance*. On this point he was emphatic: "One of the two will lose a great deal of money. But as long as the stockholders will furnish the ammunition the war will continue. When the sinews of war are not forthcoming, then there will be a survival of the fittest." [1]

To be sure, Mapleson hoped that now as before operatic selection in its evolutionary process would favor him. Seemingly he had reason to think it would. At the Academy he enjoyed the patronage of many of New York's first families, an aristocracy of old wealth with assured social ascendancy, a class identified with this fashionable home of opera since its opening in 1854 and known to social arbiters of the day as the Faubourg St. Germain set: the Belmonts, Lorillards, Cuttings, Van Nests, Van Hoffmanns, Schuylers, Astors. On many gala occasions these and other aristocrats held public court in their opera boxes, one of the epoch's symbols of New York's inner circle.

Contrariwise, many leaders of the new house consisted of the nouveaux riches: the Roosevelts, Goulds, Whitneys, Morgans, Vanderbilts. In recent years, having increased in number, the parvenus, with an aggregate wealth of more than a half billion dollars, coveted the opera boxes at the Academy. Though the older house had tried to accommodate new wealth by adding more of these, there was not enough space for all who required them and who adamantly refused to be relegated to less exalted spheres. The social invaders thereupon founded the Metropolitan, where they decreed the first three of the five tiers above the parquet the exclusive domain of boxholders.

The founding occurred in the spring of 1880, when George H. Warren, representing the boxholders *manqués*, informed the press that a new opera house was to be constructed. Fifty-two founders agreed to subscribe $10,000 each for boxes and in return received one hundred shares of stock valued at $100 a share. Thirteen more later joined as founders before the house's opening. After considerable search, a site for the new temple of music was selected, the block between Thirty-ninth and Fortieth Streets and between Broadway and Seventh Avenue. An architectural firm was awarded the contract to construct it. The design included 122 boxes, these coveted places accounting for 732 seats or approximately one-fourth of the total seating capacity of what at the time was the world's largest auditorium. The final cost of the enterprise was $1,732,478.71, well over twice the original estimate.

Meanwhile, pursing their lips at the effrontery of the plan, the Faubourg St. Germain clan remained loyal to the Academy, a distinct advantage for Mapleson in a war that promised to be perhaps more social than musical. Gratified by the loyalty of the Old Guard, Mapleson seized the moment to cast aspersions upon his rival's upstart sponsors: "My patrons . . . have eagerly taken up the

gauntlet thrown down by *les nouveaux riches*. The latter may have
the longer purses, but yet may not feel inclined to stand the drain
which will be put on them."[2]

Another obvious trump the impresario held was his agreement
with the Gyes, erstwhile competitors but since August 1882 his
partners, a relationship assuring them a dominant role in European and American operatic matters, regardless of the rival at the
Metropolitan.

Even so, Mapleson's greatest asset was his background in opera
production. Abbey's was virtually nil, as his experience had been
primarily as a manager of concert artists and in the legitimate
theater with such stars as Lily Langtry, Edwin Booth, Sarah Bernhardt.

In London and on tours of the British Isles, Mapleson had been
an independent operatic manager since 1861, the year of his thirty-
first birthday, before which time he had been a professional musician, a music agent, and an opera manager for the English impresario E. T. Smith. As an independent manager, Mapleson often
brought bursts of excitement with productions from the standard
repertoire, with revivals of works of the genre of *Robert le Diable,
Oberon, Fidelio, Iphigénie en Tauride, Semiramide, Die Entführung
aus dem Serail, Ernani, I Lombardi, Anna Bolena,* and with operas
never before produced in England, such as *Un Ballo in Maschera,
La Forza del Destino, Carmen, Mefistofele, Faust.* Legendary figures decorated the casts.

In the fall of 1878 Mapleson launched his American career,
thereafter regularly presenting opera at New York's Academy of
Music as well as on tours of the United States and Canada. Some
of the company's success may have been due to August Belmont,
President of the Academy Board of Directors, who before Mapleson's initial season there had advised him in a letter dated June
17, 1878, as to American operatic taste: "I can condense all I have
said and wish to convey in a few words: a brilliant company with
one or two stars of magnitude *is sure of complete success,* a REALLY
GOOD company *may* have a moderate success and pay expenses, an
incomplete or second rate company is sure to end in disaster, if

not disgrace." [3] Fortunately the impresario followed the first model.

Mapleson's survival thus far was due not only to the excellence of many of his productions but also to the nature of the man himself.

Mapleson was fifty-two when his siege of the Metropolitan began—urbane, peppery, guileful, garrulous, and gregarious; a veteran of twenty-one years of independent operatic management; a bon vivant guilty at times of promising more great opera than he could deliver; often a manipulator of people and events to serve his own ends, pecuniary, operatic, or otherwise; an incorrigible optimist with an irrepressible sense of humor; a shrewd manager who could placate and captivate the most contumacious and temperamental singers; an individualist jealous of his position and a formidable adversary of all who challenged it; a showman of charm and panache, given at times to rodomontades—in short, a commanding personage. Such was the gentleman determined to challenge the Metropolitan Opera House.

The siege began soon after the new year; and to counter retaliations, Mapleson adopted the principle that defense demands a ferocious offense. In the first months of 1883 he presented opera in various cities in the United States as well as in Toronto, his peregrinations extending from early January to mid-March, when the company returned to New York for the spring season.

Although such endeavors had always caused difficulties, Mapleson in Olympian anger thundered that the present labors vastly outnumbered those of the past as a result of the enemy's unremitting drumfire of attacks. Abbey's minions, Mapleson maintained, had followed the company on tour and in New York, buttonholing the chorus, orchestra, stage crew, wardrobe keepers, scene painters, call-boy, stage manager, and even his ballerina daughter-in-law, and tempting them with salaries three or four times higher than what they currently received. He threatened to send Abbey this missive: "If you wish, I will furnish you with a list of those whom I do not propose to engage for next year. This will save your agents a great deal of trouble in waylaying my people outside the stage door, and supplying them with sundry drinks in the neighborhood while it will enable you to conduct your matters in a more business-like way." [4]

Though Abbey claimed he never received the letter, its contents, published in New York newspapers, proved efficacious. Mapleson gained sympathy for his cause and succeeded in making his rival look unprincipled and foolish. Then when Abbey subsequently denied the accusations, Mapleson pooh-poohed him: "I see he has denied that he was up to those little tricks. Why he's been after every one, even down to the big drum and triangle." [5]

As for Abbey's raids on leading singers, one of the first involved Italo Campanini, a superb tenor who had been a star with Mapleson and a favorite in the United States. Last appearing in New York in the 1881–1882 season, he had then shown the strain of overuse of a once glorious voice and at the end of the engagement retired to Italy for what he said would be a prolonged rest; but Abbey changed all this with some sweet, sweet compulsion. His proposal of $1,000 a performance, with 70 performances guaranteed, so rejuvenated the ailing tenor that he announced his intention to resume his career forthwith in order to pioneer in Abbey's new world.

The incursions on leading singers continued and included others who had appeared with Mapleson. Among them were the soprano Alwina Valleria, the contralto Sofia Scalchi, the mezzo-soprano Emily Lablache, the baritone Giuseppe del Puente. Loyalty to the impresario may have been a consideration, but when Abbey offered them salaries higher than Mapleson was able or willing to match, they showed a willingness to ally themselves with the Metropolitan, and in doing so proved a director of that company correct in his evaluation of the situation: "It is a question of dollars and cents. I believe the artists will go where they can get the most money." [6]

Representatives of the press, rushing to Mapleson as each apparent defection was made known, eagerly noted his reactions. In general the purport of public statements at the time was that Abbey was welcome to Campanini, Valleria, Scalchi; but here the welcome ended. Having earlier made contracts for next season with Lablache and Del Puente, Mapleson said he would not release them and later went to court, which granted him an injunction against these two errant purveyors of song to prevent their appearing with the rival company.

Names of other singers Abbey was said to be considering appeared repeatedly in New York daily newspapers. Among these were the bass Pierre Gailhard, the baritone Giuseppe Kaschmann, the tenors Angelo Masini and Francesco Tamagno, the sopranos Etelka Gerster and Marcella Sembrich. Asked to confirm some of those reports, Abbey sidestepped the question: "I do not wish to be premature in my statements. These remarks may sound slightly Maplesonian, but I want to be quite positive of my engagements of artists before I announce them."[7]

As usual, members of the press, with fresh ammunition, charged to the Academy to record Mapleson's comments on the artists who were now potential antagonists in the opera war. One, in particular, aroused the impresario: the baritone Kaschmann. When a reporter asked whether Mapleson knew anything about the singer, he quipped: "Never heard of him. But it's a good name, and I think they'll have room for many members of that family at the new opera house."[8] At a later time Mapleson confided he had identified the baritone.

MAPLESON: "You've heard of the engagement of a mysterious baritone named Cashman [*sic*], haven't you? Well, I've been inquiring as to who he is."
REPORTER: "Have you found out?" . . .
MAPLESON: "It's Vanderbilt himself!"[9]

Weathering the assaults, Mapleson maintained that the forces on his ramparts always represented opera's best, challenging his enemy's maneuvers by negotiating with such artists as the celebrated tenor Luigi Ravelli, the sonorous baritone Antonio Galassi, and the soprano Abbey also desired: Etelka Gerster. In addition to these, Mapleson proposed to secure *the* preeminent singers who in his opinion would outshine all his rival's galaxy of stars. The artists capable of such brilliance were two of the most illustrious prima donnas of the age: Christine Nilsson and Adelina Patti. These meteors he determined to place in his constellation. Abbey of course determined the same.

What ensued made the preceding attacks seem like child's play. The war fought over Nilsson and Patti was titanic, full of sound and fury, signifying operatic survival.

During the season of 1882–1883 the two artists were in the United States, Nilsson fulfilling concert engagements under Abbey's management while Patti was appearing with Mapleson and the Royal Italian Opera. Nilsson was the first over whom they contended.

Upon assuming the managerial duties of the Metropolitan, Abbey announced that Nilsson would open the new house as Marguerite in Gounod's *Faust*. The soprano herself had insisted upon this honor, but for a while such a possibility seemed remote. In the first months of 1883 Ernest Gye maintained that Nilsson would be at the Academy, as she had made a written agreement in May 1882 on Covent Garden stationery to appear under his aegis for the season of 1883–1884; and since he was the general manager of the Royal Italian Opera and Mapleson its American director, the assumption was that she would appear at the older house. Later, however, when Nilsson's solicitor submitted the terms of a formal contract, Gye refused to accept them, astounded by her demands for special perquisites. He nonetheless continued to insist the memorandum was binding.

Meanwhile, Mapleson decided he could do without Nilsson; though he had engaged her frequently in past years, he now found his enthusiasm waning, and made this sentiment known in a number of ungenteel, acrimonious remarks attacking her personally and professionally. No doubt Nilsson's loyalty to Abbey contributed to the diminution of fervor, but one overriding factor insured it: Mapleson had determined to ingratiate himself further with, in his words, the vocal joy of joys, the singer of singers, the artist of artists, the prima donna of prima donnas he had wanted all along: transcendent Adelina Patti, at that time in the final weeks of her first American opera season under his aegis. To be sure of this superstar, Mapleson would use any means, however unscrupulous.

In the front-page brouhaha that followed, Nilsson more than held her own. As her former manager, Mapleson now confessed that her caprices as well as her lack of mansuetude had been outrageous, and that the anxiety she had caused him had made an attendant change in his appearance. Attributing his baldness to past experiences with her, he professed pious concern that Abbey's pate might soon require a toupee should he secure the prima donna for the Metropolitan: "I sincerely hope . . . that at this time next year Mr. Abbey will retain the profusion of raven locks with which I believe his scalp is now adorned." [10] Nilsson retorted: "Mr. Mapleson's head is bald from debauchery and excesses, and he never lost a hair on my account." [11] The impresario was a coward, she flared, and his posture as a colonel was ludicrous, the title being honorary. (In this revelation Nilsson was correct.) The prima donna then charged that Mapleson had become a tyrant, arbitrary and Machiavellian in his methods, with "no regard whatever for truth or justice." [12]

With these inflammatory words ringing in his ears, Mapleson made distinctly clear his response to such monumental temerity: "People never get mad unless the truth is told. And if she's going to put a lot of lies in—well, she uses pretty hot language. It's almost unparliamentary. No one outside has ever seen her temper—she's very violent at times." [13] Nilsson parried by laughing the enemy to scorn: "Yes, I am in a rage. He should see me laugh. I can't help laughing: he's so ridiculous. He can attack me, and say I've got a devilish character—I only laugh. But he must look out. The law is sometimes called upon even by women. . . ." [14]

Mapleson then attacked Nilsson as an artist. Once an admirer of her musical abilities, he now found that the present condition of her voice and art left much to be desired. He doubted whether she would be an asset to an opera company with her repertoire, he claimed, now limited to four operas; he added, " 'Swanee River' is all very well, but it is impossible to work it into an opera when the footlights are blazing and a five-act work is about to be sprung on the audience."[15] He challenged her to name a fifth opera she could still sing, saying he would offer $10,000 if she could identify another one in her current repertoire. Such comments infuriated Nilsson, who refuted the charges of vocal and artistic deterioration. The fact was, Mapleson's assertions notwithstanding, this very season the soprano had regularly included on her programs some of the most demanding works in musical literature. Nilsson concluded that the entire furor was due to Mapleson's and Gye's jealousy of her and the new opera house: "But why does Mr. Mapleson talk about me? He's no right to do so. . . . It's Gye who ought to talk, for he says he has a contract with me—not Mapleson at all. The only thing I ask of Mapleson or of Gye is to let me alone. It's the new opera house that's troubling them."[16]

Though Nilsson protested she wanted to be let alone, Gye, in particular, continued to entertain a contrary idea, insisting she would appear under his management. Nilsson and Abbey of course continued to insist otherwise, and it was not until the summer that an English court settled the issue. Mapleson in the meantime was facing one of the greatest challenges of his career: the securing of Adelina Patti. In the terrible struggle the diva, at times seemingly cold to his entreaties while apparently amenable to Abbey's, deferred a final decision until just hours before her departure for Europe.

Patti, the prima donna *assoluta*, admitted she was prolonging her choice to obtain the best possible terms in the new contract. The fact that she was currently under Mapleson's management may have prompted some to assume she would remain with him, but the diva herself was not at all reassuring. Always the prime consideration was the contract. The opera war gave her a golden opportunity in contractual matters, a situation she recognized and of which she took every advantage. Her actions reflected a highly developed business acumen: she played one manager against the other for what to them may have seemed an eternity.

In the 1881–1882 season Patti had appeared with Abbey in the United States for a series of performances. She now said that she had found the American delightful in his management and that appearing at the Metropolitan might be a most rewarding experience, words that must have sent chills up and down Mapleson's spine. At the same time, she lauded the Gyes for the part they and their late father had played in her career. Gratitude and loyalty thus seemingly were factors in the decision, as was the Gyes' control of London's Covent Garden, the scene of many Patti triumphs.

As for Mapleson, the diva maintained that the current season's experiences with him had not always been heartening, particularly in the matter of the opera war, since he had occasionally misquoted her. One such instance concerned the fate of the new house and Nilsson: "I was grieved to find myself reported the other day as having predicted a failure for Mr. Abbey's new opera house. I never said anything like that, for I've no reason for knowing anything about it whatever. I simply said that the success of the cage will depend upon the birds put in it. And it was so unkind to misrepresent me! Why, I wouldn't say such a thing any way, for I know Madame Nilsson very well indeed, and it would certainly be unkind of me to predict a failure for her in her performances in the new opera house next season." [17] Fortunately for Mapleson, the diva's displeasure ultimately dissipated, but he was taking no chances and attended to her every whim. In an interview Patti divulged something of his winning ways: "Colonel Mapleson comes here when he wants me to sing and he calls me, 'My dear child,' and he goes down on both knees and kisses my hands, and he has, you know, quite a supplicating face and it is not easy to be firm with a man of such suavity of manners." [18] All was grist for the publicity mill as well as for the new contract.

When the final days approached before the diva's return to Europe, neither Mapleson nor Abbey had secured her for the forthcoming season, a circumstance that created even more publicity, interest, and suspense. It also created what Patti had wanted all along: fantastic terms in the new contract. In the 1882–1883 season her fee had been $4,500 a performance, a fee many times higher than that of any other contemporary opera star. Patti had appeared in forty performances, thereby receiving the handsome sum of $180,000. Though these amounts were astronomical, Abbey now

raised the ante and, on April 18, went to Philadelphia, where Patti
was appearing, with a contract ready for her signature. What he
proposed was $5,000 a performance with a guarantee of 50 perfor-
mances and $50,000 security held in a New York City bank as
payment for the final ten performances. W. H. Vanderbilt was a
guarantor of the terms. Abbey offered other considerations, which
Mapleson subsequently revealed to the press: "A travelling car
was to be specially built for the Diva, which was actually to be
nickel plated. Fact 'pon honor. It was to be built with a regard to
comfort and ease never hitherto dreamed of, and would comprise;
among other new luxuries of travel, a small conservatory and fer-
nery and a Steinway piano, which would enable the sweet song-
stress to rehearse *en route*." [19] Abbey wrote Patti a letter in which
he stated his willingness to provide at once next season's guarantee.

Faced with these terms, Mapleson had no alternative but to offer analogous ones. Even so, Patti temporized. Years later the impresario remembered that she had found the contractual issue so
unsettling she became ill, and that for a time she did not speak to
her parrot, an ominous sign. Even by the afternoon of the day
before her departure to Europe, Patti had apparently not resolved
the issue and, perhaps jokingly, said so in a highly publicized interview; but hours later her decision was publicly announced. New
York operagoers learned about it that evening, April 23, during
the final performance of the spring season at the Academy.

At the end of the third act of *Aida* Mapleson appeared before
the curtain, prepared to make a speech:

Ladies and gentlemen—I feel very greatly honored by your presence here
in such large numbers considering the state of the weather, for it has
been raining for eighteen hours. I take it as a compliment to myself and
a mark of your appreciation of your—I should say my—efforts. (Laughter). This is the closing night of the opera season, and I believe I am
expected to say a few words. The management of an Italian opera company, as you may have read in the daily papers, is not a bed of roses.
Every man in this business is accustomed to be knocked about, but I
have survived it. (Cheers). I will say here that I will have next season an
array of talent which I will not extol myself, but will leave you to judge

of. I have just concluded an engagement with Mme. Patti—(cheers)—
and she will appear with my company. All I ask is your continued confidence in my efforts and your liberal support.[20]

Victorious, the impresario left the stage to a deafening roar of
cheers and thunderous applause. The enemy had suffered a resounding defeat!

Abbey accepted it none too graciously, finding in the loss an
occasion to make a public comparison of the artistic merits of Patti
and Nilsson, who he still maintained would appear with him. Such
action was unusual for this urbane American, hitherto the staid
gentleman, generally in his public utterances refraining from Maplesonian animadversions: "Patti and Nilsson are entirely different
persons in style, in the manner of singing, in voice, and in fact in
everything. Besides, Nilsson has not been heard here in opera for
ten years, and there will be a great desire on that account to hear
the great artist—for she is a great artist. Nilsson and Patti have no
equals. Then Madame Nilsson comes here with a large repertoire—Mr. Mapleson to the contrary, notwithstanding—and will
sing operas that the American people have never heard. . . .
There's a personal magnetism about Nilsson that Patti hasn't and
which is felt by all who hear and see her, either on the stage or in
private. Nilsson will be the card here next season first of all because she is new. Patti has been here, and when she comes back
it will be difficult to realize that she's been away. No, bless you;
I'm not disappointed about not getting Patti. I shall find enough
in Nilsson."[21]

The glow of the Patti coup lingered at the Academy, where the
impresario in the few days remaining until his departure for Europe attended to the myriad details incumbent upon the closing of
an opera season, finalized a number of contracts, auditioned vocal
aspirants, and, as usual, granted interviews to various reporters
eagerly awaiting his responses to Abbey's latest challenges.

Ever scorning his rival, Mapleson bristled at claims that the
Metropolitan Opera would be a true ensemble while the new edifice would provide a better setting as well as finer facilities for

staging. Interpreting these remarks as personal slurs, Mapleson retorted that he too would present a first-rate ensemble, not just stars, and that the Academy was still a superb setting for grand opera. It remained a noble house, while the Metropolitan, in his opinion—"the shop over the way"—was only a new yellow brewery on Broadway.[22] For some time he had maintained that the anterooms to the boxes epitomized the quality of the new enterprise and of the stockholders themselves: "They set great store by the anteroom adjoining the boxes, where occupants of the boxes may retire whenever they feel so disposed. The gentlemen dilate on the facilities it will afford them for playing a rubber. The fact is, the facilities are too great. It will come so that all the minor portions of the opera will be slurred and the anteroom will be fitted up with a revolving tape."[23]

Mapleson did not fear any of Abbey's challenges. Elated by the Patti contract and the continued support of the Academy stockholders, he confided he looked forward to the future with supreme confidence that the victory would be his: "I shall reappear next season as the Krupp of the operatic field and simply annihilate the whole concern with the eighty ton guns I shall import for the purpose. I am an old veteran . . . in this business, and have seen too many ambitious attempts of a similar nature fall to the ground to be in the least alarmed at the new opera house scheme."[24]

Mapleson fired his final broadside at an interview held just before his ship left New York's harbor. It was the morning of April 28, when the pier presented a lively picture of teeming humanity, many having gathered there at an early hour to wish the impresario Godspeed. Leopold's brass band entertained with such delights as "Empty Is the Cradle, Baby's Gone," and when Mapleson appeared, carrying roses and waving his tall silk hat, the musicians greeted him with "Hail to the Chief" amid cheers, tears, and handshakes. This overenthusiasm suggests the possibility that the reception had been carefully staged, but Mapleson, always the showman, knew the value of such orchestration. As usual, he was good copy.

REPORTER: "Have you made any new contracts?"
MAPLESON: "Yes, . . . here is a very important one. Print it full. I have

contracted . . . for a special train to be built expressly for the purpose of carrying my opera company around the country. There will be one beautiful palace car for the diva, Madame Patti, and it will be named after her. . . ."

REPORTER: "Is this to be something on the Barnum circus plan?"

MAPLESON: "No, not precisely. It will be far more elegant. This is not a circus but an opera company." [25]

Farewells were exchanged, and as the ship went down the bay for a time she was followed by a chartered steamer filled with some of Mapleson's friends and supporters who cheered him out of sight.

The journey homeward had begun auspiciously, with only sunshine on the horizon. In England, however, all quickly darkened, to the impresario's stupefaction. In London the directors of the Royal Italian Opera Company held a series of meetings with Mapleson, who learned to his amazement that they did not propose to ratify Patti's contract for £50,000 ($250,000) even though it had been approved by and conjointly concluded with Ernest Gye. The directors also repudiated other contracts for about £15,000 the impresario had made. Further dissatisfaction on their part, it was rumored, arose from Gye's insistence that his wife, the soprano Emma Albani, should have an increase in salary for the coming American season. Patti's had been raised; so should Albani's. Then convinced that there would be little or no profit in an American season with the high salaries Patti and others now commanded and that the Metropolitan might prove too formidable an adversary, the directors decided against another engagement in the New World. The one concluded had been financially unsatisfactory; the next might be disastrous. The directors ended the entire affair by terminating Mapleson's connection with the company while refusing to pay him his financial due, which Mapleson claimed was considerable.

Commenting on this turn of events, Mapleson declared himself glad to be once again an independent manager and sanguine about the future. The London affair he admitted was unfortunate, but not catastrophic, as he still held such resources as the Patti contract as well as other artists' contracts, a two-year agreement to produce opera at New York's Academy of Music, a lease there rent free, and a subsidy raised by its stockholders to guarantee the Patti engagement. Then, too, a resolution unanimously passed on May 4, 1883, by the Executive Committee of the Academy, called for the following assessment to be paid by the stockholders for fifty operatic performances between October 1883 and May 1884: $4.00 a seat in proscenium boxes, $3.00 a seat in other boxes, and $2.00 a seat elsewhere. This further aided the cause. Mapleson also retained the loyalty and respect of various stockholders, several of whom publicly expressed their support of his efforts and disgust at the maneuvers in London, voicing their confidence that Mapleson would return in the fall with a troupe, now called Her Majesty's Opera Company, to rout the enemy. One, Augustus L. Brown, remarked, "I can't say that I am terrified by the formidable front of Mr. Abbey's array. . . ."[26]

Others might have disagreed, for the opposition's array was indeed becoming formidable. During the summer in Europe Abbey concluded a number of engagements with a glittering galaxy of artists. Among the outstanding stars in his company, all now confirmed, were Alwina Valleria, Marcella Sembrich, Sofia Scalchi, Zelia Trebelli, Emmy Fursch-Madi, Franco Novara, Italo Campanini. Giuseppe del Puente joined Abbey after Mapleson released him and after he paid a forfeit of 15,000 francs. Like Del Puente, Lablache, ultimately released from her commitment to Mapleson, also went over to the enemy. The principal conductor of the new company was Augusto Vianesi, an eminent Italian maestro. Shining over this entire brilliant constellation was Abbey's star of stars: Christine Nilsson. During the summer an English court had declared her written agreement with Gye void. The soprano was free at last to appear in "her" opera house, which by that time was indeed impressive in its structure and in its personnel.

Mapleson had meanwhile been completing his company; and when the time came for the issuance of the official prospectus in September 1883, it contained a number of surprises which raised even more anticipation for the new season.

Patti, of course, headed the list, and joining her was another

James H. Mapleson, Impresario.
COURTESY ROBERT TUGGLE COLLECTION.

New York Academy of Music.

magnificent soprano Abbey had wanted, already a great favorite in New York: Etelka Gerster. In private correspondence Mapleson wrote: "She is a most admirable singer, and a charming woman into the bargain, and in addition a most attractive artiste and easy to manage as she has always the interest of the theatre at heart." [27] Gerster's engagement must have amazed Abbey, who had earlier thought it nearly impossible. Other sopranos Mapleson secured included Eugenie Pappenheim and Louise Dotti, two artists well known to the American public. Mapleson also announced the presence of Ida Valerga and three other ladies making their first appearances with his company: Emilia Vianelli, Josephine Yorke, and Raphéla Pattini, whose name coincidentally evoked another's. Of the nine tenors listed in the prospectus, seven were appearing with Mapleson for the first time, A. Rinaldini and Ernest Nicolini having been retained from former days. As for the baritones and basses, six were making their debuts with the company, while Ma-

Metropolitan Opera House.
COURTESY METROPOLITAN OPERA ARCHIVES.

Maestro Luigi Arditi.
COURTESY ROBERT TUGGLE COLLECTION.

pleson reengaged the glorious baritone Antonio Galassi. The ballet included three new premières danseuses: Fiorina Brambilla of La Scala, Bettina de Sortis of La Fenice, and Theodora de Gillert. Luigi Arditi was the principal conductor, as he had been since Mapleson's first American season in 1878. The impresario's regard for this man is revealed in a letter to August Belmont: "He is undoubtedly the most fitting man in all Europe that I could have selected, so we have a guarantee that the ensemble will be right."[28]

In keeping with the prevailing atmosphere, Mapleson lavished praise on all his artists, declaring that they formed the strongest ensemble he had ever assembled and that it represented the culmination of what he described as a monumental task.

In the prospectus Mapleson also announced his intention to stage operas from the repertoire he had formerly presented at the Academy and such novelties as *Roméo et Juliette, Oberon, Mireille, Norma, La Gazza Ladra, L'Elisir d'Amore, Crispino e la Comare,* all to be sung in Italian. Subscriptions were for thirty nights. The price for a balcony or an artists' box was $800, while proscenium and mezzanine boxes accommodating six persons were $800 and $600 respectively, and those holding four persons were $500 and $400 respectively. Parquette seats and the first four rows of the balcony cost $125 for the thirty evenings; the remaining rows in the balcony, $80.[29]

Mapleson was apparently fulfilling his promise to provide a company of superior strength. It remained for the public to decide.

To invite direct comparison, the two houses announced that their seasons would begin on October 22 and that performances thereafter were to be given on the same evenings. An editorial in the *New-York Times* accurately gauged the prevailing temper of opera society: "Something more than a hundred of our best families are . . . irretrievably committed to a social war of extermination. . . . For the Academy of Music on the one hand, for the Metropolitan Opera house on the other, they have pledged to each other, again like our Revolutionary fathers, 'their fortunes and their sacred honor' or the social prestige which may be taken to be a modern substitute for the same." [30]

Even before the formal opening of the rival houses it required no Cassandra to foretell disaster for one, if not annihilation.

CHAPTER 2

The Gathering, Opening Night, Ensuing Events

∽

*A*BBEY'S FORCES were the first on the field. In September and the early weeks of October 1883, personalities associated with the Metropolitan continually arrived from Europe. The press duly interviewed many of these, a circumstance prompting some later Maplesonian retorts; and by the date the impresario and virtually his entire company appeared on the scene, Abbey's artists had been rehearsing for some time, there remained but one week before the opening of the two houses, and anticipation had rocketed to apogean pitch.

It was in this atmosphere that Mapleson and his troupe disembarked in New York on Sunday, October 14, with all the principals present except for Patti, who followed several weeks later. Exuding confidence, Mapleson, though predicting to reporters an epoch season, made it clear he preferred not to elaborate: "I think the best plan I can pursue is to keep quiet and when the time comes spring my mine suddenly under the feet of my rival."[1] In the same vein he added: "I have my trumpet at my side, but I will not blow it. In fact, I have changed my tactics. My movements will be quiet, steady and sure."[2]

The pregnant silence Mapleson was imposing seemed to signal the proverbial lull; but this calm presaged a deluge.

Anxieties, solicitudes, and vanities centered on the opening of both the Academy and the Metropolitan; and though the new house, having aroused in many quarters tremendous public curiosity, held a splendid, vast audience, with many fashionables, it did not to any great extent obscure the brilliance of Mapleson's first-night ritual with its frills and flourishes. The opera at the Academy was Bellini's *La Sonnambula,* with the celebrated Hungarian soprano Etelka Gerster as Amina rapturously acclaimed by public and press, and the older house's regular habitués remained faithful, conspicuously absent from the Metropolitan. One of these, R. L. Cutting, offered an explanation: "I would not go in the other house . . . even to rehearsal. I was invited the other day but I refused. 'If you put your foot in it,' said my cousin, 'you are numbered with the other crowd,' and he was right." [3] The gentleman undoubtedly spoke for many in his social echelon.

On the memorable evening, long before the curtain rose crowds swarmed around the Academy, jammed sidewalks, disrupted traffic while lines of operagoers extending from several box offices spilled out onto Fourteenth Street. All were participating in one of the most momentous occasions in American opera history.[4] Finally the doors swung open and people surged into the auditorium. A dense mass of barouches, cabriolets, broughams, victorias, landaus rumbled upon the cobbled streets leading to and around the opera house, where from many of the conveyances blossomed sumptuously gowned, bejeweled ladies in costly wraps with escorts in the full panoply of top hats, white ties, starched shirts, opera capes, swallow tails.

These and countless others pressed down congested passages and blocked aisles until ultimately they filled the house. By curtain time it was a dazzling sight, with such society leaders as the August Belmonts, the Pierre Lorillards, the R. L. Cuttings, Mrs. Frank Leslie, Mrs. Paran Stevens, Mr. Clarence Seward, Mr. Royal Phelps, Mr. L. van Hoffmann, the W. B. Dinsmores, the Augustus L. Browns, Lady Roberts, the Marquis and Marquise Mores de Vallombrosa, Lord and Lady Carrington. Only the doyenne of Knickerbocker aristocracy was absent: Mrs. William Astor, who had prolonged her stay in the country but had sent the reassuring words she regretted her absence and intended to resume her place in the charmed circle as soon as possible. The Academy, according to some commentators, remained the bastion of culture, still representing the most worthy features of New York's social world.

Throughout the evening excitement on both sides of the footlights never ceased. It began with deafening applause and loud cheers for Maestro Arditi, who repeatedly received acclamations as the opera progressed. Under his inspired direction, the performance surpassed all expectations, being the best presentation of *La Sonnambula* New York had heard in years. It truly was an occasion "perfect in every detail."[5] Caught up in the spirit of the evening, the orchestra, chorus, and principals outdid themselves. The audience, determined to make the opening one long to be remembered, continually interrupted the proceedings with salvos of applause and ringing cries of approbation. The end of the acts saw the house in even more uproar with series of curtain calls which galvanized the ushers rushing to the footlights with floral tributes. During the intermissions, the Academy buzzed with greetings, congratulations, animated conversation; champagne corks popped for exuberant toasts; patrons in all parts of the house exchanged social calls. The crowning vocal effort of the evening occurred in the last act with Gerster's radiant "Ah! non giunge," an aria she delivered "with a lavish profusion of ornamentation which almost bewildered her hearers."[6] Soon after, the final curtain closed on this evening that had been a triumph for all, but above all, for the one who had made it possible. Though the audience again and again called for Mapleson, he chose not to appear on stage. Perhaps he knew the performance had eloquently said all.

Mapleson was willing, however, to make some comments to a representative of the press. Interviewed at the close of the performance, he expressed his delight in the gala opening: "I am pleased beyond measure . . . with this evening's success; it is really greater than I had anticipated. As far as the audience is concerned, I could ask nothing better. There were no tickets left . . . no standing room upstairs, and the hearty support accorded me by the stock-holders is, indeed, most gratifying."[7] Also gratifying was the fact that box office revenue totaled the highest he had yet experienced in a New York opening. Though now ecstatic, the impresario maintained that some hours earlier he had had misgivings.

He apparently began the evening with trepidation, concerned that three other openings on the same night—the inauguration of the Metropolitan, the opening of the National Horse Show, and the opening of Tony Pastor's variety house—might seriously affect the size of his audience, and that the new opera house might exert too powerful an influence on some of his old adherents. Fortu-nately, his fears had proved groundless. Surveying the Academy and finding it filled from pit to dome, with the boxes graced by loyal patrons of old, Mapleson did not, in his words, "miss anyone of any importance."[8]

During the performance he frequently dashed behind the scenes and over the house, attending to duties uniquely his. Whatever related to the public, box office, press, company, performance—all required his attention. He seemed to be everywhere, the ob-served of observers. Still, it was noted that despite the comings and goings Mapleson did catch portions of the opera from an up-per proscenium box in which he looked "supremely happy."[9] It was also noted he devoted considerable time to proposing and ac-cepting champagne toasts in the stockholders' room, where "wreathed in smiles,"[10] he held court with a number of his most affluent patrons who, like him, expressed delight in the opening and in the prospects for the season. In an expansive mood he shared with them contents from a letter Patti had written to Gerster: "You know by the contract *Lucia* was not to be sung except by Patti, for it is her famous role. Well, she has written to Gerster telling her she can sing in it and encouraging her to do her best and keep enthusiasm up until she arrives, when, she says, 'We'll go in and conquer everything.' "[11]

Likeminded, Mapleson made it clear the opposition held no ter-rors: "Abbey is a nice fellow and a good fellow . . . but he hasn't been an operatic manager for thirty-two years. He has fired off all his big guns at first instead of waiting till the season was well started. Now I have all my great attractions to come, and I feel confident I shall draw the public."[12] Surely the stockholders cheered, proposing more toasts to that final statement.

By any standard the impresario's evening marked a great victory. Mapleson had every reason to rejoice, and the next day's reviews and commentaries gave him even more. Of the leading artists, Gerster received the greatest acclaim. Her captivating personality, consummate artistry, magnificent voice had been creating sensations in the opera world since her debut at La Fenice in Venice on January 8, 1876, and had endeared her to such operatic centers as Berlin, London, and New York, where she first appeared at the Academy on November 11, 1878, and where she had last performed at the final matinee of the 1881–1882 season. Whether the soprano could still sing with her former beauty of tone, bravura, and command may have been questioned upon her return, but fortunately for Mapleson Gerster was in superb form, a fact critics duly celebrated.

From her singing of the first-act arias "Come per me sereno" and "Sovra il sen" to a rapturous "Ah, non giunge uman pensiero" in the last act, it was apparent, in the opinion of many, that Gerster's voice had never sounded lovelier, retaining its freshness, purity, and exquisite finish, dazzling in its phenomenal range and flexibility. The trills, leaps, swells, scales enchanted, as did staccato on high notes flung out "like stars from a bursting rocket."[13] Throughout the evening the soprano's singing electrified the audience, which gave her torrential applause and numerous floral tributes. To many Gerster remained the world's greatest Amina, the incarnation of the composer's dreams.

Critics especially praised two artists making their American debuts on this occasion. The tenor Eugenio Vicini as Elvino, "a fine, manly-looking fellow"[14] with a graceful bearing, at first seemed nervous but after recovering his composure sang and acted with assurance, frequently drawing "a round of 'bravos' from the house by brilliant efforts."[15] Some pundits detected occasional reedy tones in his singing. Vicini's first appearance nonetheless was a decided success. The bass Enrico Cherubini as Rodolfo also impressed in his debut with his handsome face, demeanor, and rich, mellow voice.

The other artists—Valerga (Lisa), Prioria (Teresa), Rinaldini (Alessio), and Bieletto (Notary)—acquitted themselves creditably, as did the enlarged orchestra and chorus, performing with "precision and vigor in a degree quite unusual for the first night of a season."[16] The few negative criticisms primarily concerned the opera itself and the scenery. One pundit considered *La Sonnambula* too old fashioned, with "its guitar-like style of orchestration and its entire freedom from anything dramatic,"[17] while another decried the settings: "It has occasionally been rumored that the Academy was to have new scenery, but such rumors must have been started by such as cannot appreciate the sweets of tradition. And so the eye dwells fondly upon that rustic scene mellowed by age."[18]

Under Arditi's direction, the entire evening left little to be desired. Interviewed after the performance, he expressed his satisfaction: "I think this evening is one of the most successful openings here that I remember. I see the boxes filled with old faces, so old friends are not deserting us, and I am very happy. I hope the public is happy too. That is all we want—for the public to be pleased."[19] His direction had been impeccable, and the orchestra a source of pride to New Yorkers, being drawn mostly from local musicians, while the Metropolitan's came from Europe.

As for the composition of the audience, critics generally considered it similar to those of the past in numbers and enthusiasm. The difference was in fashion. Though some thought it a shade less de rigueur, the journal of society, the *American Queen,* proclaimed it as lustrous as ever: "The result, socially, on Monday evening may . . . be summed up as follows: The Academy lost but little of its chief strength, and proved that its foremost social and financial backers, the Astors (although not present), Belmonts, Corses, Beckwiths and Dinsmores, still cast their lot with its fortunes."[20] The journal exulted that the glory of the Academy nobility still shone.

Though such reviews must have heartened Mapleson, the next day's accounts of opening night at the rival house undoubtedly elated him, since much of what was said vindicated his predictions. Although impressed by the vastness and fine proportions of the new auditorium, the immense stage, the mise-en-scène, costuming, some musical aspects of the performance, the size and enthusiasm of the crowd, and the elegance of the stockholders in their three tiers of boxes, many of the critics nonetheless maintained that certain social, musical, and architectural features left something to be desired.

The audience at the Metropolitan was brilliant, but in the eyes of many it was not socially analogous to the one at the Academy. Mapleson always referred to his patrons as "the best people of New York . . . the blue-blood of the city."[21] Others agreed. Still, the Metropolitan included the William H. Vanderbilts, the William K. Vanderbilts, the Cornelius Vanderbilts, the Robert Goelets, the Ogden Millses, the J. W. Drexels, the George F. Bakers, the James A. Roosevelts, the Richard T. Wilsons, the James Harrimans, the J. P. Morgans, the William Rockefellers. The splendor, grandeur, and easy arrogance of wealth almost overwhelmed. The *Evening Telegram* said: "Jewels, gems, diamonds, bright eyes and dazzling teeth flashed, sparkled, glinted, shone and shimmered in the gaslight, and lovely forms, swanlike necks, exquisitely rounded shoulders, Venus like arms and tresses that would have filled Cleopatra, Dido or Helen of Troy with envy, bewildered the beholder and made him almost a convert to the Mussulman's notion of Paradise. In the Metropolitan Opera House the scene of loveliness was almost ravishing."[22] Mere riches, however, did not admit individuals to the highest realms of New York society. The *American Queen* made that point clear: "A brilliant audience was present at the Metropolitan Opera House, and this fact cannot be denied; but there was a newness about the lustre of the gold represented there which carries not the weight of that shown at the Academy, and which of itself will never hold long the same society following, no matter how good the musical and scenic attractions may be. It was the dazzling glitter of the wealth of Vanderbilt and Gould and De Navarro and others, not the steady lustre of the Astor, Cutting and Belmont possessions."[23] In short, rank had varying connotations.

Artistically, the presentation of Gounod's *Faust*, sung in Italian, was not completely satisfactory. While some of the leading principals, the conductor Vianesi, the orchestra, chorus, ballet, settings of "fascinating beauty"[24] and superb illusion generally received praise, other features of the evening failed to arouse the enthusiasm of the critics as a whole. One concerned the late beginning and lengthy intermissions in a performance lasting over five hours. Though a boon to society activity, the waits may have proved tedious to others. They may also have shown inefficient management. Programs were unavailable until late in the evening. Occasionally the orchestra, placed almost at the level of the parquet floor, obliterated the singing of the principals; but a main source of discontent was the performance of two of Abbey's leading stars: Campanini as Faust and Nilsson as Marguerite. The prolonged rest had not restored the pristine quality of the tenor's voice. His singing sounded labored, and only at times were the wonted sweetness and golden ring evident. He nonetheless remained a superb artist. Although Nilsson was rapturously acclaimed by many critics, some maintained that she, too, no longer retained the voice and presence which had earlier enthralled New York. Mapleson could exult that in contrast his own prima donna had received nothing but glowing reviews.

Some of the loudest criticism concerned the house itself. The critics did admire the excellent proportions of the auditorium, then the largest in the world; but features of this space made a number of pundits unhappy, such as the monotony of the pale yellow decor which the *American Queen* labeled "lemon ice cream,"[25] the sage green stage curtain, the many inferior sight lines, the poor acoustics. Also regretted were the unattractive foyers, lack of a grand staircase, and undistinguished exterior. Henry T. Finck in the next day's *Evening Post* numbered himself with those who had found the new edifice unsatisfactory, but he wrote that "as the house was built avowedly for social purposes rather than artistic it is useless to complain about this or about the fact that the opportunity was not taken to make of the building itself an architectural monument of which the city might be proud."[26] An editorial in the *World* seemed to utter the last word: "A more amazing example of wealth working without taste or conviction or public spirit was never seen. The general impression made upon the observer by the Opera-house is that the capitalists instructed their architect to build as big a house as possible and not bother about its appearance or its convenience. The interior is modeled after the corridors of a state prison, and its gloomy crypts and stone aisles have a Catacomb massiveness combined with all the painful gorgeousness of color that one finds in a packing-box. . . . Looked at from the street the building appears like an enormous malt-house. Inside it has the appearance of a Mississippi steamboat."[27]

The first night of the rival enterprises had come and gone, with the prestige of the Academy socially and musically intact. Such an auspicious beginning posed a challenge for all to follow.

That Mapleson was relying on the drawing powers of Gerster and her ability to sustain the high level of the first night is evident in the fact that he presented her two more times the first week: the *Rigoletto* of October 24 and a matinee *Sonnambula* on October 27. Happily for the impresario, Gerster was singing gloriously; but it soon became apparent he was less fortunate in some of the other leading artists.

The second performance, on October 24, featured Gerster, who appeared as Gilda in *Rigoletto* with a cast that included Antonio Galassi in the title role and introduced to New York three new artists: Tobia Bertini as the Duke, Luciano Lombardelli as Sparafucile, and Emilia Vianelli as Maddalena. The evening marked another triumph for Gerster, who captivated the full house with her superb dramatic interpretation of the hunchback's hapless daughter, always singing with ease, spontaneity, warmth, elegance, and the finished style of a great artist. The critic of the *Sun* thought her rendition of "Caro Nome" had "never been given at the Academy with greater purity of tone, delicacy, or brilliancy of execution."[28] Galassi sang with his old-time "elegance of phrasing and purity and simplicity of delivery, and his acting was earnest and full of pathos and power."[29] Lombardelli and Vianelli generally impressed in their American debuts. Only Bertini received unfavorable reviews.

Nervous to begin with, the tenor never gained complete composure during the performance, which for him was disastrous. In both "La donna e mobile" and the quartet "Bella figlia dell'amore" his voice broke on some high notes, a circumstance that created laughter in the audience. One savant thought Bertini's voice lacked sonority or proper production and his acting was ineffectual, with no "dash and go,"[30] while another recommended that the tenor "would make a good end man for the chorus."[31]

The Bertini fiasco appalled and perplexed Mapleson, who when he secured the tenor, originally recommended by Gerster, had found his voice good. Since then for some reason it had obviously deteriorated to such a degree that Mapleson determined to break his contract.

Bertini thereupon consulted attorneys, who advised a $50,000 lawsuit for breach of contract and who requested that the tenor be given another opportunity to redeem himself at the Academy. Mapleson agreed, provided it was not before the public. The performance would be presented, with orchestra and chorus, before a judge of the Superior Court and a jury of individuals selected equally by the impresario and the tenor. This offer Bertini refused. The affair dragged on with legal proceedings until the tenor left for Europe, on November 14, with a financial settlement.

For the third performance of the first week, Mapleson brought forward on Friday, October 26, a revival of Bellini's *Norma*, not given in New York for a number of years. The dramatic soprano Eugenie Pappenheim assumed the title role, one of the most demanding in opera. She had appeared in New York before, though not in recent times. As Norma, Pappenheim acquitted herself fairly well vocally and dramatically. At times, however, the voice lacked flexibility and evenness, and it showed the ravages of overwork. In short, the role of Norma was beyond her present powers. Another of Mapleson's new tenors, Ernesto Falletti, made his American debut on this occasion, appearing as Pollione. Somewhat inept dramatically, he won adherents through his voice, "rich, clear and strong, especially the upper register."[32] The *Sun* maintained, however, that though a valuable artist, he had not sustained himself acceptably through the entire performance. Cherubini as Orovesco confirmed the good impression made in his debut, singing and acting with the finish of a fine artist, while Dotti as Adalgisa was creditable. The chorus and orchestra under Arditi did well. The opera undoubtedly needed more rehearsal and was, according to the *Evening Post* critic, an outdated work, "tiresome to a modern audience."[33]

Mapleson concluded the week with a repetition of *La Sonnambula* at the Saturday matinee of October 27 with the same cast as on opening night. Marcella Sembrich, one of the leading new sopranos from the rival house and an excellent Amina herself, occupied a box and in a magnanimous gesture heaped praise upon Gerster, always the consummate artist.

In the second week Mapleson presented *Lucia, Trovatore,* and *Faust,* and at the Saturday matinee repeated *Norma* with the same cast as on October 26. Gerster appeared twice in *Lucia:* first on October 29 at the Academy, and again three evenings later at the Brooklyn Academy of Music. The repertoire, like the Metropolitan's, leaned heavily on the traditional, and thus provided a direct comparison with the productions of the same works at the Metropolitan, where Abbey had already given the three operas Mapleson introduced into the repertoire that week. Mapleson was taking a chance, but he may have been angry or vainglorious enough to think the comparison would be in his favor.

The *Lucia,* on October 29, starred Gerster as Lucia, Vicini as Edgardo, Galassi as Ashton, and Lombardelli as Raimondo, with Arditi conducting. Abbey had presented the opera with Sembrich, Campanini, Kaschmann, and Augier in the same roles. Mapleson's production, spirited and smooth, was remarkably good. Singing with brilliance and taste and encored for several arias, Gerster impressed not only with her voice but also by her involvement in the dramatic aspects of her role, constantly adding intensity to her acting. The intensity disconcerted one critic, who warned that not "everything can be done on the operatic stage that would be in place in a purely dramatic representation."[34] Vicini, who seemed to be gaining in public favor and whose performance was vocally effective, gave "a very excellent impersonation"[35] of the fated Edgardo. Galassi and Lombardelli were most satisfactory. The large house enjoyed the performance immensely, encoring the harpist, Gerster, and the sextet and recalling the artists for a number of curtain calls.

Two evenings later Mapleson brought forward *Il Trovatore* with Pappenheim as Leonora, the ubiquitous Vicini as Manrico, Galassi as Di Luna, Lombardelli as Ferrando, and Rinaldini as Ruiz. The Azucena was Gemma Tiozzo, making her American debut on this occasion. The past week at the Metropolitan these parts had been portrayed by Valleria, Stagno, Kaschmann, Augier, and Grazzi, with Trebelli as Azucena. The audience at the Academy reveled in Verdi's melodies and in the artists, enthusiastically applauding their efforts. Pappenheim's Leonora was better than her Norma, "her forcible delivery of the music, together with her impassioned acting, frequently calling forth unrestrained plaudits."[36] Vicini, though at times somewhat hoarse, was vocally effective, dramatically less so. Tiozzo's presence was commanding, her voice far above the average, with rich, full notes in the lower range but with a top that at times sounded metallic. The other artists contributed vigorous interpretations to a performance that often thrilled the house.

Having been fortunate in *Lucia* and *Trovatore*, Mapleson turned, on November 2, to *Faust*, which he hoped would compare favorably with the Metropolitan's production of the same work. On paper Mapleson's cast looked interesting, as he announced four debuts: Ernesto Sivori as Valentin; Josephine Yorke as Siébel; Raphéla Pattini as Marguerite; and as Faust the tenor Giovanni Perugini, a New York singer whose original name was John Chatterton and whose claim to fame, perhaps, was his brief marriage to Lillian Russell. Cherubini and Valerga also were in the cast. Un-

fortunately for the impresario, the evening was a disaster, one daily
on the morrow declaring that "there never was a performance quite
like it in the Academy." [37] The only one of the new singers critics
generally favored was Yorke, a contralto and a native of Cincinnati
who had appeared with the Carl Rosa Company and whose mellow
voice and acting pleased. The others were mediocre or worse. By
contrast Cherubini's Méphistophélès loomed as a definitive interpretation.

By now it was apparent that the comparison of Abbey's and
Mapleson's performances of the same operas was not exactly in
the latter's favor and that Mapleson's main strength lay in only
two of his artists: Gerster and Galassi. Though they had risen to
the challenge, the other performers did not possess the magnificence of voice or the overall ability of artists of the highest rank.
As a whole, they were not a sufficient counterattraction to their
counterparts at the rival house. How Mapleson must have longed
for Patti's return! Then, too, a scenic comparison of the productions at the two houses was in Abbey's favor. Since the mise-en-
scène at the Metropolitan was new, the antiquated sets at the
Academy elicited more and more caustic comments in reviews.

By this time it was also apparent that Abbey was having problems. In the first two weeks the Metropolitan presented *Faust*,
Lucia, and *Mignon* twice each and *Trovatore* and *Puritani* once with
generally strong casts, an excellent chorus and ballet, a capable
orchestra under an energetic music director, superb costuming and
sets. Of the new leading artists, the Polish soprano Marcella Sembrich made the deepest impression in her appearances as Lucia,
the role of her American debut, and as Elvira in *I Puritani*, while
reliable, conscientious old favorites as Nilsson, Scalchi, Trebelli, Valleria, Del Puente, Campanini provided pleasure in their
roles. Musically the new house offered much, as did the Academy,
one critic maintaining that the musical fare of the two companies
was virtually equal. Even so, attendance at the Metropolitan was
sparse for most of the first eight performances. At Sembrich's debut, on October 24, the *World* reported thirty-two boxes empty,
the balcony not full, and the parquet only moderately occupied.

The soprano herself said: "I have sung never before such an empty house in my life. I suppose, though, that the same number of people it takes to fill only half that house would make an ordinary opera house uncomfortably crowded."[38] It was not, in fact, until the third week that the presentation of *Lohengrin*, on November 7, attracted a house comparable in size to that of the opening-night *Faust*. It was said that Abbey at this time was losing approximately $15,000 a week.[39]

What was hurting the new house was not only, of course, the competition from Mapleson but also the publicity concerning poor sight lines, long waits between acts, the acoustics. This last flaw seemingly created the most havoc. One critic suggested that for the benefit of the public "in course of time someone will probably publish an acoustic Baedeker, showing intending purchasers of tickets in what parts of the house they can hear the soloists to the best advantage."[40] Many insisted that the acoustic difficulty resulted primarily from the orchestra's not being sunken. To keep the pit at almost the parquet level overpowered some of the singers and impaired the stage view for a number of patrons; to lower it robbed, in particular, the strings of brilliance and, according to the principal conductor Vianesi, precluded the musicians from hearing one another. The management experimented with different levels without complete success.

Mapleson began the third week by adding on Monday, November 5, still another opera to the repertoire: Donizetti's *Linda di Chamounix*. According to the *Tribune*, it was the best performance the impresario had yet presented that season. Again demonstrating exquisite art, Gerster sang Linda's music with the "notes falling from her mouth as light and clean as dewdrops from a shaken flower."[41] Galassi (Antonio) added another triumphal success to his impressive gallery of portrayals, displaying his rich baritone, grand style, and finished acting. As Carlo, Vicini was beginning to show the strain of overwork, having sung at virtually every presentation since opening night, and some of his tones sounded reedier than before. Others in the cast were Lombardelli and Yorke, whose contribution strengthened the good impression made at her debut. In all, it was an evening reminiscent of Mapleson's best past performances at the Academy.

It also was an evening of surpassing suspense, if not one of suspended animation. Mapleson expected momentarily to receive a telegram that would precipitate a major event in New York's opera world: an elaborate celebration in honor of Patti's return.

For some time the impresario had been making arrangements to welcome the diva with a spectacular befitting her exalted rank. While flattering the soprano, he would give the new house's troglodytic tyro a lesson in operatic protocol. Since his rival apparently did not understand such esoteric matters, he, Mapleson, would further Abbey's education.

Mapleson's plans were suspiciously reminiscent of Barnum. As soon as Patti's steamer, the *Gallia*, appeared off Fire Island, the impresario was to be sent a telegram; at Sandy Hook pilots had promised to fire a gun salute. Upon entering New York harbor, the ship was to be greeted by sixteen tugboats flying banners appropriately emblazoned, which would then range themselves eight on each side to provide a right royal progress, with loud steam whistles and military bands, all the way to the Twenty-second Street Wharf, where Arditi, the opera house orchestra and chorus were to hail the sovereign in a ceremony worthy of the occasion. On October 31 Mapleson said: "Arditi has written a hymn which the chorus are rehearsing now, and the whole orchestra and all the chorus will be present to greet her. Such a reception never was before and never will be again."[42] Strangely enough, the reception that never was before remained unrealized.

Because of fog or human error or otherwise the *Gallia* steamed by Fire Island early the morning of November 6 unreported, with the consequence that Patti disembarked in New York without any fanfare whatever. On the pier she had the greatest difficulty in keeping warm and in finding transportation to her hotel, but fortuitously a friend was at the dock and assisted her into a four-wheeler. The *Herald* commented: "To smuggle the brightest star in the operatic firmament into town without a solitary hubbub to its back was a blow under which even the impresario's military heart saddened."[43]

The contretemps unsettled both Patti and Mapleson who, full of contrition, later called upon her at the Windsor Hotel. Though still miffed, the diva preferred not to linger on the annoyance, happy to be back in the country she had known since childhood, eager for future musical events.

Patti had selected Rossini's *La Gazza Ladra* as the vehicle for her first appearance of the season on Friday, November 9. During the past summer it had been revived for her at London's Covent Garden, where she had extended her engagement to nine performances instead of the original six in her contract, and where her appearances in this rarely performed opera had been a success. Patti of course hoped she would succeed with it at the Academy, since there, as at Covent Garden, it was a novelty. Thus the unfamiliar work itself, as well as the fact that it gave the diva a role in which New York had not seen her, created much interest. In short, the opera seemed an excellent choice for her reentrance. Mapleson averred he would provide Abbey with some laborers "to keep the walls of the Metropolitan Opera House from falling down like the walls of Jericho."[44]

Whether Patti could exert Joshua-like force remained to be seen. At least, the challenge was one of the greatest in her extraordinary career, a career that had long intrigued a vast public.

The daughter of Italian opera singers, Patti made her debut as Lucia on November 24, 1859, at New York's Academy of Music, instantly creating a furor. Sixteen, attractive, and exceptionally winning in her ways, her voice "fresh and full and even throughout,"[45] she created a sensation and became a national celebrity virtually overnight. Triumphs abroad duly followed. On May 14, 1861, London, sensibly following the American example, capitulated when the young star made her debut as Amina in *La Sonnambula* before a critical Covent Garden audience. To their amazement and delight they found her a revelation.

After this momentous beginning Patti conquered one Old World music center after another, until finally from the Atlantic to Moscow and from St. Petersburg to the Mediterranean her radiance emblazoned the operatic firmament. Thus did Patti apotheosize her art, and thus did she attain the title *diva*. Others contending for her crown remained at best penumbral princesses.

Patti enthralled the public in her private life as well. As a favorite of royalty, the possessor of enormous wealth, the chatelaine of a castle in Wales, a physically alluring woman, she was ever a fascinating personality; but perhaps what created the greatest sensation was her marriage in 1868 to the French aristocrat the Marquis de Caux, followed some years later by a prolonged separation and the diva's living "in sin" with the French tenor Ernest Nicolini, a married man and father. Some pillars of propriety as well as certain publications duly adopted a high moral tone over the affair, one California periodical maintaining that people now went to her performances "not to hear a great artist, but to see a great wanton—a beautiful sensualist the fame of whose adulteries has overspread the globe." [46]

At the time of the liaison a divorce in France was virtually impossible. Still, though the relationship horrified many in the Victorian world, the fallen one's career never suffered nor did the intake at the box office.

Presumably in the titanic operatic struggles of 1883–1884 the glamorous, vocally peerless, highly publicized diva would play the decisive role. Perhaps it would be the most eventful one in her entire career.

CHAPTER 3

The Queen and
the Princess

∽

OR MANY in New York the evening of November 9, 1883, the
Academy of Music radiated an intense splendor, with all else
seemingly revolving around it. An ineluctable glory emanated from
the luminous presence within—Patti!

Since opening night the Academy had not held such a house,
with every available space occupied and with the bon ton, led by
the Astors, out in force. Mapleson must have been overjoyed by
the magnificence of the purple, as well as by the vast numbers
massed to revel in the diva's matchless art and to see her in what
must have been for many an unfamiliar role: Ninetta in Rossini's
La Gazza Ladra. Needless to say, the assemblage hummed with
excitement.

When Patti appeared on stage the full house greeted her with
paroxysms of rapture, applauding and cheering for almost five
minutes. Here before them stood a legend—in the words of the
Daily Tribune critic, "the last perfect representative of the old art
of beautiful singing—a charming woman whose graces of face, figure and action were only ornaments to a perfectly balanced and
divinely inspired musical nature."[1] Finally the tumult subsided
and Patti launched into her opening cavatina, immediately dispel-
ling any possible doubt of her right to the exalted rank she held.
The phenomenal range, haunting purity, and extraordinary ex-

pressiveness of her voice, the seamless scales, brilliant fioriture, flawless trills—all enthralled the audience as it heard the soaring exhilaration of the aria. The house interrupted with tumultuous applause, and at its end gave Patti an ovation crowned by the presentation of a laurel wreath.

As the performance continued, the diva repeatedly proved that her voice remained unrivaled in its "wonderful carrying quality, its certainty of intonation, and its ease of execution in rapid staccato or legato passages." [2] She still sang, according to the *Sun*, with "that certainty, ease and marvellous finish of execution that marks all her works and makes it a constant pleasure to listen while she is on the stage." [3] Then, too, critics noted the authoritative way the diva led the ensemble and the improvement in her acting. All in all, it was Patti's night.

Vicini as Giannetto acquitted himself fairly well vocally, though he sounded tired, but did not impress dramatically, one critic remarking that the magpie in the opera "was made of wood, and the tenor was wooden, also." [4] Galassi as Fernando and Cherubini as Podestà generally satisfied in the vocal and dramatic treatment of their parts. Extremely nervous, Emilia Vianelli as Pippo executed the florid passages creditably, but her voice lacked the breadth and strength the part required. Rinaldini as Isacco and Lombardelli as Fabrizio completed the cast. Arditi conducted.

The opera itself failed to arouse much interest, now deemed too old-fashioned for modern taste, and undeserving of repetition. Some pundits also observed that the presentation needed more rehearsals. The performance, in short, had not been a complete success.

Because of the cool reception of the opera itself, rumors soon circulated that Patti intended to leave the Academy, dissatisfied with the current state of affairs there; and her nonappearance at her second scheduled performance seemed to confirm the gossip.

The diva was to have appeared on November 12 in one of her favorite parts: Violetta. That evening people thronged to the Academy, expectant of a wondrous performance, but upon arrival found this disappointing notice: "Mme. Adelina Patti is suffering from a cold which will render it very imprudent for her to sing this evening."⁵ The substitution, *Il Trovatore*, failed to interest, with the consequence there were many empty places in the auditorium.

Despite Mapleson's assurances that the diva would again sing on November 16, rumors of her imminent departure to the Metropolitan persisted until Patti, Abbey, and the impresario himself publicly denied that possibility. The diva conveyed her future operatic plans in a letter published in the *Sun:* "I have never thought for a moment of leaving Col. Mapleson. I have got a cold, and will sing when it gets better. I will sing at the Academy when I do sing."⁶ Abbey replied to the hearsay in an interview: "I have not seen Mme. Patti . . . since her recent arrival in this city, nor have

"The Operatic War in New York," cartoon in Puck.
Mapleson to the left versus Abby to the right.
COURTESY NEW YORK PUBLIC LIBRARY.

I made any negotiations with her since the end of last season, when I tried to secure her for my present opera season. There is not the remotest prospect of her singing with my company this season." [7]

Mapleson used the rumor to his advantage, making light of it while offering the enemy some advice: "This Patti story made me laugh all day. I sent it to Patti. She laughed. My friends laughed. It would make a cat laugh. It was a desperate canard started by the enemy. I tell you what it is . . . that new-fangled arrangement for Abbey's orchestra under that vast wilderness of stage is my salvation. They spent $120,000 blasting out rocks to get a stage with a cellar depth of thirty feet, and put the orchestra in the cellar. The result, in addition to breaking them up financially, is that all the sound is swallowed up by the cellar—singers, band, and everything. I am magnanimous enough to suggest a remedy to save Abbey, who is a pretty good sort of fellow. It is a well-known fact in acoustics that if you put glass saltcellars under the legs of a piano it increases the sonority of the instrument. The same thing is true of singers. If Abbey will shoe his tenors and prima donnas with saltcellars their voices can be heard. This improvement can be made readily—he can get the saltcellars anywhere—and the public will be mystified and gratified by the great change. Science is a wonderful thing. Abbey needs its aid to enable him to give opera up town in that Broadway pitfall." [8]

Patti's appearance in *La Traviata*, on November 16, with Vicini (Alfredo) and Galassi (Germont) stirred the house to frenzied enthusiasm and the critics to superlatives, one declaring her the greatest exponent of the part ever heard in New York. The recent illness had not harmed her voice, which soared over the orchestra and thrilled with its rich tones, remaining flawless: "One might as well attempt to criticize and analyze the warbling of the nightingale as to discover defects in her voice. Her notes are pure as silver; her vocalization marvellous, and she possesses the rare power of imparting expression to her notes—a quality in which nearly all sopranos are more or less deficient." [9] Her acting also impressed. Over the years it had improved immeasurably: "One of the most remarkable things about Mme. Patti is the fact that every year she seems to become more proficient as a tragic actress. . . . The mobility of her features is extraordinary, and in the death scene in particular her whole aspect last evening was so completely altered that if she had come on the stage with that expression her oldest friends would have scarcely recognized her."[10] In short, Patti infused into the music, including florid passages, sentiments appropriate to the character, not using them for mere vocal display; realized the dramatic requirements of the role; and instilled into her listeners a response that kept them on the edge of their seats.

Patti further impressed by her magnificent gowns and her jewels, with ladies peering through opera glasses to catch a better glimpse of the riches. What they saw stupefied:

In the first act she wore a pair of mammoth solitaires, a glittering dog-collar formed of squares of diamonds, a girdle to match, a diamond-studded fan-chain, three sparkling bracelets on each arm, half a dozen ornaments in her hair, and her dress was literally studded with diamond-set gems of various colors. . . .

But in the ball-room scene all the famous diamonds came to the fore. The wonderful necklace, with its long rivières of huge sparklers; the great horse-shoe shoulder-brooch with its long trail of diamonds running across the breast; a long shoulder-clasp, and another pair of matchless bracelets; diamond pins to stay the draperies of her dress—diamonds, diamonds everywhere![11]

Following the fantastic success of *La Traviata*, Patti appeared on three more occasions during the month of November. On the nineteenth she triumphed as Lucia, and four evenings later again received raves when she assumed the role of Elvira in *Ernani*, critics particularly citing her perfection of method and magnificent breadth of tone. The enthusiastic full house not only cheered her but also Galassi (Don Carlos) and Cherubini (Don Ruy Gomez). It did not respond well, however, to Bello (Ernani), who found his role uncongenial, too demanding for his light voice and histrionic limitations, and whose performance was "tame and colorless."[12] On the twenty-eighth Patti crowned her previous efforts in many people's opinion, while amazing some of her warmest adherents, when she introduced New York to her interpretation of a role in which the city had yet not seen her: Aida. Her assumption of this part created much interest, raising great expectations. Nor did Patti as Aida disappoint the many who reveled in the expressiveness of her singing, the perfect vocalization, the incomparably beautiful tones, the power of her voice. Others maintained, however, that the part was too heavy for her talents. Nicolini as Radames so outdid himself that "those who had declared that his upper notes were worn and that he was afflicted with the vibrato were loud in their declarations that they had never heard the part sung so well."[13] Galassi as Amonasro surpassed himself, while Tiozzo's Amneris was generally satisfactory. The orchestra, under the direction of Maestro Arditi, performed admirably, but the ballet did not, with dancers jumping up and down, each, seemingly, guided only by an individual will.

In the first week of December Patti appeared but twice: the *Ernani* of December 5 and the *Aida* of the December 8 matinee. By the latter date Patti's plans as well as Mapleson's had considerably altered. Disquietude in the company and the competition with the new house were taking their toll.

Though still distant, rumblings of a gathering storm were disturbing the atmosphere at the Academy. They would in time intensify. At the moment much of this static emanated from the Princess.

Between Patti's reentry of November 9 and the December 8 matinee Mapleson brought forward three operas starring Gerster: *Marta* on November 14, *I Puritani* on November 30, and *L'Elisir d'Amore* on December 7, Vicini sharing the honors with the prima donna in each of these productions. Gerster captivated in two of these, the one in which she did not receive complete critical acclaim being *Marta*, a work with limited opportunities to reveal the soprano's range or flexibility. Though these continuing successes must have heartened and reassured, Gerster was nonetheless finding her position in the company increasingly untenable.

The celebrity of Patti, the publicity she constantly received, the adoration of the critics and public, the deference paid to her by

Mapleson and the company, the fee of $5,000 a performance—all must have galled the hardworking, volatile Gerster who reportedly received a mere $1,000 each time she sang, and who though a formidable artist was unable to make any substantive headway against the diva. Then, too, until Patti's return Gerster, with the Academy virtually her own territory, had been Queen, but once the diva reclaimed her domain the younger woman found herself relegated to a less prestigious rank, that of Princess. As such she exemplified the Shakespearean axiom of a substitute's shining as brightly as a queen—until a queen be by, and as such she was now smarting from a rather severe case of lèse majesté.

The successful debut of another soprano the latter part of November posed a new factor with which Gerster had to contend. The artist, an American of approximately her own age, sang some of the same roles and at her first appearance evoked considerable public and critical enthusiasm.

On November 26, 1883, the Academy had the honor of presenting the American operatic debut of one of the greatest singers the United States has produced: Lillian Nordica. At that time to many she was known as Lillian Norton Gower, her married name, or simply as Lillian Norton, a Yankee maiden reared in Farmington, Maine, who possessed a phenomenal high C and who shook the rafters using it in such music as "Inflammatus" from Rossini's *Stabat Mater*.

The soprano received her early vocal training in Boston, studying with an Irishman named John O'Neill and at the New England Conservatory of Music. In time she joined the distinguished bandmaster Patrick Gilmore and his brass band in a tour of the United States and England, where in 1878 she gave over seventy concerts with this group. In that year she also appeared at the Trocadéro in Paris. Operatic engagements in Europe followed, the first being in Italy, where she adopted the stage name Nordica. Later she sang in Russia and France. Among the parts she essayed at the Grand Opéra in Paris were the heroines of Gounod's *Faust* and Thomas' *Hamlet*, roles she studied with the composers.

Such a background stood Nordica in good stead at her American debut, considered "an occasion of much social and artistic interest." [14] Some of the social interest related to her husband's Frederick A. Gower's wealth, high societal position, hauteur. The publicity surrounding the debut, said to be inspired by this man, made it distinctly clear that Nordica was appearing at the Academy only for artistic, not pecuniary, reasons. To Gower, his wife's appearance in opera seemingly was an act of noblesse oblige. To Nordica, it was her raison d'être.

At her American operatic debut as Marguerite in *Faust* the soprano impressed with a superb appearance, winning personality, charming manner, originality in the characterization, which, according to the *Evening Post*, "nowhere called for serious censure and often for high praise." [15] The *Sun* disagreed, finding "too much self-restraint, too much of the refined lady, and too little of the artist." [16] The same critic found her singing quite another matter: "a winning, tender, and sympathetic voice of great purity, and it is always used correctly and with much grace and refinement of style." [17] According to the *Herald*, Nordica's voice shone in the highest notes, with the medium somewhat "veiled" [18] and the lower notes deficient in resonance. The other principals were Vicini as Faust and Cherubini as Méphistophélès.

The soprano's presence provided more than usual interest in New York's opera world. At the same time her successes increased the volume of the gathering storm.

La Patti was also contributing to the tumult, once again making even more than the usual havoc of Mapleson's sangfroid when the impresario heard of possible developments between her and the Metropolitan. Rumors proliferated. This time it was said the rival house intended to offer Patti a contract for $6,000 a performance and $40,000 for the damages Mapleson might require were she to break her contract. Signor Franchi, Patti's agent, confirmed that such an offer had been made. Outraged, Mapleson called the offer "an unexampled piece of villainy." [19]

Questioned about this, Patti equivocated in her responses; but among these was one pregnant with territorial peril: "I am very happy in the academy. It is like an old home to me. My audiences are splendid, and we get along very well down there. Mme. Gerster is a very nice lady; she stays in her corner and I stay in mine. There is no trouble of any kind." [20]

The matinee of December 9 concluded Mapleson's seventh week of opera at the Academy, three weeks remaining in the subscription series. These he determined to defer until January, meanwhile beginning the annual tour to avoid Abbey, who had announced appearances of the Metropolitan in some of the same cities and at the same times as those scheduled by Mapleson. In changing plans, he intended to have the field to himself, thereby hoping to survive financially, since receipts in New York had not met expenditures. Mapleson later confessed that early in the season he had used up his own funds as well as the subscription sales, that his losses had been approximately $6,000 weekly, and that his present survival was due to a $24,000 voluntary assessment guaranteed by some stockholders to the Bank of the Metropolis with the stipulation he might draw from it up to $3,000 a week while in New York.

To the public Mapleson provided a novel explanation for the revised peregrinations, citing Philadelphia as an example: "In such a peaceful city as that of Brotherly Love one of the leading papers, foreseeing the tumult that will arise from the introduction into that city of two rival bands of hot-blooded Italians, urges all respectable citizens to stay at home during the visit of the opera companies, to lay in a stock of provisions for a siege and barricade their doors. . . . I don't want to go to the Quaker or any other city for the purpose of making a boom in condensed milk or any other canned goods. I think there is good cause for alarm among the peaceful residents of suburban cities, and therefore I have decided to avoid the foe wherever possible." [21]

After six performances in Philadelphia (December 10–15), the company journeyed to Boston, where Mapleson presented a short season (December 17–22). The New England metropolis rejoiced in the return of a virtual native daughter when a crowded house, on December 19, greeted Nordica as Marguerite in *Faust*. The *Boston Daily Globe* found her promising, considering her singing "marked more by brilliancy and purity than expression, yet . . . far from being unsympathetic."[22] Though triumphing in the Jewel Song, Nordica, said this paper, surpassed herself in the duet with Faust and in the last scene of the opera. The *Advertiser* was less generous, flatly stating that the artist was not yet ready to assume the part of Marguerite. The *Boston Morning Journal* thought otherwise, particularly praising her voice.[23]

Nordica was but one delight, however. Of the other leading artists, Boston especially reveled in the voices of Gerster and Patti. The season in Boston thus provided much aural pleasure; but for Mapleson it provided, above all, further enlightenment in the ways of La Patti with her performance in *La Traviata*, on December 18, the source of special illumination.

That afternoon when Patti's agent attempted to collect the $5,000 fee for the evening's performance he found Mapleson unable to oblige, with only $4,000 in the box office. Informed of this, Patti decreed she would be at the theater, prepared to go on stage except for a missing element—her shoes. When the remaining $1,000 was in her tiny hands, then and only then would she appear as Violetta. Hours later just before the beginning of the performance the impresario turned over $800 more to the agent, hoping this would suffice. Of course it did not. Soon returning with the cheerful news Patti had put on one shoe, the agent assured Mapleson she would don the other upon receiving the remaining $200. Finally that sum was realized and the divine one, now in full panoply, proceeded to the stage, all smiles.[24]

From Boston the company headed north to Montreal, where, though business was light, the public responded favorably to four presentations, perhaps again unforgettable artistic experiences; but one event there, as in Boston, the impresario long remembered. Once more it related to Patti and money. Putting them in the foul clutch of irony, myrmidons of the law had seized her for a debt she did not owe!

On their arrival railway car officials had demanded $300 more for the Patti traveling car attached to the train. Low on funds, Mapleson hastened to the theater to obtain the amount, not then realizing that sheriffs had meanwhile seized the diva's car, rolling it into a stable and locking iron gates behind. Unaware of her imprisonment, Patti slept through the entire episode, while Mapleson, returning with the requisite cash, felt understandably relieved at rescuing her from bondage.

Mapleson resumed his season in New York on December 31 with one of the earlier successes: *Aida*. He immediately enjoyed a monopoly, as the Metropolitan was on tour in Boston.

During the three weeks at the Academy (December 31–January 19) the house was not always full. Perhaps the city had already had too much opera, or the repertoire failed to intrigue, though Mapleson added two new works: *Crispino e la Comare* on January 4, and *Les Huguenots* on January 11. As Annetta in the former work, Patti carried off all honors with droll humor, vivacity, and glorious singing, some critics maintaining that in this role she surpassed her Rosina, always considered her greatest part. Caracciolo also earned kudos for his excellent characterization of the cobbler in a performance critics contended was one of the most brilliant of the season. *Les Huguenots* with both Patti and Gerster attracted a huge crowd that reveled in the two artists and in the opera itself, which received "a finished and symmetrical rendering—such a one, indeed, as to reflect the highest credit upon the company." [25] Patti as Valentine and Gerster as Marguerite de Valois seemed perfection in their respective roles, singing and acting with excellent effect. Nicolini as Raoul also sang admirably and acted "with a vigor that must put to the blush some of our later tenors." [26] The cast included Galassi (St. Bris) and Yorke (Urbain).

This opera with the same cast served as the vehicle for Mapleson's annual benefit on Friday, January 18, a performance that roused the crowded house to stormy applause. Marking the end of the subscription series, it seemed an appropriate time for the impresario to make a speech. Standing before the footlights in evening dress and nosegay, Mapleson favored the audience that had repeatedly called for him with well-chosen remarks, after which he retired from the stage amid cheers and thundering applause. Moments later a reporter accosted him in the lobby, questioning him over rumors from Cincinnati. Was Yorke leaving the company, and had Patti and he quarreled over the $20,000 reportedly owed her? The response, though reflecting annoyance, contained joyful financial tidings: "Pooh! Hoo! That, my boy, is simply B-O-S-H, in big letters. . . . It is superlatively silly. Why . . . how would Patti and Yorke be singing to-night if it was true? . . . Stuff! This is positively the grandest house known to American opera. The receipts to-night were $19,200."[27]

Two days later, on Sunday, January 20, the grand tour began, with scenery, costumes, stage properties, Patti's thirty-two trunks, the diva herself entraining for the first stop on the extended journey. The impresario, finalizing last-minute arrangements at the Academy, nonetheless found time to grant an interview to a *Times* reporter. Reviewing the past months, he expressed satisfaction with his series of performances, which he said inspired for the future: "My Winter season . . . has been successful far beyond my wildest expectations. I came here prepared for almost any kind of—I won't say defeat, for I am not the man to anticipate defeat or to yield to it tamely—but to be knocked down occasionally, or something of that kind. I formed a very strong army, however, and I have conquered with it, and now I am going out into the open to defeat the enemy."[28]

Both Mapleson and Abbey were now on the road, while behind them the smoke of battle in New York gradually receded, a lull giving time for a review of operatic activities, results in comparison to those of former seasons, and future implications for opera in the metropolis.

The season just concluded featured few novelties in either company's repertoire, with traditional works retaining their hold on the public. The resuscitated *La Gazza Ladra* at the Academy was not a success, receiving only one performance, and the American premiere of *La Gioconda* at the Metropolitan, on December 20, created no profound impression except for its spectacular scenic effects.

Of the singers, those who had been before the public a number of years achieved the greatest successes. Patti remained peerless, critics enskying her every performance. Gerster, Nilsson, Campanini, and Scalchi held high places in the operatic hierarchy, in many ways unequaled. The last three were inimitable in some of their roles, eclipsing the efforts of their colleagues at the Metropolitan with the single exception of Sembrich, who at her New York debut immediately established herself as a superior artist and who then and thereafter received critical and popular acclaim.

With regard to the other principals, Nicolini impressed as Raoul and Radames, while the remaining Maplesonian tenors worthy of notice, Vicini and Falletti, possessed resonant voices but lacked requisite experience or artistry. The contraltos Yorke and Tiozzo were merely acceptable, whereas the participation of Galassi, Caracciolo, Cherubini, and Lombardelli always was "a source of satisfaction."[29] At the Metropolitan Alwina Valleria, Emmy Fursch-Madi, and Del Puente pleased; Zelia Trebelli had not been sufficiently heard for a complete critical judgment, while the tenors Roberto Stagno and Victor Capoul and the baritone Kaschmann disappointed.

As for the leading conductors, Arditi with his experience, musicianship, command overshadowed Vianesi. As the *New-York Times* put it, "The sense of absolute confidence in the magnetism and authority of the conductor—a feeling without which the dilettante cannot completely enjoy a representation of opera—has possessed the audiences at the Academy of Music as continuously as it has been missed from the auditorium of the Metropolitan."[30]

Of the performances, Mapleson provided the most cherished ones, with Patti carrying all honors in a galaxy of extraordinary portrayals. Abbey's most notable feature, aside from his leading singers, was "the visible magnitude of the performances."[31] The new scenery, new costumes, the large chorus and orchestra impressed. What did not please all was the auditorium, failing to satisfy in every respect.

The season, in the opinion of the *Times* critic, merited this summation: "We have had as good singers in previous seasons, and the stage attire of the operas presented in previous years, although less costly, has been such as no European opera-house would have blushed to own. We have had efficient choruses and efficient orchestras, and the only advantage that might have been regarded from the increased numbers of the masses has been neutralized by the defects of the new house. Hence we have learned practically nothing from the season just ended." [32]

Despite such critical opinion directors of the houses professed satisfaction with the presentations, the principal artists, the public response, as well as the management of the two companies. Speaking for the Academy, director Augustus L. Brown said: "We furnish the Academy to Col. Mapleson free of rent, lighted, warmed, and cleaned. The fixed charges of the house to the stockholders amount to $30,000 per year. Naturally, in contending against opposition, we expected it to cost us more. . . . But we have done better than we anticipated, and we have every reason to feel satisfied with Col. Mapleson's management." [33] James A. Roosevelt, President of the Metropolitan's Board of Directors, expressed a like satisfaction: "As we have to foot the bills, it seems to me that if we are satisfied with our house and with Mr. Abbey for a manager, that ought to be quite sufficient." [34]

The duration of such satisfaction depended upon events in the near future. Mapleson resolved it would endure. While away from New York for months, the impresario determined never to relent in his efforts in the cause of opera or in his siege of the Metropolitan. The temporary withdrawal from his headquarters had a strategic value. Mapleson retreated to advance.

CHAPTER 4

Grand Tour

∽

*T*HE EXTENDED tour began on January 21 in Philadelphia, where the Metropolitan had just concluded a series of performances (January 14–19) and where Mapleson presented Patti in two operas and Gerster in one. The public crowded to see the diva in *Aida* (January 21) and *Crispino e la Comare* (January 23). Though superior in both, Patti as Aida created a furor, astounding those who had hitherto seen her only in roles for the light soprano.[1] A less than full house greeted Gerster in *L'Elisir d'Amore* on January 22, a circumstance no doubt annoying her as did also her rival's critical and public reception. Gerster's dissatisfactions soon became public knowledge, the long-tried Princess no longer able to repress resentment. The anticipated storm now burst in fury.

Various factors fueled the explosion in Baltimore, the next stop on the tour. Rumors said Mapleson by now owed Gerster $10,000 in back salary payments. Then upon arrival the soprano noted a playbill on which Patti's name was larger than her own, a further humiliation. More psychical damage followed when she discovered that tickets to her rival's operas cost twice those for her own appearances. The final sparking affront was an article Gerster saw in the January 24 issue of the *Baltimore American*: it listed the expenses of a hypothetical man and woman attending a Patti performance. The cost, needless to say, was excessive.[2]

Livid with rage, Gerster demanded to see the impresario, who, arriving at her hotel, needed all his battery of diplomatic skills.

Mapleson nonetheless finally succeeded, so he thought, in calming the feral prima donna; but later Gerster determined to leave the company for good and entrained for New York. Unable to find her, her husband became alarmed and alerted Mapleson to the disappearance. Fortunately for the two men, a member of the chorus had seen Gerster making her way to the railway station and informed them of this fact. Mapleson immediately telegraphed to Wilmington, the first stop after Baltimore, that all would be amicably settled were she to return on the first available train. Meanwhile it had been arranged for the express from New York to be detained in Wilmington until her train arrived. Unfortunately for a quick resolution to the affair, Patti was on the express and, discovering the reason for the delay, became enraged that she, the prima donna *assoluta*, should be inconvenienced by a lesser's folly. Nicolini found his emotional state complementing Patti's, furious, perhaps above all, that the gourmet dinner awaiting in Baltimore would be ruined by the time they arrived. Then when Gerster's train appeared, the prima donna absolutely refused to enter the express, as she had found out it held Patti. Without further ado she went on to New York. Mapleson thereupon changed the opera: *Ernani* in place of *L'Elisir d'Amore*.

To a representative of a local paper, Mapleson expressed regret for Gerster's nonappearance, and to avoid a scandal offered this explanation: "Ah, you see, Madame Gerster is a very devoted mother and a very impulsive woman. She has a two-year-old child in New York, and she heard that it had the croup or a cold or something like that, and nothing must do but she must rush off to consult Dr. Jacobi. You may know how sudden and unexpected was her departure when I tell you that she left here all her baggage, and that her husband and her maid are still here." [3]

Hours later Mapleson took the midnight train to New York, determined to bring the soprano to her senses. Not having had anything to eat since morning and unable to satisfy his hunger en route, the impresario himself was by now enraged. In the city he finally located Gerster at her brother's residence, and after a time and presumably much palaver succeeded in persuading her to return to Baltimore, whereupon Gerster sent this telegram to her husband: "Get dinner ready this evening for 9 o'clock; baby quite recovered."[4]

To attain the rapprochement, Mapleson no doubt made a number of concessions, and whether or not the rumor that Abbey had offered to negotiate with Gerster was true, Mapleson could not afford dalliance.

Peace once again apparently reigned. Still, though hostility in the company might momentarily be camouflaged, it was a live coal which could at any time flare up to a red hot flame.

Though fearful the Gerster scandal had reverberated throughout the United States with dire effects on the box office, Mapleson found upon his arrival in Chicago that the two-week engagement at McVicker's Theatre (January 28–February 9) was actually heavily patronized. He also discovered he did not have the field to himself. Since Abbey's forces had already entrenched themselves at Haverley's Theatre for a two-week season beginning January 21, the operatic giants were again in combat on the same terrain. What made the situation potentially devastating was their proximity. Both companies lodged in the Grand Pacific Hotel with (horror of horrors!) Patti, Gerster, Nilsson, Fursch-Madi, Sembrich, Trebelli, and Scalchi on the same corridor.

The impresario led from strength when he presented Patti in *Crispino e la Comare*, on January 28, with the usual cast. Not having seen the diva in this opera before, Chicago knew not what to expect, but her glorious singing, charm, and vivacity evoked wild enthusiasm. Abbey countered with the novelty *La Gioconda*, featuring Nilsson, Fursch-Madi, Stagno, Del Puente. The *Tribune* critic considered this production superior to those of the Metropolitan's previous week, saying "its performance also showed careful preparation and moved more smoothly than any previous performance of the season."[5] The following evening Gerster pleased in *L'Elisir d'Amore*, as did Vicini, Caracciolo, the chorus, orchestra, costumes, stage settings; at Haverley's Theatre Sembrich and Campanini enjoyed a success with their portrayals of Amina and

Elvino in *La Sonnambula*, though the Metropolitan's chorus, orchestra, stock scenery, slovenly stage business did not. Within twenty-four hours Chicago had thus heard three of the greatest sopranos in the world, a fact not lost on the *Tribune*, which commented that of those "Patti is to this day without an equal."[6] It is to be hoped Gerster did not read this.

On Wednesday Mapleson offered Chicago his pièce de résistance: *Les Huguenots* with both Patti and Gerster, scheduled in opposition to Nilsson in *Mignon*. Thousands of people packed the two theaters, with over one thousand unable to gain admittance to Mapleson's offering. Speculators received as much as $25 a seat, and those who crowded every available space counted themselves fortunate to witness the presentation that by all accounts ranked as an exceptional musical experience, one critic considering it "by far the most sensational opera performance that ever occurred in Chicago."[7] Mapleson later divulged that it had certainly been "sensational," though what he had in mind did not relate to the critic's use of the word. The sensation concerned, as might be expected, the Queen and the Princess.

A number of expensive bouquets and set pieces for Patti had been received at the theater. The diva's agent Franchi customarily informed the usher of the appropriate time to present such tributes, but on this occasion he was absent. When the first act ended and applause thundered upon the principal artists, the uninformed ushers, galvanized by the opening, rushed to the footlights with all the floral arrangements. A contretemps then ensued. In this act Patti as Valentine sang little while Gerster as Marguerite had the stage to herself, vocally speaking, electrifying the house with brilliant singing. It had been her act; and such tributes rightfully belonged to her. Unaware of this, ushers handed many bouquets and set pieces to Arditi, who, as he read attached cards, passed them along to the addressee. As Patti constantly received the tokens of admiration, the audience became restive then annoyed. For Gerster there was not even one! Then finally when Arditi handed Gerster a small basket of flowers, the house went wild, cheering for minutes, much to the diva's annoyance.

The ludicrous affair so angered Patti that at the end of the performance she vowed never again to appear in the same opera with her rival. Later, according to Mapleson, Patti attributed the embarrassment to the impresario himself, facetiously maintaining he wished to humiliate her publicly to obtain her services at a lower fee. Then in a serious vein she blamed Gerster for the misadventure, convinced her rival possessed an evil eye. For this reason, whenever thereafter Patti heard the name Gerster or whenever a mishap occurred in Patti's presence, the superstitious diva immediately extended her first and fourth fingers in the sign of a horn to avert the maleficent powers of her rival's evil eye.[8]

On January 31 Mapleson brought forward a new opera in the repertoire, *La Favorita*, with two artists making their American debuts: Andres Anton as Fernando and Maria Bianchi-Fiorio as Leonora. The cast also included Galassi (Alfonso) and Cherubini (Balthazar). The debuts failed to impress vocally or dramatically, critics deeming it an off night. The same evening Abbey delighted Chicago with *La Traviata*, starring Sembrich. Mapleson concluded the first week with Gerster in *Linda di Chamounix* on February 1 and Patti in *Lucia* at the February 2 matinee with Nicolini (Edgardo) and Galassi (Ashton), while Abbey ended his financially unsuccessful engagement in the Loop with *Robert le Diable* on February 1, *Marta* at the February 2 matinee, and *La Gioconda* that evening.

Though admiring many of Abbey's artists, critics could not forgive the inadequacies; invectives directed toward him generally concerned the stock scenery he had used and the far from satisfactory work of the chorus and orchestra. The *Lohengrin* on January 23 especially disappointed, and after that, according to Quaintance Eaton in *Opera Caravan*, "Abbey never recovered ground in Chicago. The performances were termed listless."[9]

In the second week Mapleson introduced still another opera into the repertoire: *Roméo et Juliette*, sung in Italian on February 5 with Patti as Juliette, Nicolini as Roméo, Cherubini as Friar Laurence. Patti sang gloriously but the *Tribune* critic wrote a scathing review of the production, maintaining it had not been faithful to the composer's score. Mapleson, incensed by this, refuted the charge in a letter to the editor.

Another sensation occurred the following evening, February 6, when Mapleson introduced Nordica as Gilda in *Rigoletto*. She triumphed in a most emphatic way, creating such tremendous excitement that the house lavished upon her "the most enthusiastic applause given any singer during the present Mapleson season." [10] These words may have disturbed the Princess as much as the Queen. Nordica's success, however, generated so much interest that leading citizens of the town urged Mapleson to present her again. Responding to their pleas, he scheduled *Rigoletto* for the last evening of the engagement, on February 9, with Nordica once more assuming the role of Gilda. Captivating a full house on this occasion, the soprano ended the Chicago engagement in a blaze of glory for herself and for the company, but the blaze apparently had not warmed all. Nordica, so gossip buzzed, had created considerable jealousy. Her departure from the company soon followed.

Nordica's biographer, Ira Glackens, in *Yankee Diva* suggests another reason for difficulties: her husband, who held an exalted opinion of himself and thus disapproved of the soprano's being second to any other artist, or for that matter pursuing an operatic career at all. [11] Alexander Graham Bell's brilliant business manager and a millionaire, Frederick Gower apparently had a superiority complex as well as Svengalian drives, requiring his wife's undivided attention, angry if this was not forthcoming, pathologically jealous of anything denying him his due. He now aimed a shaft at another artist, the unassailable one. The press quoted him as saying there was only one reason for his wife's sudden withdrawal: Patti's demand Nordica be given subordinate parts.

Responding to Gower's charges, Mapleson said there was no trouble and defended Patti, who he maintained felt no jealousy of the young soprano. Nordica's reason for leaving the company did not warrant the publicity; it was, according to the impresario, simply a matter of her having concluded her contractual agreement. Still, it must have been more than this, as he did not refrain from making some vitriolic comments on Nordica's prima donna airs.

After the Chicago engagement Mapleson added Minneapolis to the tour. While there (February 14–16), he may have heard of Abbey's increasing personal financial losses, which it was later said totaled approximately $600,000, a sum representing deficits in New York and on tour; he must also have heard of his rival's decision to retire from the management of the Metropolitan at the end of the spring season. The announcement probably came as no surprise, though it must have startled those who did not anticipate such a swift surrender, barely four months after the October 22 opening.

The February 14, 1884, edition of the *New-York Times* announced the rout, while also carrying a lengthy summary of the Metropolitan's financial picture, revealing that the anticipated deficit by the opening of the 1884–1885 season would be $238,478.74. This figure of course did not include Abbey's loss of his own hundreds of thousands of dollars. The cost of the Metropolitan's property, building, and contents totaled $1,835,833.41, while anticipated additional disbursements by the fall of 1884 raised the figure to $2,019,478.74. At the end of January the directors requested each of the seventy stockholders to purchase $3,500 more stock in order to raise $245,000 for payments of all outstanding accounts and for needed funds to improve the interior appearance of the house. Otherwise, the directors proposed taking a second mortgage on the property.[12] The stockholders were learning the costliness of opera. The future of the Metropolitan remained to be seen. Meanwhile its archenemy continued on tour.

After completing the short season at Minneapolis on February 16, Mapleson's troupe entrained some thirty-six hours to St. Louis, where the Metropolitan had recently concluded its engagement (February 4–9), and where Abbey's box office average had been the lowest in his tour: $2,333 per performance.

Opening with *La Sonnambula* on February 18, Mapleson presented seven operas during the one week in St. Louis, with Gerster starring in three of these while Patti sang in only one, *La Traviata*, on the nineteenth; but on February 21 the city luxuriated in an evening with both prima donnas, this despite the Chicago episode. Since the diva had vowed never to appear with Gerster, the impresario's program reflected his genius at diplomacy.

Mapleson had announced *Les Huguenots* with the two stars, but the Chicago affair precluded this. The two artists, however, apparently harbored no objections to appearing in a mixed bill on the same evening, which found Gerster thrilling in the first two acts of *Rigoletto* and Patti overwhelming in the last two acts of *Lucia*. Patti brought the performance to an unforgettable ending when she added as an encore "Home, Sweet Home," a ballad she always rendered with plangent tones, tenderness, deep feeling. The audience left the theater reveling in the experience, but some critics did not entirely share this euphoria. Both *The Missouri Republican* and the *Globe-Democrat*, though enthralled by the prima donnas, nonetheless criticized the operatic truncation, with the former newspaper commenting that a piece of a work "will not answer as sample of the whole, like cheese and cloth."[13]

Even so, the evening had been memorable, but actually it was not until the next day people realized just how memorable! Hours after the performance a portion of it sparked an event producing tremors subsequently felt in various parts of the world. The morning of February 22 Patti at her hotel graciously received individuals eager to make her acquaintance and to pay homage. Among these was Governor Thomas Crittenden of Missouri, who had apparently felt transported by her singing of the previous evening, especially the incomparable rendition of "Home, Sweet Home." Now in her presence he committed a horrendous faux pas. To put the matter as delicately as possible, the horror was an osculation, which flung Victorian propriety to the winds. Such audacity scandalized sensibilities, with Patti, Governor Crittenden, and Gerster contributing to the subsequent furor.

The diva's version appeared soon afterward. Interviewed by a St. Louis reporter, she said: "Your Governor—Crittenden, I think his name was—yes, Gov. Crittenden, came to me after that night, and what do you think he did? . . . Well, he kissed me. He said, 'Madame Patti, I may never see you again, and I cannot help it,' and before I knew it he threw his arms around me and was kissing me. . . . Now it wouldn't do, you know, to have everybody washing my face, but an old gentleman and a nice-looking old gentleman—I think he was nice-looking, but the truth is, he kissed me so quick I didn't have time to see—and especially when they do not give me time to object, what can I do?" [14]

The Governor's remembrance differed from the diva's: "I called next day in company with some friends, and as I approached Patti's room, I met in the corridor of the hotel a party of young girls, who said to me that they had just been given that which I should never have—a kiss from Patti. After the introduction to the lady I repeated what those happy young creatures had said, to which she laughingly replied that she did not see why that should never be. No sooner was this said than I had my kiss. I then remarked that this was better than even 'Home, Sweet Home.' The joke of it all is that in telling on me afterwards the friends with whom I had gone in declared that I said the kiss was . . . better than anything at home." [15]

What became known as the Patti kiss ultimately elicited some choice Gerster comments spiced with her characteristic flavor:

MODEST REPORTER: I suppose, Mdme Gerster, you have heard about that kissing affair between Governor Crittenden and Patti?

MDME GERSTER: I have heard that Governor Crittenden kissed Patti before she had time to resist; but I don't see anything in that to create so much fuss.

REPORTER: (interrogatively) You don't?

GERSTER: Certainly not! There is nothing wrong in a man kissing a woman old enough to be his mother. [16]

After St. Louis the company appeared in Kansas City, Missouri, St. Joseph, Denver, Cheyenne. Of these the last locale provided several special experiences.

For hours on March 4, citizens of Cheyenne, the Magic City of the Plains, waited for the "army of the victorious Colonel Mapleson . . . with his brilliant battalions under the lieutenancies of

Gerster and Patti, the sweetest nightingales who ever piped a note." [17] The townspeople intended to greet them with ceremony. Earlier that day dignitaries from the legislature and others of eminence began the welcome, boarding a special train to meet the operatic caravan. When the train with the conquerors and their welcoming committee rolled into Cheyenne about two in the afternoon, several thousand excited people roared a welcome. The Ninth Infantry Band struck up festive music, and after Mapleson appeared, introducing Gerster to the throng, the crowd rent the air with cheers. The Princess, accompanied by Mapleson and the band, then proceeded to the Inter Ocean Hotel, where she again received an ovation, finally in response to the tumult outside appearing with Mapleson on a balcony, bowing to the multitude.

Patti had meanwhile ordered her special car detached from the train. The diva thus assured herself of her own special reception. In due time and with Gerster away from the scene, Patti's coach was drawn into the station, where crowds cheered and the band members played, though apparently not so expertly as several hours before. Mapleson explained the fall from musical grace: "they had taken 'considerable refreshment.' " [18]

Patti's private car, costing tens of thousands of dollars, attracted extraordinary attention with its silk damask curtains, gilded tapestry on the walls and ceilings, elaborate furnishings, sandalwood trim, costly Steinway piano, and white and gold drawing room.

The evening's performance of *La Sonnambula* with Gerster, according to a local historian, reached "the high-water mark of theatrical activity in Cheyenne during the nineteenth century," [19] an $8,000 house with each seat priced at ten dollars.

Marching westward, the company crossed vast territories en route to Salt Lake City, where Mapleson arranged for a performance of *Lucia* with Gerster. Upon arrival Patti, Nicolini, and Mapleson visited the great Mormon Tabernacle, a structure that amazed with its acoustical perfection and seating capacity, inspiring Mapleson, though the inspiration perhaps was due neither to religious associations nor to an inner light. The building was an ideal setting for a concert! Unfortunately, the impresario's inspiration did not fire those whose consent he needed. Mapleson did not give up, so unbelievably moved was he, and enlisted the aid of the diva.

Attuned to his pleas, she invited the Mormon Prophet John Taylor and his twelve apostles for a déjeuner on her private railway car. At this gathering Patti demonstrated that she, like the impresario, possessed gifts of persuasion and guile, going so far as to declare an interest in joining the Mormon Church. The elders, favorably impressed, thereupon agreed to her appearing at the Tabernacle several weeks later.

That same evening, March 6, a large house contributed some $3,750 to the exchequer, cheered Gerster as the hapless Lucia, and, discovering Patti and Nicolini in a proscenium box, vociferously applauded the diva. Though seemingly full of bounce and vigor, Patti apparently subsequently tired, departing long before Gerster's mad scene.[20] By then the Princess may indeed have been mad.

The opera train, leaving Salt Lake City, moved with dignity across Utah and Nevada, here and there greeted by denizens of small settlements anxious to catch a glimpse of at least one of the prima donnas, thrilled when they succeeded in doing so. Reno intended to pay homage and when the troupe arrived there, some thirty hours after leaving Salt Lake City, a splendid reception awaited the company, loudly cheered by townspeople, Indians, and Chinese while the Renoites who had initiated and prepared the welcome ceremony beamed with pleasure.

At long last the train reached California, and all went well until the arrival at Truckee, where a washed-out culvert and snowslide on the tracks delayed transportation for hours. Countless Chinamen labored to repair the road, as well as to construct a temporary passage over which the cars moved one at a time. Meanwhile, a crowd surrounded the opera carriages, one Indian woman with a papoose on her back in moments working a miracle on the diva. Waiving the usual $5,000 fee, Patti, accompanying herself at the piano, sang nursery rhymes to the little one and then to the child's delight whistled a tune.

After hours of delay the company left Truckee, accompanied by a spine-tingling war whoop from the Indians. Loud cries from the Chinese, miners, and cowboys swelled the volume.

Finally on the morning of Sunday, March 9, the caravan arrived at Oakland, whence the diva was among the first to embark across the bay to San Francisco, landing there amid acclamations and exultant strains.

Opening its gracious portals wide, the city welcomed the divine one with hosannas, its golden gates, financially speaking, gleaming as never before.

CHAPTER 5

Golconda

༌

OR WEEKS a topic of conversation, Patti graciously acknowledged the royal welcome, while a band of twenty-five entertained with a march written by its director and dedicated to her. The news that she would appear with the company had exploded earlier that day. Exhilarated, Patti expressed keen pleasure in being in San Francisco: "According to every physical rule I should be a very tired little woman to-day, but, *au contraire,* I am so filled with the electricity of novelty and excitement that I really haven't time to grow weary. Everything possible has been arranged for my comfort in travelling, but the weather has been so very naughty that it gave me no rest at all last night. Then these wash-ups—wash-ins—wash-outs—how is it you call them?—have made such long delays that it really seemed as though we should never reach this Mecca of our hopes. . . . Ah! If you but knew how much has been done to prevent my coming; but I have come, and am consequently in humor to smile on everybody and everything."[1]

The diva was not wholly in humor, however. Had Patti been completely candid, she would have added that presently she was willing to smile on all except Mapleson, piqued he had not announced a definite date for her first appearance. Perhaps the impresario had equivocated to placate Gerster. Very well, Patti determined to take the matter into her own tiny hands and, asked by a journalist the date of her first appearance, stated it would occur in four days' time: "There is a great deal of '*Je ne sais quoi*' about me just now, but you can put down that I am going to sing *Traviata* on Thursday." [2] Hours later Mapleson confirmed her statement, by then having no doubt mollified Gerster, who, apparently believing her arch-rival would appear only once, made no vehement protest, content with the advance sales for her own performances, the attention and adulation of the press, and, it is presumed, the impresario's platitudes.

Meanwhile, following other members of the company, Mapleson arrived in San Francisco about noon to find a representative from the *Morning Call* waiting for an interview. In an expansive mood, he informed the reporter that both Patti and Gerster were in excellent health, voice, and spirits. Only the day before, he said, Patti, waiting for breakfast, accompanied herself at the piano, singing in the original key one of the Queen of the Night's difficult arias from *Die Zauberflöte* until "Nicolini rushed in, and tearing his hair, implored the diva, if she loved him, not to thus tax her wonderful organ, especially in a railway car." [3] Mapleson then denied the allegation that he had released many of his company while in Chicago. Questioned about Abbey, Mapleson bristled, indulging himself with several choice comments: "I look upon Abbey as a very able theatrical speculator—a speculator in the fullest sense of the term, as he will take up anything from which money can be extracted. Why he entered the Italian opera field to ruin himself I cannot for a moment imagine. I predicted his downfall at the very outset. . . . Abbey knows nothing whatever about operatic management and when he finishes his ten nights in New York commencing to-morrow, he quits the operatic arena for good." [4] A further comment concerned the rumor that Metropolitan directors intended to secure Ernest Gye as the next manager of their house. Such a likelihood held no terrors for Mapleson.

The highlight of the company's first day in San Francisco was the evening's entertainment in honor of Patti, with Wetterman's Band serenading her in the brilliantly illuminated courtyard of the Palace Hotel, a magnificent enclosure with six galleries rising to a stately dome of crystal. A crowd of approximately one thousand richly dressed ladies and gentlemen thronged the court and lined the corridors of each gallery to catch a glimpse of Patti, who, appearing after the third selection amid cheers and applause, acknowledged the enthusiasm by bowing and waving her handkerchief. The diva and Nicolini thereafter retired to their suite of rooms, where she held a levee.

Some blocks away Patti received yet a further tribute, this one from season subscribers, who Mapleson decreed had first choice of tickets for the diva's San Francisco debut.[5] They early began forming lines in front of Sherman & Clay's music store on Kearny Street, from time to time fortifying themselves with liquid as well as solid sustenance, while others joined them simply for the purpose of later selling their places to the highest bidder. The police, ultimately having difficulties with several, arrested the offenders, one of whom made himself, according to the *Chronicle,* "conspicuous by language not found in religious works."[6] Obviously the Adelina Patti fever had struck; in hours it would become a raging epidemic.

The next day, March 10, when the sale began, season subscribers retained their places for the special occasion with a 20 percent discount, a generous policy for patrons and a clever, lucrative one in that it impelled many others to subscribe to the entire season in order to attend the Patti gala. Mapleson had meanwhile scheduled ticket sales for nonsubscribers for Tuesday, March 11.

The season opened on Monday with *Lucia* at the recently renovated San Francisco Grand Opera House on Mission Street. Throughout the performance the full house listened raptly to the singing of Gerster, lauded the rich baritone and artistry of Galassi, but thought Anton, substituting for the ailing Vicini, a failure as Edgardo, one reviewer lamenting that in the first act duet with Gerster the tenor sounded "like a scratchy violin after a Wilhemj solo."[7] As for the audience, a pundit maintained it was the most enthusiastic seen in many years.

In short, the season began with a boom, amazing Californians and reassuring Mapleson, who said he had felt some qualms in undertaking the Western venture; but the impresario's greatest reassurance at the time no doubt related to the next day's sale of

Patti tickets to nonsubscribers, which caused a panic. It got under way long after the announced hour of ten, but what ensued maddened the hundreds who had waited and waited. When Mapleson's business manager Louis Nathal opened the box office window, supposedly there were some four hundred places available to the general public. According to the *Chronicle*, however, after the first five in line purchased twenty-two tickets, Nathal closed the window, declaring the entire house sold out. Stunned, people protested and howled, uncontrollable in their indignation, all clamoring for admission.[8]

Many of the dailies subsequently maintained that tickets had previously been sold to speculators, and that Mapleson himself had employed these speculators, while others said they worked for Nathal. A San Francisco journal the *Wasp* declared the "management called the ticket speculators to their banner, heeled those sharks with tickets, and then turned them loose to prey upon the public."[9] And "prey" was a mild word for what they did. What some demanded was a 400 percent advance on the regular prices, with a mezzanine box at $100, seats in the dress circle, orchestra, and family circle at $20, $15, $10 respectively.

Later, hearing rumors Nathal and he were involved in the swindle, Mapleson vehemently denied the allegations, by now mushrooming into character attacks. As for Nathal, he would discharge the business manager if he found him guilty of wrongdoing. Rumors nonetheless persisted.

Whether Mapleson was privy to the bilking of the public is now impossible to say. Contemporary San Francisco newspapers unanimously accused him of such involvement, and in his memoirs Mapleson, desiring to clear himself, stated that at a later sale of tickets he was responsible for the detaining of some speculators. What he did not reveal, however, is the date of this action: March 20, the halfway mark of the season.

During the day of the diva's first performance in San Francisco, on March 13, the entire city seemed to suffer from opera madness resulting from that pernicious Patti fever, the symptoms of which were an endless chant: "Patti, Patti, Patti, Patti! The word rang all day long, all up and down the streets, and within the houses. . . ."[10] The diva disease had unleashed mass hysteria.

As the hours passed, hundreds upon hundreds of people flooded the area of the opera house so that by seven o'clock it was virtually impossible to pass through. A little after the hour the first carriage arrived, and the crowd in a festive mood warmly greeted it with cheers. Other affluent topliners followed in rapid succession as did ticketholders on foot, some dodging between carriages, risking their lives, fighting a way to the main entrance. Some ladies maintained that "their feet had never even touched the ground from the time they got out of their carriages. . . ."[11] Struggling to keep open a passageway for the surging mass, police found they could not cope, and reinforcements had to be pressed into service. More and more the scene became chaotic, frightening but fantastically exciting, the atmosphere charged with an all-compelling force, enveloping in its intensity.

Once inside, patrons struggled through the crowded vestibule and into the auditorium, threading a precarious way to their seats. The house's seating capacity was 2,200, but by the time the opera began it was estimated over 4,000 were in attendance. Hundreds were standing and blocking the aisles, in which some were sitting on stools they had surreptitiously brought with them. Standees also included a number of irate individuals, said to be as high as two hundred, who discovered their places already occupied, duplicate tickets having been printed and sold. These blazed in righteous indignation, as did Chief of Police Crowley, who engaged Mapleson in acrimonious dialogue concerning the overcrowding, ending a heated discussion with the announcement he would press charges the following morning for violation of the fire ordinance.

Crowley proved to be a man of his word, and when the case came to court on March 21 after a series of clever delays and more crowded performances, Mapleson's attorney based the defense on the premise that since the impresario was not the manager of the opera house, he personally could not be held responsible for any violation of the fire ordinance. Unconvinced, Judge Webb convicted Mapleson but, apparently an opera enthusiast, fined the impresario less than he might have and as a beau geste collected the settlement in opera tickets.

Meanwhile during the hubbub at the opera house, while Chief of Police Crowley was berating Mapleson something was occurring in the auditorium which the impresario recalled with horror in his memoirs years later: "In the top gallery people were literally on the heads of one another, and on sending up to ascertain the cause, as the numbers were still increasing, the inspector ascertained that boards had been placed from the top of an adjoining house on to the roof of the Opera-house, from which the slates had been taken off; and numbers were dropping one by one through the ceiling on the heads of those who were seated in the gallery." [12] A journalist described the scene this way: "They stood upon stools, they sat upon steps, they hung on to balcony rails by their eyelids. They were five deep in the back of each circle of the auditorium, and fifty deep in the vestibule. They were uncomfortable, hot, cross, nervous, weighted with the importance of the occasion. . . ." [13]

The auditorium by curtain time was a dazzling cornucopia with the hall seeming from pit to dome a mass of colors and jewels, with full dress de rigueur even in the family circle, and with "so many society faces seen on all sides it seemed like one vast salon." [14]

Though some no doubt feasted on these splendors, what magnetized ever was the stage, now hidden by the great curtain. The *Chronicle* recorded the following sequence of events when the curtain rose: "The last notes of the orchestra sounded and then the curtain went up, disclosing the banquet scene set for the first act of *Traviata*. The opera is not a familiar one here and by very many the bright-eyed, trim little figure in light-blue silk and white brocaded petticoat seated at the center table was not recognized as Violetta, the giver of the feast. Some one, however, saw that it was Patti and started to hand-clapping. Then others took it up, rattling it from right to left like a *feu de joie,* and then the applause went off like a platoon of musketry. The figure rose and bowed and as she did so she seemed to sparkle like a thousand prisms shaken in the sunlight. They were Patti's diamonds. They glistened in her hair, blazed about her neck, shone in her ears and flashed from her hands and wrists."[15]

With her eyes flashing like her diamonds, Patti gloried in the overwhelming reception as the cheering mounted, smiling, radiating happiness, acknowledging the wild enthusiasm with many bows, looking from boxes to parquet, dress circle, family circle, gallery, taking it all in with infinite grace and charm. But this tremendous acclaim paled beside the demonstration at the end of the act: "Cheers and cries of bravo went up from all over the house, and ladies, standing up in their places, flung their bouquets on the stage. Again and again and again she was recalled, each time going off the stage laden down with bouquets and set pieces."[16]

The rest of the performance was as memorable. To many Patti eclipsed every other artist, in the opinion of a local journalist her conquests now complete: "In all the history of the world, there is no history like the history of Adelina Patti, who is left, since Thursday night, like Alexander, with no more worlds to conquer. She has come to the uttermost west, by the shores of the sundown sea, and she can go no farther."[17]

The following day's press lavishly praised Patti, virtually every critic's giving her the full diapason. Several also devoted space to her costumes and jewels. Not all praise was unequivocal, however. The *Argonaut* expressed ambivalent feelings, lauding her voice and personality but considering her more a curiosity than a great artist:

What is there to say of Patti's voice that people have not been saying for twenty-five years? And how many went to hear her voice? She has become a spectacle, like Jumbo or any other freak, and the world goes to see rather than to hear.

I doubt if twenty women in the house heard the music in the ballroom scene. *La diva* treated the house to a view of as many of her diamonds as she could carry without being brought in on trestles.[18]

The day after the gala dawned to a state of internecine warfare, with Patti partisans pitted against Gerster zealots. The rivalry created tremendous publicity and havoc at the box office, as was evident that very day, March 14, when the tickets went on sale for Patti's second appearance. There was bedlam—unprecedented demands for admissions, with the police as frantic as the desperate crowd, with property damage to the opera house's entrance and lobby, with all, in the words of the local press, characteristic of a "first-class Kansas cyclone in one of its worst moods." [19]

Newspapers later called the proceeding unsatisfactory. Having earlier promised to superintend it to prevent speculators from obtaining tickets, Mapleson apparently failed to keep his word, for once again many who had waited for hours to secure seats found few available, while soon after scalpers blatantly peddled tickets. It was also noted that Nathal presided at the box office. His continued presence prompted some suspicions of graft. One of the speculators later swore under oath he had paid the business manager sums higher than the ticket prices for the first Patti appearance.

Still, in the midst of charges and countercharges performances went on as scheduled. Also going on as if scheduled was the Patti-Gerster feud, with the morals of each now publicly scrutinized. A local publication, the *Wasp*, led the way in the comparisons, focusing on a social event. The wealthy owners of the *San Francisco Chronicle*, the M. H. de Youngs, had entertained Patti, Nicolini, and others at a soiree in their mansion, where Patti seemingly outdid all the ladies present in the sumptuousness of her dress and gems. Particulars of the evening as well as the names of those attending duly appeared in the press, with the *Chronicle* of course leading in coverage and in vivid, complimentary details. Not all publications applauded the affair, and the *Wasp* was especially stinging in its disapproval: "In the breakneck efforts of Mr. Mike de Young 'to get into Society', San Francisco has . . . been treated to a spectacular extravaganza of a singularly lively sort. This execrable and detested person . . . has the unthinkable effrontery to fancy that by grasping the scant skirts of strolling play-women

he can obtain entrance at doors hermetically sealed against themselves. . . ." [20]

Just as San Francisco's highest social echelon, according to the
Wasp, snubbed Patti's host and hostess, so it turned against the
diva while receiving Gerster with open arms: "The women of good
society in San Francisco honored themselves when they recognized in the one the womanly virtues, and in the other did not
condone the practices of a life at war with the proprieties of American civilization." [21] Then in the second week a societal triumph
evolved from tragedy, cementing Gerster's social standing and
lessening Patti's even more.

After the performance of *Rigoletto,* on March 14, the bass Lu-

"The Operatic Whirlwind in San Francisco," cartoon in
The Wasp. Gerster on the left, Mapleson, Patti.

ciano Lombardelli contracted pneumonia and, late the evening of the seventeenth, died. Various members of the troupe, aware of the widow's lack of funds, contributed sums on her behalf. Mapleson gave $600; Patti and Galassi, $150 each; Nicolini, Arditi, and others, smaller amounts; but of the leading artists Gerster, learning of Patti's gift, contributed the most, $1,000, not only thereby, in Mapleson's ironic words, showing she was the greater artist but completing her social conquest. The press of course listed the sums contributed, much to Patti's chagrin. At the moment Gerster was winning so much approbation, critical and social, that it seemed she was about to assume Patti's mantle, scepter, and crown. The wily Queen, however, determined otherwise, biding her time, secure in a power sustained by countless past victories.

Of the second week's six performances, the greatest glory radiated from Patti, who, emboldened by adverse forces, resolved to overshadow her rival in all operatic respects and to show conclusively that *la Diva* and only *la Diva* carried the scepter. It still was her shapely head, exquisitely poised, that glorified opera's golden round.

Police took no chances when Patti made her second appearance, with forty outside and twenty inside dedicated to keeping order. Fortunately they stabilized the wild forces on this occasion that in many ways duplicated the turbulent Patti first night—enormous crowds, excitement, frenzied enthusiasm.

As Leonora in *Trovatore*, on March 18, the challenged Queen did indeed rally her forces, exerting a tremendous power over the audience and effacing the memories of other artists in this role. She sang effortlessly, running "the gamut of emotion from natural simplicity of affection to dramatic grandeur with the greatest ease,"[22] ever involved in the action on stage. The authenticity of the final act brought the house down; it was "the kind of Italian opera which sets the excitable natures of the South and the artistic circles of Europe generally wild."[23] Afterward some Gersterites may have questioned the wisdom of their allegiance. The *Chronicle* the following day emphatically decided its: "Mme. Patti can feel secure of her place for a long time yet if Gerster is the second prima donna of the age, great as that artiste is." [24] Nicolini as Manrico drew good reviews, in the opinion of some dividing the honors of the evening and being infinitely better than other tenors in the company. Galassi as Di Luna, Tiozzo as Azucena, and Cherubini as Ferrando had marked success.

It was in her third appearance, however, as Annetta in *Crispino e la Comare* on March 22, that Patti achieved the ultimate triumph. From the beginning she enthralled the crowded house. Throwing herself into the part with complete abandon, she so scintillated and enchanted that the audience responded fantastically to everything provided. Thunderous applause, encores, recalls, cries of *"Viva la Diva,"* bouquets thrown from all parts of the house celebrated the glory of Patti. Then when she interpolated Arditi's "Il Bacio" into the proceedings, the house went wild: "The singing of it by Patti simply carried everybody away. Brilliant is a mild description. It went through light and shade, through forte and pianissimo, like a superb musical whirlwind, clear and telling in every note, and it was impossible for Mme. Patti to resist the wild demand for its repetition . . . Patti simply took San Francisco by storm last night as she has taken other places." [25]

Yes, the Queen still reigned in solitary splendor, the force majeure, her scepter, crown, and regal mantle firmly in place.

Since enthusiasm for opera remained unabated, Mapleson added an extra week. A few apparently regretted this extension. The *Argonaut* maintained that "even the most steadfast pillars of the church have swayed somewhat from perpendicular during this season of opera and Lent. What is positive delight to some has become actual dissipation in others; and pastors are already beginning to sermonize about it to their wayward flocks," [26] giving the company invaluable publicity.

To foil speculators and to avoid censure regarding ticket sales, Mapleson put up to auction, on March 21, every place in the house for the four evening performances and matinee. Only series tickets were auctioned, with a bidder allowed to take up to ten tickets. For each place the purchaser had to pay a premium as well as the regular box office price. When, for example, M. H. de Young successfuly bid on a proscenium box, he paid a $70 premium and the regular price of $210. The sale began after twelve noon in the presence of approximately one thousand people and went on for hours. Diagrams of the seating plan of the house were placed before the curtain on the stage. With auctioneer Eldridge presiding, in time virtually every place was sold.

The first highlight of the extra week occurred on the second night, March 25, when Patti captivated in the title role of *Linda di Chamounix*, all her notes in descending scales "like a rain of pearls on a many-runged silver ladder." [27] What no doubt remained longest in memory, however, was her interpolation of an air that had become her signature: "Home, Sweet Home," her interpretation bringing "tears to most eyes in an irresistible way." [28]

That Patti sang at all this particular evening must have reassured Mapleson as to her stamina and dedication. Only a few hours before San Francisco had had an experience that could have been devastating. Two minor earthquakes shook the city, a phenomenon immediately ascribed by the diva to the malign influence of a human element—Gerster! [29]

Patti's concert at Mechanics' Pavilion on Thursday, March 27, with prices ranging from $1 to $3, was also of more than usual interest, attracting an audience of approximately nine thousand. The evening provided much vocal pleasure, though not all were fortunate in seeing the diva clearly. In the gallery a number resorted to the use of telescopes. Assisted by other artists in the company, Patti favored the crowd with four numbers, only one of these from the operatic repertoire: "Bel raggio" from Rossini's *Semiramide*.

The season drew to its close with Gerster's last appearance scheduled for the final evening performance and Patti's for the following day's matinee. Both presentations promised the extraordinary.

Gerster's farewell as Adina in *L'Elisir d'Amore*, on March 28, drew a responsive house and wrung only superlatives from the critics. *The Daily Alta California* said: "The scene at the fall of the curtain . . . was an ovation in the fullest sense of the word.

The applause was deafening. Cheers rent the air, hats were waving, and handkerchiefs were fluttering in the air, while the favorite artist . . . bowed and bowed her acknowledgements. Such a leave-taking of such an artist is a credit to both the public and the artist."[30] Such a farewell posed an arresting question. Would tomorrow's prove anticlimatic?

Patti's Annetta in *Crispino e la Comare*, on March 29, ended the season in a cyclonic demonstration without parallel in the city's history. Hours before the matinee people formed long lines for standing room and waited for a seemingly interminable time. Though hundreds were later turned away, the police permitted more in the house than before, with many standing in the auditorium and blocking the aisles and many more overflowing into the vestibule and the wings backstage.

From the beginning to the end of the performance Patti enthralled a house that followed her every effort in rapturous attention, lavishing upon her tumultuous applause, cheers, flowers thrown from all parts of the auditorium. Patti had never impressed during the season so much as on this occasion.

In the last act, the opera was interrupted to present her tokens of admiration, the first being a large floral offering of a lyre of camellias and azaleas supported by a column with four wings, all on a floral pedestal. Each wing symbolized in flowers a role she had sung during the season: Annetta in yellow pansies, Violetta in violets, Leonora in Japanese quince blossoms, Linda in cinerarias. On this design rested an autograph album made of highly polished California woods and Russian leather. In it many of the diva's friends and admirers had inscribed their names. Crowning those tokens, however, was a most appropriate gift: a loving cup in gold and silver with the words and music of "Auld Lang Syne" engraved on the front.

Between the end of the opera and the departure hour the company bustled about in preparation for the return to the East. One of the busiest was the impresario himself, settling the payment of bills at the Palace Hotel, where a reporter engaged him in dialogue.

MAPLESON: "Never saw such an extraordinary town in all my life. . . . Here I've been arrested seven times since 4 o'clock this afternoon."

REPORTER: "What for?"

MAPLESON: "What for? Well, I don't know myself. My head is all in a whirl. . . . Here's a sample—for advertising in the *Evening Post*, $412. Now, I never authorized that; don't know anything about it, but here I'm hauled up by the Sheriff and have to enter protest against these things and put the matter in the hands of my attorney. Here's another—for 80 gallons of eau de Cologne, $200. What in the world does that mean? Most extraordinary thing I ever heard of. Then here's a bill for advertising in *Le Petit Journal*. Never authorized the advertisement and, in fact, never heard of the paper before."

REPORTER: "What were your receipts for the season, Colonel?"

MAPLESON: "Receipts, receipts. . . . Were there any receipts? Oh, yes. Well, I can't give you the figures now."[31]

If so disposed, Mapleson might have informed the reporter that receipts had totaled approximately $200,000, and of this sum his profit, it was said, was between $55,000 and $65,000.[32]

Later that evening on a train of nine cars, the company left behind a city that, though it keenly felt its loss on the morrow, nonetheless rejoiced in a wealth of memories the season had abundantly provided.

The eagerly anticipated Patti concert at the Mormon Tabernacle in Salt Lake City took place on Tuesday, April 1, with the same program as the one given at the Mechanics' Pavilion in San Francisco. According to the *Deseret Evening News,* approximately six or seven thousand people attended, enthusiastically applauding all provided by La Patti, who, sumptuously gowned, glittered in diamonds from head to foot. The church received one-sixth of the proceeds, with seats at $1.50 and $2.00.[33] John Taylor, President, no doubt contributed sufficiently with admissions for his five wives and seven children.

Three evenings later at Omaha Mapleson brought forward *Lucia* with Gerster. Though expressing admiration for the soprano and some of her vis-à-vis, a local music critic did not extend compliments to all, with the ladies in the chorus especially arousing his spleen, he considering them "undoubtedly the homeliest and most awkward lot of femininity that ever trod the boards at the Boyd."[34]

From Omaha the impresario ordered a return to home base, which surely awaited with accolades. Heads held high, members of the company entrained for New York, returning as conquerors from the clash of arms.

CHAPTER 6

Victories and
Vicissitudes

〜

*T*HE COMPANY arrived in New York the evening of Monday, April 7, exhilarated by the Western tour, with Mapleson entering the city a hero. To reporters bombarding questions, the impresario maintained he looked forward to the annual spring presentations at the Academy, where the opening promised to be a gala occasion with the diva in an opera not given during the fall-winter New York season. At that time she would sing "Home, Sweet Home," the rendering of which Mapleson predicted would make those who had roamed to the other house cry like babies, thankful for once again finding their way home.

Also assailed with queries, Patti said the Golden Gate had highlighted the entire tour. Jubilant over the final performance, she recalled her emotions: "Indeed I cried like a child, but soon recovered sufficiently to sing 'Home, Sweet Home,' to which the audience responded with such cheers as I have never heard. Five carriages were inadequate to carry the floral offerings. . . .' "[1] Inquiries of a more personal nature were then fired at her. Had Governor Crittenden really kissed her? Did not Nicolini challenge the Governor to a duel for taking such a liberty? Was the rumor true she intended to return to the Marquis de Caux? The question prompting the longest response concerned the reported troubles with Gerster. Though at first seeming hesitant, Patti soon warmed to the topic, apparently believing this the time to wreak her wrath.

Such press coverage was no doubt valuable publicity for the fortnight's coming attractions, which promised to be eventful.

In the first week Mapleson presented four operas, with Patti and Gerster each starring in two. The season opened on April 14 with Patti in *Linda di Chamounix,* her appearance as usual accompanied by a crush outside, crowds in the corridors, society out in full force, a house filled. The *Herald* noted that at her entrance Patti's face "lighted with a $5,000 look of delight at being home again"[2] and that throughout the evening rapturous applause echoed. It was also noted that a number of the Metropolitan seceders had returned to the Academy fold. The week's pièce de résistance occurred on April 18, when the impresario brought forward *Roméo et Juliette* with Patti and Nicolini as the star-crossed lovers, a performance creating more than usual interest. New York had not heard the opera in a number of years, Abbey had promised to produce it at the Metropolitan but had failed to do so, and the casting of the principal parts seemed deliciously ideal.

During Mapleson's second and final week opera seemed to generate a climactic excitement in New York, with two debuts at the Academy, Abbey's benefit at the Metropolitan, the seasonal farewells of Patti and Gerster, and a presentation of *Semiramide,* considered the outstanding occasion of the entire 1883–1884 musical season.

The week began with *La Favorita,* presented on April 21 and introducing New York to two artists about whom there had been much publicity at the time Mapleson secured them: Anton and Bianchi-Fiorio. Mapleson had then called the tenor a phenomenon. His said-to-be fantastic top notes prompted the impresario, who had not yet heard him, to comment, "Why, bless you, they've been selling tuning-forks in Havana, so that when the people went to hear him in *Il Trovatore* they could strike the forks on the arms of their orchestra chairs, hold them to their ears, and test the pitch of the note he was singing."[3] Anton's appearances on tour had not merited such celebrity, and at his New York debut he achieved only a moderate success. Bianchi-Fiorio met a similar critical fate. All in all, it was not a red-letter night at the Academy.

That distinction this evening belonged to the Metropolitan, where virtually the entire company as well as the great English thespians Henry Irving and Ellen Terry contributed their talents to Abbey's benefit, which drew an immense house. It also revealed Sembrich in a new light. At the gala she not only sang but also performed superbly as a violin soloist in the adagio and finale from De Beriot's Violin Concerto No. 7, and thereafter played brilliantly a Chopin mazurka at the piano. All, however, were at their best on this occasion, which subsequently became a part of New York operatic legend.

Though the Metropolitan held a number of distinguished individuals at the benefit, few perhaps received the attention bestowed upon a lady in a box near the stage. The occupant and cynosure of many eyes was Patti, though no doubt there were those preferring to look the other way, reminded some hours earlier of the notoriety over the diva's marital affairs.

The morning of the benefit the New York *World* published an interview the Marquis de Caux had granted to a French reporter in Paris. In the article he denied any possibility of a reconciliation, rumors to the contrary, stating that for the past seven years his wife had addressed him neither directly nor indirectly and that the French courts had found her the guilty party in the separation granted him.[4] The article and Patti's presence at the benefit may thus have disturbed some pillars of Victorian society; but the subject herself gave no signs of any moral trepidation, declining to say anything to the press about the marquis' interview.

During the performance she enthusiastically applauded the proceedings and after one of Nilsson's arias threw a bouquet at her sister-artist's feet. Later, accompanied by Mapleson's son Charles, she went backstage to pay her compliments to the soprano, a courtesy subsequently eliciting some observations from young Mapleson, who had a special reason for bringing the two artists face to face.

As the victor in the opera war, his father intended his triumph to be complete. To make it so, he intended to secure his rival's greatest asset: Christine Nilsson! Mapleson planned to offer her a contract for the coming season, provided that Patti and she could co-exist in the same company. Mapleson was not renewing Gerster's contract, her rivalry with Patti having become intolerable, and he did not purpose to be embroiled in another similar hazardous undertaking. Bringing Patti and Nilsson together at the benefit was thus a way of determining possible future moves. Of the meeting Charles said: "They both spoke of singing together in the same company, and both seemed to be pleased at the notion that they might do this in the future."[5] Such phatic communion apparently reassured the impresario.

Of the four final performances at the Academy, one outshone, in the opinion of many, all the other operatic presentations of the 1883–1884 New York season. Heading the cast of course was Patti, and assisting in the superlative evening was none other than one of the Metropolitan's greatest artists: Sofia Scalchi, her association with the rival house having by now ended. The opera which these two stars glorified was *Semiramide;* the date, April 25. The presence of two such names in the same cast Mapleson knew would lure thousands to the Academy while providing a fitting climax to the closing days of an epoch season.

Earlier in the day, however, rumors spread that Patti did not wish to make her farewell in *Semiramide,* unhappy about dividing the honors with Scalchi. Patti later confided she would have preferred *Traviata,* but after listening to Mapleson's plea, she acquiesced. Another rumor concerned Scalchi, who it was said might not appear, terrified that Abbey might have placed some of his minions in the audience to heckle her. Since she had failed to fulfill her final engagement at the Metropolitan, he was presently suing her for damages. Abbey had wanted her to appear in *Le Prophète* at the April 12 matinee; but having been informed of this fact only a few hours before the performance and having by then devoured an enormous breakfast, wrecking control of the diaphragm, Scalchi refused to assume the role of Fidès, one of the most demanding parts in her repertoire. Abbey ultimately canceled the performance and went to court, suing her for the money he lost by the cancellation. Scalchi supposedly feared that her appearance at the Academy gave him an opportunity to seek public vengeance on her. A further rumor related to Mapleson, said to be in such financial difficulties with the Academy stockholders that officers of the law intended to stop the performance. In short, New York this day blazed with crossfires of assertions and counterassertions.

The evening itself crystalized as one of those splendid theatrical experiences at which all elements coalesce to create an unforgettable musical occasion. The diva sang gloriously, while nothing that Scalchi had done at the Metropolitan equaled her magnificent interpretation of Arsace, ravishing to the ears. The house responded with the wildest enthusiasm. In the many recalls Christine Nilsson from a box threw flowers at the diva's feet, reciprocating Patti's courtesy at the Metropolitan. Then at the end of the performance enthusiasm passed all bounds, the artists again and again appearing before the footlights to take innumerable curtain calls. In the midst of this the audience did not forget Mapleson, calling his name until he came on stage with Patti and Scalchi at his side to say a few words.

Afterwards, as Mapleson began walking off stage, from the wings advanced Judge Shea with some other gentlemen who intended to memorialize the evening. Patti and Scalchi seized Mapleson's hands, drawing him to center stage. After addressing the impresario in a speech laced with accolades, the Judge handed him a jewel case containing a gold watch and chain, a locket, diamond shirt studs, and a pair of diamond cufflinks.[6]

Expressing thanks, Mapleson left the stage but with an unexpected development, which he related in his memoirs: "I . . . with difficulty left the stage amidst ringing cheers and waving of pocket-handkerchiefs: I say with difficulty, because at that critical moment, as I was picking up a bouquet, the buckle of my pantaloons gave way; and as my tailor had persuaded me, out of compliment to him, to discard the use of braces, it was only with great difficulty that I could manage to shuffle off the stage, entrusting meanwhile some of the jewellery to Patti and some to Scalchi."[7]

Hours afterward Mapleson brought the season to its triumphant close at the matinee of *Faust* with Gerster. Though he should have rejoiced in this and in future possibilities, several recent happenings in New York's opera world precluded an exuberance of enthusiasm.

According to documents in the archives of the Museum of the City of New York, Herman R. Le Roy, Secretary of the Academy Board of Directors, wrote Mapleson a letter dated April 14, 1884, which stated that the impresario owed the Bank of the Metropolis $24,101.27 with interest from January 24, 1884, and August Belmont & Company, which held the $30,000 Patti contract guarantee, $10,852.12 with interest from December 31, 1883. Mapleson had drawn on these sums in his struggle against the Metropolitan. After receiving the letter, he replied the same day, writing, "Yours received. Do you intend it as a joke?" Le Roy apparently had written the letter at the behest of several of those who had guaranteed the Patti contract and the fund raised after the opening night, and who now insisted that the impresario must pay back his debts. After all, he had made, so the story went and the press reported, large sums on the tour. Mapleson, however, did not respond, maintaining he had never been legally bound to repay these sums. The affair climaxed at Patti's farewell, when sheriffs appeared at the Academy for the purpose of attaching the receipts in the suit of the Bank of the Metropolis. Mapleson later said several Academy directors had directed the bank to take this action.

The public first heard of the development on April 27, when in an interview one of the Academy directors explained the reasons for the notices served on Mapleson: "Those who stand behind the fund and who placed their names to the paper which secures the bank were personal friends of the Colonel and some of them are men who never go to the opera. They, of course, will make the account good, but . . . the gentlemen mentioned thought it well to try and squeeze some of the money out of the Colonel. Hence the papers and notices served upon him. He will, in all probability, pay no attention to them, and the guarantee fund will be made up by the guarantors." [8]

Then on that day the public heard of another startling development: a possible merger of Academy and Metropolitan interests. Information now surfaced that at the Academy J. Coleman Drayton had spearheaded the movement, collecting proxies for an amalgamation of the two houses. Apparently the union was most desired by the Astor vote and other Academy stockholders with an interest in the new house; but those pressing for it actually found little support, suffering a resounding defeat at the annual stockholders meeting, held at the Academy on Monday, April 28, when out of 200 votes Drayton mustered only 38 in favor of the amalgamation.

This meeting held other surprises. August Belmont announced his decision to resign as President, maintaining that business interests precluded him from remaining in his present position at the Academy. The announcement was received with regret, and in his place the stockholders subsequently elected Augustus L. Brown. Thirteen directors were also elected. Then, as if the evening had not already held enough excitement, Mapleson, though in absentia, now contributed his bit to the proceedings when in a letter read by Belmont he requested for next season a guarantee fund of $50,000, and $30,000 to $40,000 for new scenery and repairs at the Academy. The request fell, to say the least, somewhat flat. Since Mapleson had done nothing to cancel his present debts, how dare he ask for additional funds?

For a time nothing was done to assist the impresario. With the presumed tour profits he alone, so some ever insisted, should repay the guarantee fund. If the profits did not exist, there remained scenery, costumes, and other properties that would have to be sold. Only after he exhausted his property should the guarantors fulfill their obligations.

On April 30 sheriffs at the behest of the Bank of the Metropolis seized all the impresario's scenery, costumes, and other assets at the Academy, moving them to the adjacent Nilsson Hall in preparation for a public sale. Mapleson, whose contract extended for one more year, thereupon accused the Academy directors of Machiavellian designs as well as moral turpitude: "I have been shamefully treated, but I am going to let matters take their own course. . . . These directors think they can have opera without paying for it." [9]

Though some directors may have thought this way, the majority publicly stated their willingness to help Mapleson and to relieve his property from attachment. While no doubt grateful for such verbal support, Mapleson made it clear he needed concrete action. He responded to a communication from one of the directors: "I have received a letter from Mr. Robert L. Cutting telling me not to mind what the newspapers say, that the directors are all gentlemen and will do what is right. It reminds me of the man that was being pelted with rotten eggs and his attorney came to him and said, 'Don't mind them, they can't do it.' Just then another egg hit him in the eye and he said, 'But they are doing it.' 'But they can't do it legally,' said the attorney, and so Mr. Cutting comes and soothes me with gentle words, but they have done it all the same. . . ." [10] Mapleson later wrote a letter to Augustus L. Brown, requesting a meeting with the Academy Executive Committee in the hope of attaining a quick settlement. The impresario's request was granted, and the committee met on Saturday, May 3.

Apparently Mapleson now believed the matter would soon be settled to his satisfaction, and after the special meeting entrained to Long Branch on the Jersey shore for a much-needed respite. It is to be hoped he found just that, for upon his return to New York on Monday, May 5, he heard the directors had not yet resolved the affair but were in fact entertaining another idea for settlement. Informed of the plan, Mapleson determined to have no part in it:

Well, I got back from Long Branch this morning with two crabs, which I caught myself. I tell you I wanted all the ozone I had sniffed in when I got to New-York and found the directors were still to be fought single-handed. I understand that their talk of final settlement amounts to just this: they want to buy up the judgment against me. But that is not my way of doing business. I should be working for five or ten years like one of those poor beggars at Sing Sing with a shotted chain tied round my waist. Fancy running an opera in opposition to the new house, with a debt of $35,000 hanging over my head like the sword of Damocles. I am not going to do anything of the sort. I shall remain passive like one of those old turtles you see outside a fishmonger's shop till they bring me the judgment with a pen drawn through it. . . .[11]

Fortunately Mapleson did not have to give up opera in New York, for in several days' time the fuss ended when all the guarantors paid their portions. Mapleson beamed with pleasure: "Righteousness and peace have kissed each other. . . . I am to go with a blank check in my pocket from the directors. Of course I shan't fill it up. It will be like the sovereign the Vicar of Wakefield gave his daughter—something to look at but not to spend. But think of the confidence it will inspire. . . . There will be no talk of guarantees when I flutter that in the artists' faces." [12]

Mapleson brought about this happy resolution after having induced the Bank of the Metropolis to contact each of the guarantors. In doing this, he was following the advice of one of the Academy directors. Various factors contributed to this settlement, some not of an eleemosynary nature.

During the entire crisis Mapleson spoke volumes: the result, publicity that made the guarantors look like pikers and that aroused a great deal of public sympathy. The Metropolitan also entered the picture when one from that house sniffed: "We have recognized the fact that if we want good opera we must pay for it, and in the face of opposition, pay for it handsomely, and they ought to become aware of the same thing." [13] Such comments from the enemy were embarrassing to the stockholders.

What mattered most was their determination to remain at the Academy. For that reason they agreed to retain Mapleson, who best served their interests. Also important were rumors as to the possibility that he would assume the directorship of the Metropolitan; but even with the squabble at its height, Mapleson denied there had been any such maneuvers. The rumors nonetheless persisted; and some time later it was publicly acknowledged the rival house had indeed made overtures to Mapleson. To secure him for the Metropolitan would be a devastating coup. Again it was in the stockholders' interest to settle difficulties; but in the immediate days that followed, they did little to reassure Mapleson as to his future at the Academy. Perhaps some were still smarting from the financial assessment just redeemed, or from a suspicion they had been outsmarted, the ostensible profits from San Francisco still fresh in memory. At any rate, the stockholders did not respond to Mapleson's persistent pleas for $30,000 to secure Patti's contract.

Mapleson meanwhile prolonged his stay in the hope of a subsidy for the coming campaign. The blank check earlier promised had not materialized. Losing patience, the impresario announced, on May 16, his imminent departure, already having deferred his return to Europe on several occasions. The following day he embarked for the continent, roseate about the future but concerned that the recent financial difficulties would undoubtedly escalate the artists' guarantees, and that under these circumstances he might have problems securing the best.

While a multitude gaped, friends surrounded him, extending best wishes and presenting flowers, among which one display formed into a design of his initials and the word "Invincible." Adjusting a monocle, Mapleson philosophized: "I have become reconciled to the non-appearance of the banquet at Delmonico's . . . and feasted with a contented mind on the two crabs I caught at Long Branch, but I certainly thought the strains of 'See the Conquering Hero' would greet me as I came on board. However, I am used to the cold ingratitude of the world in general and Academy directors in particular. Thank God, I've got the public at my back. I have a whole portmanteau full of letters expressing sympathy with me which I received from total strangers." [14]

Saying *au revoir*, Mapleson reiterated his determination to return with or without a guarantee. Then waving to all with his silky top hat, he finished dramatically: "If any one says I'm not coming back, don't believe a word of it. Mapleson may die, but he never surrenders. God bless you!" [15]

To the last moment the impresario remained good copy.

CHAPTER 7

A Long, Hot Summer

∽

*F*OR CONSIDERABLE time after Mapleson's departure directors of the older house continued to procrastinate in furnishing the impresario with a guarantee, seemingly apathetic to the Academy's immediate operatic future, while the new house, recovering from the trauma of defeat, cast about for a manager to fill Abbey's place. Here, too, the directors seemed to act neither with dispatch nor with resolution.

At various times it was said the Metropolitan directors were again approaching Mapleson, while also considering Maurice Grau, Italo Campanini, the variety-house entrepreneur Tony Pastor, and Mapleson's son Charles; but nothing definite transpired until the end of June, when on the twenty-seventh Edmund Stanton, the Metropolitan's Secretary of the Board of Directors, announced that Ernest Gye, currently presenting opera at London's Covent Garden, had been secured and that the directors had agreed to subsidize him $1,700 for each of the 52 performances in a series of thirteen weeks, the total amount of the subsidy being $88,400.

Receiving word of Gye's appointment and the proposed subsidy, Mapleson must have bitterly contemplated the reluctance of his own directors to assist him with such largesse. For a while he averred that next season he would present only concerts at the Academy, not opera, a policy proposed to arouse indignation in

New York. At the same time he informed his patrons that if they would guarantee $50,000, he would secure both Patti and Nilsson. Interviewed in London on July 18, he said they had failed to act: "But although hourly expecting an answer, the directors are as slow as an Arctic whaler. Yes, I am really afraid they will again spoil their staunch ship for the sake of a pen 'orth of tar. I am sorry my directors (not to make a pun) are so tardy. If they should lose Nilsson and this glorious opportunity of sinking the other line-of-battle ship, they will duplicate that other blunder of allowing a sheriff to come into the Academy without a spark of reason and so to expose their weakness—at a time, too, when practically they had won last Winter's battle. However, if Gye gets Nilsson there will be the usual rows. . . ."[1] Despite all entreaties the Academy directors failed to respond, a circumstance Mapleson said aided the enemy.

The Metropolitan, however, soon suffered a severe setback when on July 23 its directors received word that Gye was not signing the contract, unable to meet the fiscal demands of the singers he had wished to engage and already financially embarrassed as the result of a disastrous season at Covent Garden.

Stunned, the Metropolitan directors began negotiations all over again, but it was not until almost mid-August that their search ended: Dr. Leopold Damrosch, a prominent New York musical figure, who proposed a season of German opera.[2] Since his emigration to the United States from Germany in 1871, this musician, in his homeland a founder of the Breslau Orchestral Society, had conducted the Männergesangverein Arion in New York, where in 1874 he also founded the Oratorio Society and four years later the Symphony Society, for both of which he served as conductor, as he did for the Philharmonic Society. The Metropolitan Opera directory appointed Damrosch musical director at a salary of $10,000, and in this capacity on August 13 he left for Europe to recruit a company.

In adopting German opera, the directors were meeting a musical need long felt by various New York music critics. Several days after the stockholders founded the Metropolitan, on April 15, 1880, *Musical Review* commented that the New York public wanted German opera, which "would be heartily supported by a class of people which is already large and whose number is constantly increasing."[3] In 1882 *Music and Drama* also promoted such a repertoire: "German opera is the opera of to-day. It must be given here where there is such an enormous German population who will support, by their presence and their purse, any adequate representation of the great works of the German masters."[4] In November 1883 the *Tribune* critic maintained that "the patrons of the opera in New-York are ripe for something better and nobler than the sweetmeats of the hurdy-gurdy repertory," and that "a winning card to play in the game now going on between the rival managers would be a list, not necessarily large, of the best works of the German and French schools."[5]

Advocating the change and agreeing with such comments, Damrosch, according to his son Walter, had dreamed of sweeping "away forever the artificial and shallow operas of the old Italian school with which Mapleson . . . and others had until then principally fed our public."[6] Whether he would realize this dream was problematic, for Mapleson's competition remained formidable.

In Europe, Mapleson stated that German opera at the Metropolitan posed no threat to him. At the moment his greatest challenge was not the enemy without but the enemy within—namely, recalcitrant Academy board members, seemingly unwilling to levy an assessment on the stockholders to ensure the Patti contract.

Damrosch in Europe meanwhile was so successful in gathering together a company of German artists that by mid-September he provided the Metropolitan directors with the names of leading singers he had secured, while also informing them the season would open on November 17 and continue for at least thirteen weeks. Among the principals were Auguste Kraus, Anton Schott, Marianne Brandt, and, above all, Amalia Materna, one of Wagner's favorite sopranos. Having the enemy (or was it Patti?) in mind, Damrosch claimed his singers were not only outstanding artists but also pillars of propriety: "In selecting my company I was, of course, governed primarily by artistic merit, but I also kept in view social requirements and picked out ladies and gentlemen."[7] Damrosch said he intended to use the services of players from his own Symphony Society and as choristers singers from his Oratorio Society.

Finally reacting to Damrosch's challenge and the renewed activities uptown, Academy stockholders met to decide whether to grant Mapleson's request for a $30,000 guarantee. Of the 200 shares, 117 were represented. The vote itself revealed 86 favored the assessment, which for forty nights in the fall and spring seasons amounted to $4 per share for seats in the proscenium boxes; $3 in the other boxes; and $2 elsewhere. In this way the stockholders provided the $30,000 the impresario had requested, though they did so with a stipulation: "The conditions are that either Mme. Patti or Mme. Nilsson shall appear on each of these nights, and that Col. Mapleson shall only be allowed the assessment for representations in which Mme. Patti or Mme. Nilsson shall take part. The assessment is to be paid to the Executive Committee, and at the close of each week that body will hand over to Col. Mapleson the amount due him for the performances given by Mmes. Patti and Nilsson."[8]

On October 20 New York received Mapleson's prospectus, which contained some startling surprises. Though listing such known artists as Patti, Dotti, Scalchi, Nicolini, Vicini, Caracciolo, Cherubini, and Arditi, it also included other persons unknown to New York, a quantity that for some may not have been reassuring, while the omission of one great name created a furor. Nilsson was not included! Mapleson later explained that she had decided to remain in Europe for a prolonged rest; but the greatest shock no doubt was the announcement that in the coming season Patti was making her farewell appearances in the United States.

A letter from Patti dated September 25, 1884, now in the Pierpont Morgan Library, seems to relate to these startling developments concerning Nilsson and the diva. In this letter, the handwriting and tone of which suggest a highly agitated emotional state,

Patti says she wishes she had Mapleson in her presence, apparently furious that he, "this fool of a worm,"[9] had dared (twice underlining the verb) to dictate to her what to do or say. Several lines later she states she had heard the impresario planned to engage Nilsson for the new American season. Such, in her opinion, would be a misfortune. The announcement of Nilsson's nonengagement and Patti's American farewell followed approximately a month later.

Arriving in New York on October 25, Mapleson's son Charles with his wife, the dancer Malvina Cavalazzi, prepared the way for his father, unfurling seasonal plans, thereby whetting appetites for the promised musical feast. He praised the new singers: the dramatic soprano Ida Riccetti, the contralto Emma Steinbach, the baritones Innocente de Anna and Antonio de Vaschetti, the tenor Franco Cardinali, "second to none of the tenors of the Old World,"[10] and especially the young American soprano Emma Nevada, "the next best singer in the world after Patti."[11] He also mentioned the novelties planned for the season, citing particularly the production of *Lakmé:* "The Colonel and Arditi . . . were dining with Delibes, the author of *Lakmé,* on the day when I sailed, getting final instructions from him in regard to the first production of his opera in this country."[12] Asked whether there was any truth to the rumor Patti had deserted Mapleson, Charles denied it. The diva's appearances should be to houses with standing room only, as this season, the younger Mapleson asserted, absolutely was her final one in the United States. It also was a special time in her life, as it marked the twenty-fifth anniversary of her operatic debut at the Academy in 1859. The Silver Jubilee warranted a gala.

As for the Metropolitan, Charles Mapleson said the impresario feared nothing: "I hear that my father has been accused of speaking disparagingly of this enterprise. Of course I don't know what he has said since I sailed, but I know that up to that time he was rejoiced to know that German opera was to be given at the new house. I can't suppose that since then he has said anything disparaging of the new enterprise, because it is for his interest to see

German rather than Italian opera at the new house, and far from discouraging it, it is his business to encourage it." [13]

Charles Mapleson had masterfully set the stage for forthcoming events. Soon the leading artists would take their places, each a spark in a conflagration meant to destroy the enemy.

Adelina Patti—Mapleson's Greatest Star.
COURTESY HARVARD THEATRE COLLECTION, HARVARD COLLEGE.

Patti as Marguerite in Faust.
COURTESY ROBERT TUGGLE COLLECTION.

Patti as Harriet in Marta.
BY PERMISSION THEATRE COLLECTION,
MUSEUM OF THE CITY OF NEW YORK.

Patti as Juliette.
BY PERMISSION THEATRE COLLECTION,
MUSEUM OF THE CITY OF NEW YORK.

Ernest Nicolini as Roméo (?).
COURTESY ROBERT TUGGLE COLLECTION

Etelka Gerster as Amina in Sonnambula.
COURTESY ROBERT TUGGLE COLLECTION.

Antonio Galassi as Ashton(?) in Lucia.

Lillian Nordica as Marguerite in Faust.

BY PERMISSION THEATRE COLLECTION,
MUSEUM OF THE CITY OF NEW YORK.

Enrico Cherubini as Assur (?) in Semiramide.

Sofia Scalchi as Frederic (?) in Mignon.
BY PERMISSION THEATRE COLLECTION,
MUSEUM OF THE CITY OF NEW YORK.

Emma Nevada as Lakmé (?).
COURTESY ROBERT TUGGLE COLLECTION.

Giuseppe del Puente as Nevers (?) in Les Huguenots.

COURTESY ROBERT TUGGLE COLLECTION.

Minnie Hauk as Carmen.
COURTESY ROBERT TUGGLE COLLECTION.

Luigi Ravelli as Edgardo (?) *in* Lucia.
COURTESY ROBERT TUGGLE COLLECTION.

CHAPTER 8

A New Campaign

~

ARLY SUNDAY morning, November 2, 1884, the *Blackbird*, with a huge welcome sign and a band playing festive music, steamed down New York bay to hail Mapleson and virtually the entire company on board the steamship *City of Berlin*, the two artists missing being Patti and Nevada, scheduled to arrive later.

As newsworthy as ever, Mapleson immediately expressed delight in returning to the United States, eager for the new campaign. At his side attracting considerable attention were two bawcocks, sergeants of the British army in austere uniforms decorated with a number of gold medals on each officer's chest. Mapleson explained the decorations: "Won at Tel-el-Kabir. In India, and in China in any number of famous battles for personal bravery, by Jove, and they don't give medals for nothing in those countries." [1] He maintained the officers had been removed from active duty to assist him in his operatic battles.

Contemplating the coming struggles and recalling some recent ones, Mapleson spoke with amazing candor, attributing many difficulties to the Academy directors, chiding them for begrudging the financial support opera required.

Mapleson nonetheless intended to present Italian opera with what he called an extraordinary company and, if the repertoire did not include sufficient novelties, the quality of his artists would more than make up any deficiency. He had not rested in his efforts to secure the best. Italian opera remained supreme, he told a reporter from the *Sun* who had questioned whether the impresario thought it waning in popularity, German opera perhaps now to the public taste: "Italian opera will never die. They are a parcel of idiots who insist that the music of the future is to take its place. In this modern music, as they call it, they can introduce discordant rumpuses which make even a dumb animal whine and curl about, and yet everything may be in accordance with the laws of music. Why, once I heard a tenor in German opera sing half a note flat and he made a horrible discord, but all the people near me clapped their hands and said to each other that there were always discords in the best music. Now, what is the effect of pure Italian opera? It just makes everybody happy." [2]

By eleven A.M. the impresario secured his usual lodgings at the New York Hotel, greeted there various members of the establishment, then with a rose in his buttonhole strode to the Academy, where for a number of hours he worked on strategies.

What perhaps provided the day's greatest excitement evolved from the arrival of a telegram stating that the steamship *Oregon*, on which Patti and Nicolini were passengers, had been sighted off Long Island. Mapleson immediately made arrangements for a military band to greet the diva, but hours passed without further word. The musicians were meanwhile quaffing such quantities of williewaughts that by the time Mapleson and his party boarded the welcoming craft *Blackbird* the players had seemingly forgotten their duty to entertain with a little light music.

The musicians were not the only disappointment. About to board the *Oregon*, Mapleson, eager to escort Patti to shore, was informed by the captain that she would not be allowed to leave the ship without permission from the health officer. Several hours later the impresario secured the necessary paper and, returning to the *Oregon*, handed the captain the permit that freed the diva, who shrieked for her parrot, Ben Butler by name, which was soon found, though one of her maids was not. The passengers subsequently cheered as Patti boarded the *Blackbird* followed by Nicolini, a maid who had not dallied, Ben Butler, and the diamonds. [3]

With the most valuable member of his company in New York,

Mapleson was again in a position to so dominate the scene that the enemy's defeat seemed inevitable.

Several days later Mapleson heralded the operatic first night with far from glad tidings. God was not in His heaven: all was not right with the world. The directors had refused to furnish sufficient war funds.

On November 7 the impresario loudly complained he had not received the stockholders' guarantee for Patti's contract, reminded the directors that two hundred of the best seats at the Academy, those reserved for the stockholders at every performance, provided no revenue at the box office, and finally asseverated his need of funds to launch the forthcoming series. It was said Mapleson had written the directors a letter in which he stated Patti might not sing unless the guarantee money were provided. Sad to relate, all pleas fell on deaf ears. Then declaring Patti might not even appear at the opening, Mapleson ruefully wondered aloud whether malign forces had organized what he called a Society for the Suppression of Italian Opera.

Although for a time all signs were ominous, the impresario duly began the season with Patti in one of her greatest roles, Rosina in *Il Barbiere di Siviglia,* and on the date originally announced, thereby anticipating the Metropolitan's first performance by a week.

Opening night at the Academy on Monday, November 10, drew an immense house with the boxes graced by such stalwarts as the Dinsmore, Belmont, Cutting, Beckwith, Astor families. Society ladies carried colorful bouquets, while their dress and jewels epitomized high fashion. Escorts complemented in the sartorial splendor of formal attire. Though most likened the opening to those of the past, socially speaking, the *Times* maintained it was "a trifle less brilliant than an opening performance of bygone days,"[4] citing as reasons a slight business recession, other theatrical counterattractions, a lack of interest in the opera selected for the occasion; but the diva's magnificence cast its usual spell.

Patti mesmerized as Rosina, her vocal gems coruscating, singing with spontaneity, exquisite taste, and verve. Many of the next day's reviews echoed the one in the *Times,* in which the critic said that as a vocalist and as an actress, she played the part with charm, "lightness, coquettishness, and mischief,"[5] reveling in its humor and dramatic possibilities. In the lesson scene she introduced the bolero from *Les Vêpres Siciliennes,* afterwards in response to wild ovations bringing down the house with "Home, Sweet Home." For Patti the evening was one long triumph. Others in the cast fared less well, the critic of the *Tribune* unequivocally stating that they were "utterly unworthy"[6] of the diva or the Academy. The *Times* and *Herald* disagreed, the latter maintaining that Vicini as Almaviva, Caracciolo as Dr. Bartolo, De Pasqualis as Figaro, Cherubini as Don Basilio, Saruggia as Berta, Rinaldini as Fiorello, and Bieletto as the Sergeant "did justice to the music."[7] De Pasqualis, making his debut, at once won favor, according to the *Evening Post,* for his "vivacious acting and easy, fluent, pure vocal style."[8] As always, Arditi led the orchestra with authority and enthusiasm.

For the second presentation Mapleson brought forward *Il Trovatore,* on November 12, with two of his artists making their first New York appearances: Riccetti as Leonora and Cardinali as Manrico, in a cast that included De Pasqualis (Di Luna), Scalchi (Azucena), Saruggia (Inez), Manni (Ferrando), and Rinaldini (Ruiz). Arditi conducted. Of the two new artists, the tenor made the more favorable impression, singing after initially marked nervousness with ease, beauty of tone, and fervor. Cardinali, like some tenors earlier and later, occasionally overemphasized the power of his loud high notes and courted popular favor over artistic considerations. But he was a decided success with the Academy audience and, in general, with the critics. The *Herald* was especially impressed, claiming he had dethroned Campanini and calling him a "tenor for the ladies. A tenor handsome as Apollo. A tenor tall and straight, with coal black hair and steel blue eyes. A tenor in the prime of youth, full of warmth and emotion. A tenor who will catch the town."[9] Riccetti, who began a bit tentatively, in time pleased a number of the critics with her resonant soprano, though there were those who found little to admire in her use of it, while most considered her dramatic efforts amateurish. De Pasqualis failed to make so favorable an impression as on opening night, the *Evening Post* saying his voice was "better suited for the rapid parlando style of singing than the cantabile style."[10] While Scalchi did not find Azucena the most congenial of roles, her mellow tones gave pleasure to the crowded house that applauded her to the rafters.

Two evenings later Mapleson presented Patti in *La Traviata* with Vicini as Alfredo and a new baritone, De Anna, as Germont, and concluded the week at the Saturday matinee with *Il Trovatore*, which featured the same cast as on Wednesday. Continuing to delight, Patti's Violetta, said the *Times*, as "a combination of voice, lyric execution, and histrionic skill . . . had and has no rival on the operatic stage."[11] That Patti sang at all on this occasion was due to Mapleson's pleas, for she was suffering from a cold. Under such circumstance she usually would not have appeared. Knowing her cancellation would be interpreted as a move on his part to intimidate the directors, Mapleson earlier in the day had exhorted her to make every effort. Otherwise, the season might just as well end. Realizing the seriousness of the situation, Patti agreed to sing. How well she succeeded is evident in Mapleson's comments: "Why, in the death scene in the last act half the audience and even the orchestra were in tears."[12] Vicini and De Anna generally received praise, the latter at his debut adjudged a valuable accession. A second hearing of Riccetti at the next day's *Trovatore* did not win her new critical acclaim, but Cardinali held his own, confirming the generally good impression made at his first appearance.

Though these various popular and critical successes must have heartened Mapleson, the continued refusal of the Academy directors to provide the Patti guarantee so embittered him that early in the first week he again announced the possibility of the diva's withdrawal. On his dignity, he refused to be handed a $600 assessment each time Patti sang, telling the stockholders to keep their money, and on November 11 wrote Augustus L. Brown,

President of the Academy Board of Directors, to the same effect.

Relations between the impresario and directors swiftly deteriorated. In the midst of charges and countercharges, Mapleson confided to a reporter: "I'm glad of one thing—what I said about
them will never appear in print. . . . You see when I get above
112 degrees I let things slip."[13] On November 12 Mapleson asserted that the directors were like "a chorus of masked conspirators sent by the Metropolitan people to ruin the Academy."[14] Dr.
Damrosch with the New York Symphony and the conductor
Theodore Thomas were monopolizing the stage for their own rehearsals in what Mapleson considered a deliberate harassment tac-
tic. The Academy directors, he claimed, had "let the building for
every hour of daylight, and what with Damrosch building up a
great place for his orchestra and Thomas tearing it all down again
and building up an arrangement of his own, we have had no rehearsals. . . . We must have midnight rehearsals. But that will
kill my artists. These great crowds use up all the oxygen, they
leave a vitiated atmosphere, and artists cannot sing in such a
place. . . ."[15] Mapleson then zeroed in on the real cause of his
problems: "It's not the directors as a body; it's a clique among
them. You know those fellows in the play with slouch hats, cloaks
and daggers and a scowl on their faces. I call them Metropolitans
now, not villains."[16]

Matters unresolved, rumors proliferated that Patti intended to
return to Europe; but Mapleson denied this: "It's the old story of
the three wishes. . . . I have secured Patti for forty nights. Like
the man's first wish for a pudding, so are the . . . nights I have
billed her to sing in New York. Shall I throw away my other two
wishes, as the man did, in wishing the pudding on his wife's nose
and then having to wash it off again? Not much; not if I can help
it."[17]

Faced with opposition at the Academy and the reopening of the
Metropolitan, Mapleson began the second week with a warning:
"I hope that the masked conspirators will not attain their fell pur-

pose."[18] To counter opening night at the Metropolitan, Mapleson introduced the same evening, November 17, a new artist: Emma Steinbach as Leonora in *La Favorita,* in a cast including Vicini as Fernando, De Anna as Alfonso, and Cherubini as Balthazar. The large audience throughout the performance expressed pleasure in Steinbach's vocalism and interpretation of the role. Though the critic of the *Herald* subsequently thought the debut only a succès d'estime, his counterpart at the *Times,* generally in agreement with his colleague's evaluation, nonetheless maintained that Steinbach's voice possessed "a sympathetic quality which went far . . . to atone for minor defects in the timbre."[19] Unfortunately there was evidence of hard use of the voice as well as a "decided vibrato."[20]

The first night at the Metropolitan drew an immense crowd, reported by the *Tribune* as approximately five thousand. The new decoration of the auditorium pleased, with a more elegant background for occupants of the boxes and with so much gold applied to the box fronts that they seemed all gilt. The house now possessed "a richness and cosiness about it which were sadly needed last season."[21] The performance of *Tannhäuser,* under Dr. Damrosch's direction, elicited much praise for the superb new scenery and costumes, chorus, orchestra, and principals. Kraus as Elisabeth, Slach as Venus, Robinson as Wolfram, and Schott as Tannhäuser "worked well together"[22] and generally produced a favorable impression.

Although the next day's New York newspapers devoted considerable space to reviews of the preceding evening's two performances, the return of the young American soprano Emma Nevada, on November 17, created such interest that its press coverage virtually overshadowed all other operatic news. Perhaps Mapleson had planned it that way.

Accompanied by her father, Dr. William Wallace Wixom, her manager, Dr. Palmer, and a French maid, Nevada expressed keen pleasure in returning to the United States after an absence of eight years. While away, she had studied singing with Mme Mathilde Marchesi in Vienna, adopted the stage name Nevada after the city of her birth, Nevada City, California, made her operatic debut in *La Sonnambula* with Mapleson at Her Majesty's Theatre in 1880, and afterwards sang extensively in Italy and France.

Nevada's arrival in New York was not the only newsworthy feature of the second week, however. The directors now allowed Mapleson financial assistance for the times Patti sang. Also of interest during this time were the reviews of performances and a comparison of the competing companies.

Following the opening-night *Tannhäuser*, the Metropolitan presented a *Fidelio*, on November 19, that according to the *World* eclipsed all earlier productions of the work in the United States; it had "never before been presented to an American audience in so complete and satisfactory a manner." [23] Brandt's Leonora highly impressed the critics, who considered the impersonation powerful, and who ranked her as a great artist. Schott as Florestan sustained his part creditably while the orchestra and chorus performed admirably under Dr. Damrosch's inspired direction. *Les Huguenots*, on November 21, and the following day's matinee of *Tannhäuser* also received favorable critical comments. The operas, all sung in German, attracted large audiences.

On November 23 the *Tribune* reviewed the two companies, asserted that both had been well patronized, found assets and defects in each. Those "who love beautiful Italian singing," said this paper, "will crowd to Mr. Mapleson's representations," whereas for individuals "to whom the higher, or—not to quarrel with anybody—the broader ideal of the modern German school makes appeal, there will be continued keen enjoyment at the Metropolitan." [24] In the final outcome fashion, not art, might be the determining factor in the competition.

Though the two companies apparently were equally successful, the coming week's series might alter this; and as events unfolded the bill of fare at the older house did indeed attract, focusing the limelight on Mapleson's activities.

CHAPTER 9

A Banner Week

∽

$\mathcal{T}$HE THIRD week's program at the Academy created a sensation in opera circles. Mapleson gloated as he contemplated its attractions: "We have arranged a most magnificent programme . . . I tell you . . . they can't beat that even with Miss Brandt and the other German beauties at the Metropolitan." [1] In arranging the series he outdid himself, presenting Nevada in her American operatic debut and another superb performance of *Semiramide* with Patti and Scalchi, but, above all, a production of *Marta* honoring the diva's silver anniversary in grand opera.

The week began with the debut. Nevada appeared at the Academy for the first time on Monday, November 24, as Amina in *La Sonnambula* with Vicini as Elvino, Cherubini as Rodolfo, Rinaldini as Alessio, and Saruggia as Lisa. The soprano's artistic reputation had preceded her, and Mapleson had hyperbolized, with the consequence that expectations skyrocketed.

Since her debut under the aegis of Mapleson in London in 1880, Nevada had grown musically and, if the words of her vocal mentor, Mme Mathilde Marchesi, are accurate, she had done so only after having overcome various obstacles. Marchesi said that Nevada's health, in particular, had caused concern. For example, though engaged for three years at the Royal Berlin Opera, Nevada did not fulfill her contract, "fearing she was not physically strong enough for the German stage." [2] Hopefully she would be strong enough for the American stage.

Throughout the first act the audience listened in rapt attention to the young artist who, according to the *Times*, immediately impressed by "the extreme purity of her voice . . . and the ease and precision of her delivery of florid measures."[3] When the curtain fell at the end of the act, the house went wild, repeatedly demanding recalls and heaping many bouquets and set pieces upon her. Standing before the prompter's box, Nevada gestured to Arditi, who led the orchestra in the opening bar of "Home, Sweet Home."

In the succeeding portions of the presentation the soprano sang with wonderful flexibility, looked fetching, and managed the transition from a shy country girl at the opera's beginning to a ecstatically happy woman. All efforts reaffirmed the good impression she had made in the first act and the audience cheered rapturously, especially demonstrative after the rendition of "Ah! non giunge." At the end of the opera they gave the young artist a standing ovation. According to the *Herald,* no other recent performance had stirred such enthusiasm.

Virtually all the next day's reviews praised Nevada with few reservations. The *Evening Post* marveled that she was "now in the position, so enviable by one in her profession who has sufficient talent to sustain it, of having every new appearance watched with favorable interest, though with close and even anxious regard."[4] The *Herald* raved that Nevada had "at once taken rank among the very first singers of light opera,"[5] while the *World* wondered at the voice, "capable apparently of any feats in alt and all manner of florid exhibitions."[6] Typical of the more tempered reviews was the entry in the *Times:* "Mlle. Nevada's execution is rather facile than labored; her scales are clean and fluent, her staccatos neat, if not precisely brilliant, her trill passable, and her ability to sustain a tone in half-voice somewhat exceptional. . . . Her defects are less numerous, but they are no less distinct. There is absolutely no light or shade in Mlle. Nevada's singing; there is neither pathos nor sparkle in her tones; her execution as well as her acting is wanting in freedom . . ."[7]

The diva appeared twice this week: the *Marta* of November 26 and *Semiramide* at the Saturday matinee three days later. Of the two performances, the first was by any measure the memorable one, as it celebrated a milestone in Patti's career: the twenty-fifth anniversary of her operatic debut, on November 24, 1859, at that time she a mere lass of sixteen. Since it had occurred at New York's Academy of Music, to celebrate the silver jubilee in the same surroundings was most fitting. Krehbiel, writing in the *Tribune,* struck the right note: "Stars of great brilliance have flashed across the firmament and gone out in darkness, but the refulgence of Patti's art remains undimmed, having only grown mellower and deeper and richer with time."[8]

The Academy held an enormous audience for the anniversary, with society fashionables out in great numbers. It was an evening of legend. The house was gladdened by the performance, continually expressing pleasure, encoring, lavishing applause, cheers, flowers on the diva. Assisting Patti were Vicini as Lionel, Scalchi as Nancy, Cherubini as Plunkett, and Caracciolo as Tristan; but they hardly mattered. All eyes were riveted on the diva, who sang as magnificently, and looked as young, as ever.

Musically, the gala reached its climax after Patti's rendition of "The Last Rose of Summer," which she sang in Italian but, encored, repeated in English, "enunciating the English words . . . with delicious richness which made one almost believe they were Italian."[9] The air occasioned more floral gifts; ladies threw bouquets from the boxes; Arditi handed over the footlights immense offerings, and a deputation of the chorus brought two huge floral arrangements on stage. In all, the tributes "formed a small mountain,"[10] including a silver basket of roses and rare blooms, a floral lyre, silver wreaths, a harp of blossoms, a flowery star with Patti's initials and the dates 1859–1884.

Ceremoniously, the climax of the celebration occurred at the end of the last act, when the curtain remained open. From backstage sounded the rattle of snare drums, and the Seventh Regiment Band in blue and gold uniforms, led by Carlo Cappa, marched out ten abreast. The chorus and principals made way for the musicians, positioning themselves at the wings. At the footlights Cappa turned and faced the band. At that moment the scenery at the back opened, revealing one hundred gas jets blazing in the shape of an American eagle with the word *Patti* below and the dates 1859–1884. The house went wild. The group played a march, and at its conclusion Patti rushed forward to the band director, grasped his hands, and in a voice shaking with emotion said:

> My dear friends, it is twenty-five years ago since I sang here for the first time. The reception you have given me to-night is a tribute I shall never forget. It overcomes me. I am so overwhelmed I can say nothing more.[11]

The house was pandemonium all over again, with ladies and gentlemen standing and the former waving handkerchiefs, cries of *brava* filling the auditorium, thunderous volleys of applause. As the band resumed playing, Patti kissed Scalchi upon the cheek, shook Cappa's hand, bowed to his players, repeatedly threw kisses to the many admirers in the audience, and then disappeared from view.

The celebration, however, had not ended. Mapleson's special part in it now began. Always the showman, he had arranged for a triumphal procession from the Academy to the Windsor Hotel, where the diva resided. It got underway just before midnight, but only after a squad of police officers cleared the way. Ultimately it numbered some two thousand celebrants.

At the end of this banner week Mapleson must have been optimistic about the remaining series of performances in New York and about his coming prolonged tour of the United States. According to the *American Art Journal,* at the moment he was holding his own against the Metropolitan's competition: "The two rival opera-houses appear to be dividing the honors of the season rather evenly. If the fine ensemble, even performances, splendid scenery and the attention accorded to the minor details . . . attract toward the Metropolitan, the brilliancy of the world-renowned Patti, assisted by Mme. Scalchi, [is] a powerful magnet for the Academy, and even little Nevada possesses considerable drawing qualities, and is proving quite a success. The tide did not turn quite as strongly as was sanguinely expected in favor of German opera. . . ."[12] Hopefully the week would serve as a preview of the future.

At the moment the prospects looked bright.

CHAPTER 10

New Princess Problems, Among Others

〜

*T*HE STATE of euphoria at the end of November rapidly evaporated during the first two weeks of December, when Nevada, on whom Mapleson now relied heavily, canceled three of her scheduled performances as Gilda in *Rigoletto*, a circumstance creating bad publicity as well as a loss of confidence with resultant dire effects at the box office.

Mapleson had advertised the first *Rigoletto* of the season for December 3, with Nevada as Gilda. Though Mapleson had cast her in this role, the artist herself apparently had never agreed to such an undertaking. There followed a battle of wills.

By two in the afternoon of the third the impresario had ordered a notice placed that Nevada was indisposed and that Dotti would replace her. Before the evening's performance ushers distributed slips of paper carrying the name of a medical doctor who certified Nevada's illness. Mapleson offered a refund to those not caring to attend the opera with her replacement. To a reporter from the *Tribune* he gave a brief explanation: "I think the sea voyage affected Mlle. Nevada to such an extent that she has not been quite herself since."[1] But when Mapleson made this statement there was nothing physically wrong with Nevada.

Interviewed at her residence, the soprano made this clear while offering an explanation for the nonappearance: "I was by no means in good voice when I arrived, and felt that the date of my first appearance was a little early for me to do myself full justice. However, as *Sonnambula* had been advertised, I sang, and, as it is a light opera, managed to get through quite well. To my surprise, however, Mr. Mapleson, without even going through the form of consulting me, advertised me to sing in *Rigoletto,* a task which I felt at present beyond me." [2]

Indignant, Mapleson thereupon advertised Nevada as Gilda for the December 6 matinee, but, perhaps in response to importunities, ultimately changed the offering, substituting the opera of her choice: *Lucia.* Still, while momentarily placating, he remained resolute, once more announcing her in the Verdi opera for Wednesday, December 10; but the young artist again canceled the performance, pleading illness.

After this third disappointment Mapleson, confounded and exasperated, threatened to sue Nevada, unwilling to believe she had suffered from any malady, convinced the problem stemmed from an inflated ego. Then on Thursday, December 11, Nevada, still suffering, in his opinion, from curiously bad health, canceled her performance as Amina in Brooklyn. This time the impresario exploded, stinging the young artist with the remark there would be no playing of "ducks and drakes with him," [3] following this with a letter demanding compensation that, of course, he could not collect, as there was no proof she had been devious.

Despite the cancellations Nevada did appear twice the first two weeks of December: as Lucia in the matinee of the sixth, and as Amina in *Sonnambula* on the thirteenth. At each, though impressive, she failed to efface the memory of others in these roles. Generally she sang with fluency, purity of tone, faultless intonation, delicacy, but at the same time without abundant color, expression, or brilliance. In short, while remarkable, Nevada could not assume the role for which Mapleson had intended her: that of another Gerster. In Nevada, Mapleson held a star but no meteor.

By now, two other singers also disappointed: Riccetti and Cardinali. Since the soprano had failed to arouse much critical or popular acclaim, Mapleson broke the contract, replacing her with an artist whose contributions to the Metropolitan's first season had been highly acclaimed: Emmy Fursch-Madi. As for Cardinali, the tenor was superb as Manrico, but subsequent appearances as Ernani, Edgardo, and the Duke in *Rigoletto* impressed less, he being at times defective in intonation and unmusical, occasionally a law unto himself.[4]

Then, too, poor attendance at some performances created a terrifying drain on the treasury, the December 13 matinee of *Sonnambula* with Nevada being one of these. Mapleson maintained that the light demand for tickets resulted from the public's loss of confidence in the singer. Several hours before even he did not know whether Nevada would sing. Informed she was ill, Mapleson sent a messenger to her hotel to ascertain the truth, but the emissary returned empty-handed. The impresario knew only that the soprano had gone driving. Nevada did appear, however, on this occasion.

Another serious drain on resources was the competition of the Metropolitan, which increasingly attracted New York's nouveaux riches, German-speaking residents, Academy regulars. By early December, opera in German was receiving considerable critical and popular acclaim. The *World* lavished praise upon the German artists who had infused "a meaning and depth"[5] into their December 3 performance of *Lohengrin* unequaled by any Italian company in New York; the *Tribune* marveled that *Der Freischütz* had "never before been sung"[6] in New York with such perfection in all the roles; the *Times* exclaimed over a number of performances, enraptured by the unity, the attention to details, scenic and musical, and emphasis on ensemble performances, the esprit de corps, the artists' dedication.

Also by this time, the younger house was attracting not only the German-speaking and the nouveaux riches but also members of the Faubourg St. Germain set, not solely for musical reasons. Some months before, the warmth of Vanderbilt hospitality had begun to thaw Knickerbocker gentry's iciness, and members of the Old Wealth were gradually acclimatizing themselves to atmospheric social changes.

Mrs. William K. Vanderbilt, to celebrate the opening of her

fabulous new Fifth Avenue mansion costing millions, had extended invitations for a fancy dress ball the evening of March 26, 1883, to more than one thousand guests, aware that *the* Mrs. Astor's ballroom accommodated a mere four hundred. The architect Richard Morris Hunt had designed the great house after a sixteenth-century French Renaissance château. Its inauguration unleashed tremendous excitement in the elegant world, planned by the toweringly ambitious Mrs. Vanderbilt. For weeks New York's fashionables spoke of little else but the costume ball that promised to be the greatest ever given in the metropolis. The question of what to wear, according to the *New-York Times,* "disturbed the sleep and occupied the waking hours of social butterflies, both male and female. . . ."[7] Further occupying the waking hours of some was the organization of quadrilles to be performed at the ball. The expenses for the affair also created talk. According to the *World*'s calculation, such items as flowers, costumes, catering, music, champagne totaled at least $250,000. To be excluded was to be out of Society; yet the one representing that august body at its grandest found herself for a time in just that position. Mrs. Vanderbilt had not invited *the* Mrs. Astor, Society's queen.[8]

Meanwhile this venerable lady's daughter and friends had arranged a quadrille that met the approval of the mother, who ever assumed an invitation was forthcoming; but as the time approached for the spectacular affair the assumption proved false. Mrs. Astor, increasingly alarmed and miffed, determined to press the issue, commandeering a confidant to deal with the situation.

Duly informed of terpsichorean efforts by the emissary, Mrs. Vanderbilt regretfully stated to the gentleman that she could not possibly invite any individual who had not as yet recognized her socially. The response came quickly: the Vanderbilts' time had arrived. Without further ado Mrs. Astor ordered her coachman to drive her to the Vanderbilt residence, where a footman presented her calling card. Soon after the invitation arrived.[9] A major part of the Old Guard's bastion had collapsed. Symbolic of the victory were subsequent invitations requesting the honor of the Vanderbilts' presence at the Astors' annual ball. Then in time, following the Astors' lead, other portions of the Old Wealth capitulated before the New Wealth's irresistible force.

Still, it was not the Metropolitan's competition and Society's socialization alone that alarmed those sympathetic to Mapleson. Also of concern was the impresario's discord with individuals all-powerful in his present and future movements: the Academy directors. Signs pointed to a severance of ties.

Mapleson's greatest fault, however, lay in his inability to provide an overwhelming challenge to the Metropolitan, gradually emerging as the vital force of opera in New York. Mapleson's repertoire, except for the Patti operas, did not lure full houses, and his company disappointed at certain key points, the paucity of quality tenors being particularly noticeable. Italian opera itself no longer seemed to satisfy.

Despite disappointments in the fourth and fifth weeks of the New York season, Mapleson found enough to hearten. The continuing successes of Patti inspired, her appearances providing much-needed revenue. Then, too, the fortnight ended with a brilliant affair: a reprise in commemoration of Patti's silver anniversary in opera, festivities due to the initiative of the *Tribune* music critic Henry Edward Krehbiel and his counterpart at the *Times*. After gaining her consent, these two savants with other eminent gentlemen invited a number of prominent New Yorkers to a banquet in her honor on Saturday, December 13, at the Hotel Brunswick.

Unfortunately the hosts overlooked an absolute in the Victorian world: their wives refused to attend a banquet honoring a fallen woman. Embarrassed, Krehbiel and the *Times* critic, squaring their shoulders, resolved to approach Patti anew for her approval of another plan: to be the guests of only gentlemen, representatives of New York's legal, artistic, and literary professions. Unperturbed, she immediately acquiesced, perhaps enjoying the new arrangement more than the original.

The evening of the celebration Patti, enthroned upon a divan, received her hosts, about fifty, in a room adjoining the banquet hall, smiling on all. Radiant in an elaborate gown and diamonds,

Patti plumed herself on the admiration, luxuriating in the gentlemen's rapt attention. After a Lucullan feast Judge Joseph F. Daly, who presided, began the formal program by eulogizing Patti as a person and artist. Then, though speeches of a similar vein followed, the remarks of the eminent maestro Max Maretzek perhaps made the deepest impression. Of those present, this elderly gentleman may have known the diva the longest; and as the conductor when at the age of eight she amazed New York's music world in her first public concert on November 22, 1851, he held a unique place in her life.

"The Decline of Italian Opera in New York—Will It Have to Go A-Begging?" cartoon in Puck. Arditi and Patti.

The following day the *Times* paraphrased his speech:

Max Maretzek said he made Patti's acquaintance when she was about 3 years old, (laughter,) in the Astor-Place Opera House, and she then kissed him and called him uncle. Two or three years after Patti's mother sang Norma in the Howard Athenaeum, and the child appeared in a child's part, though she was troublesome, for she wanted to sing her mother's part. (Laughter.) When 8 or 9 years old she first appeared as a prima donna, but when about to go on she wanted to know what she was singing for, and would not sing until she had received a hatful of bonbons as her price. She was not yet demanding $5,000 a night. (Laughter. Patti joining and Nicolini appearing pleased.)[10]

The banquet ended with a charming endearment. The eight-year-old Patti had rewarded Maretzek for the candy not only by singing but also by giving him a kiss. After the toastmaster's adjournment, the diva went straightway to her old conductor, saying, "Max, if I gave you a kiss for a box of candy then, I'll give you one for nothing now!"[11] The diva was a lady of her word.

The last two weeks of the New York season abounded in contraries, touches of the ridiculous and the sublime. The former concerned Scalchi and the breakfast that had upset the Metropolitan's past season, while the latter related to artistic activities at the Academy.

The court proceedings concerning Scalchi's April 12, 1884, repast and her subsequent failure to sing at the Metropolitan's final matinee created some comic relief. Abbey sued her for $5,000 in damages for her nonappearance, while Scalchi claimed $1,441 in back pay, as well as money for last spring's passage to Europe. The crisis had begun after a number of principals reported inability to perform, whereupon Abbey had turned to Scalchi as his savior, requesting her to assume the role of Fidès in *Le Prophète*. According to the artist, he had solicited her aid only a few hours before the matinee, after the hefty meal. Though she had offered to sing less demanding roles, Scalchi maintained, Abbey refused to compromise, adamant it would be Meyerbeer or nothing. The singer, likewise adamant, had refused, whereupon Abbey had closed the house, taking her to court for the amount he lost by the cancellation.

In pursuit of justice a number of witnesses, on December 17 and 18, supported Scalchi, who tempered her remarks while several others spiced theirs, one of these being Mapleson.

LAWYER: "Let us assume that she had not eaten for 18 hours previously, do you think she could have sung the part?"

MAPLESON: "She would have given a very feeble performance of it . . . She would have been disabled for a considerable time. . . ."

LAWYER: "Have you ever met Mr. Abbey?"

MAPLESON: "Once or twice." . . .

LAWYER: "Do you consider him a good manager?"

MAPLESON: "No. . . . His experience, you know, was only obtained in 1883 and 1884. Before that he knew nothing of operatic management."

LAWYER: "Is it usual to close a house when a prima donna refuses to sing?"

MAPLESON: "It is not. . . . I think by deliberately closing the theatre Mr. Abbey pulled his nose at the expense of his face." [12]

By December 23 the court reached its momentous decision: Scalchi won the case.

Other events of the final two weeks sobered and inspired, as they generally related to some excellent productions. Mapleson had originally announced the December 20 matinee as the end of his New York fall-winter season; but since the engagement in Boston did not begin until December 29, he added four New York performances beginning the week of December 22. Highlights of these final presentations included Patti as Marguerite in *Faust* and Annetta in *Crispino e la Comare,* two roles she had not hitherto essayed this season; a production of Gounod's *Mireille,* or *Mirella,* as it was sung in Italian; Mapleson's benefit performance of *Semiramide;* Emmy Fursch-Madi's engagement, and that of the gifted tenor Francesco Giannini, who had created a sensation in New York that fall as a member of the Milan Opera Company. Of these, the Gounod opera was especially newsworthy, as a needed novelty.

After first presenting *Mireille* in Brooklyn on December 18, Mapleson brought it forward in New York at the December 20 matinee. The cast, headed by Nevada in the title role, was satisfactory, with Scalchi as Taven, Vicini as Vincent, De Anna as Ourrias,

Cherubini as Ramon. Arditi conducted. Of the artists, Nevada received the most attention from the *Times* critic, who admired her vocal flights, especially extolling her for the waltz-song in the last act, in which a "D in altissimo was touched in a series of brilliant staccatos"[13] and which "deserved the demonstration of delight it elicited."[14] The *Tribune* critic objected to revisions of the score and the reduction of the opera's five acts to three in Mapleson's adaptation. He also found fault with the ending. In the original the heroine died, but in the performance at the Academy the critic confessed he was somewhat bewildered by the last portions of the presentation, in which he was not too sure of the ultimate outcome, noting that Nevada "recovered from the sunstroke, trilled her dying waltz, was gathered into the arms of her lover, and the curtain fell; but only to rise again that she might repeat the waltz, and bow herself either into eternity or the basket-maker's hut—it was not plain which."[15]

With the matinee of December 27 the fall-winter season came to a close. In retrospect, its greatest financial successes were due to one artist: Patti, the *Tribune* critic estimating that the diva in her 13 appearances of the 28 representations was responsible for nine-tenths of the box office receipts.

Artistically, except for Patti, Scalchi, De Anna, Nevada, Fursch-Madi, the season was neither outstanding nor sufficiently brilliant, with the operas too often hurriedly produced and underrehearsed. Though the *Times* critic now evaluated the troupe as one of "considerable efficiency,"[16] he, like his *Tribune* colleague, expressed disappointment in the series. As for the repertoire, it, too, disappointed, the only novelty being *Mireille*, despite the fact Mapleson had promised a production of *Lakmé*. Krehbiel noted: "A review of the list is not calculated to inspire one with either surprise or admiration at the achievements of the manager and his artists. It is the familiar list. . . ."[17]

Krehbiel concluded his review of the season with an evaluation of the present relationship between Mapleson and the directors: "There seems to be considerable indifference to Mr. Mapleson's fate among the directors, for which, of course, the manager has himself largely to blame. The supporters of Italian opera have always been willing to discount managerial promises heavily and accept them nevertheless, but there must come an end sometime to even their patience. It seems to have come this season, and the natural desire to save themselves as much money as possible prompts the frequent leasing of the Academy for all manner of entertainments. The condition of the house gives evidence of an unwillingness to sink money in an unlucrative enterprise." [18]

Though Krehbiel believed the Academy no longer lucrative, the financial report for the year, released in late April 1885, revealed that expenses amounted to $36,750 and the receipts to $45,882, a tremendous gain over the year before. Also, advance bookings in late April surprised, being at $26,165, in contrast to about $7,000 at the same time the past season. As for the comments concerning the Mapleson-directors relationship, Krehbiel absolutely was on target. It had deteriorated seriously.

Generally in the past Mapleson had been fortunate in his dealings with this governing body and particularly with its president. From the time he appeared on the scene in 1878 until the spring of 1884 there had been but one in this office: August Belmont, who, as correspondence reveals, was well aware of Mapleson's pecuniary needs and business practices even before approving the first contract with him.

In 1878 correspondence from London, Baron Ferdinand de Rothschild wrote Belmont that Mapleson had no financial resources and for that reason advised extreme care in any contractual matter. In later correspondence the summer of 1878 Bernard Ullman, a former Academy impresario, offered Belmont similar advice: "He will promise anything very boldly, very well knowing all the time that he cannot keep it. You ought to aid him, as much as you can, *mais, toujours, restant sur vos gardes.*" [19] Another missive from Ullman, dated September 6, 1878, revealed further tactics: "Mapleson is very foolish, to announce, that he will have new artists in January—He cannot get any—All he could get this year, he *has* got—He knows it—but such is the man and in that, he is incorrigible." [20]

Though so forewarned, Belmont, determined to have opera at

the Academy on a sounder, higher artistic level, duly recommended Mapleson as the new manager, hopeful he would do the job well. Once the decision had been made, Belmont assisted Mapleson in many ways; and regardless of any subsequent adverse comments he loyally supported the impresario.

Under the new regime with Augustus L. Brown as president, Mapleson obviously fared none too well, with fault on both sides. Except for the $600 assessment provided each time Patti sang, the directors refused to furnish him with any additional funds in his competition with the Metropolitan, whose directors were munificent by comparison. Mapleson was keenly aware of the difference in generosity and of his own directors' apparent indifference to his plight. Too often the unavailability of the Academy stage for rehearsals resulted in inadequately prepared productions. Revenue from rentals apparently now meant more to the directors than did first-rate opera. On the other hand, Mapleson did little to ease the situation. When the directors failed to meet his demands, he turned on them in public utterances, abrasive in his remarks on egos no doubt as large as his own.

Why he followed this course is not clear, though there are certain intimations. Perhaps overweening pride, financial/managerial responsibilities, resentment of the insufficient pecuniary assistance affected his behavior; but these factors do not explain all. Perhaps Mapleson's mad method was a signal of availability to the rival house. After all, in a few months his contract with the Academy would end.

As Mapleson had purposely antagonized Nilsson in wooing Patti, so in alienating some of his own directors, he may actually have been courting the Metropolitan powers who in the near past, he surely had not forgotten, had found themselves unable to secure suitable places in the Academy's enchanted circles and who this past spring, bearing Mapleson himself no grudge, had urged him to assume the new house's management. At that time, his contract with the Academy precluded him from considering their offer. Were they in the near future to approach him anew, nothing would stand in the way of his assuming such a responsibility.

Mapleson's movements in December and January prompted the

Metropolitan directors to give him consideration. His announcement on December 24 concerned them. On that date he stated that he and a number of wealthy men proposed to erect an opera house, music hall, and ballroom as part of the Madison Square Garden complex. If realized, the undertaking might pose a threat to the Metropolitan. Finally, a direct Mapleson overture occurred in mid-January, when it was made known that Mapleson's son Charles had offered to assume the Metropolitan management. Whether he, probably a front for his father, would secure it remained to be seen.

Meanwhile the impresario himself was in the midst of a transcontinental tour, the success of which would perhaps determine the final outcome of the rivalry as well as the future of opera in the United States. As ever, he thought that future lay not in German opera, which fashion, in his experience, had failed to support. The "experiment" at the Metropolitan, he believed, would eventually be abolished.

Such a turn of events seemed likely. At the moment, the *American Queen*, the journal of Society, reported that the repertoire did not appeal to all those who really mattered: the wealthy owners of the house. According to the January 3, 1885, issue of this publication, German opera was unpopular with the majority of boxholders. Wagner especially displeased. Elizabeth Drexel Lehr in her reminiscences noted that at this period "it was considered fashionable to be unable to understand Wagner and to despise him accordingly. He was described as 'vulgar and immoral.' "[21]

It was moot whether the Metropolitan boxholders would countenance German opera's continuance.

CHAPTER 11

Transcontinental Journey

〜

*I*N THE 1884–1885 season vast stretches of the United States
surrendered to Mapleson, his company the only major opera
organization transcontinentally touring, while the Metropolitan
tours extended only to three cities. With Patti as the standard-
bearer and with her farewell emblazoned on the company's banner, Mapleson overwhelmed the republic, which yielded quantities of gold to the invincible forces.

Mapleson opened the prolonged national tour in Boston, from
December 29 to January 10 giving thirteen performances and, on
January 7, introducing another opera into the repertoire: *I Puritani* with Nevada (Elvira), Vicini (Lord Arthur), De Anna (Sir
Richard), Cherubini (Sir George), Saruggia (Henrietta). Arditi
conducted. Afterwards the company presented highlights of the
repertoire in Philadelphia, an engagement extending from the
twelfth to the twenty-first of January. As in Boston, so here Mapleson introduced another opera for the first time that season: *Lucrezia Borgia*, on January 17, with Fursch-Madi as the title heroine
in a cast including Scalchi (Maffio), Cardinali (Gennaro), Cherubini (Don Alfonso), Caracciolo (Astolfo), and Arditi conducting.

From Philadelphia the troupe entrained to New Orleans, arriving on Sunday, January 25. The fine climate cheered the artists as
well as the city, which before this time had had rainy weather for
weeks. Mapleson no doubt considered the weather change a pro-
pitious sign for the operatic fortnight due to begin Monday, January 26, and end on Saturday, February 7.

The repertoire included many of the operas given in Boston and Philadelphia except that Mapleson brought forward *Crispino e la Comare* for Patti, introduced Nevada in a new role, Marguerite in Gounod's *Faust,* and concluded the season with an opera hitherto not presented on the tour: *Les Huguenots.*

The engagement began auspiciously enough, on January 26, with Nevada in *La Sonnambula;* but the return of the beloved Patti as Violetta the next evening brought the house down rather more literally than anyone could have wished. Before the last act plaster fell from the front of the dress circle, creating a panic during which many left the theater, fearing for their lives. The next day, the city surveyor with various architects examined the building, the St. Charles Theatre, from pit to dome and found it in satisfactory condition, findings duly released to the public by permission of Mayor J. V. Guillotte and David Bidwell, the manager of the playhouse. Even so, Mapleson determined the company, while remaining in the building until the end of the week, would move to other quarters for the last performances: the old French Opera House.

From New Orleans the company journeyed to St. Louis, opening on Monday, February 9, in *Sonnambula* with Nevada and the usual cast. Though Mapleson had originally scheduled *Lucia,* inclement weather so delayed the train with the scenery and costumes for this opera that he had to offer a substitution. That he was able to open at all seems miraculous, for the troupe arrived in the midst of a blizzard. The change from the above-seventy-degree temperature of New Orleans to a temperature below zero tried the endurance of all, and soon affected the health of various members of the company.

Despite this introduction to St. Louis, Mapleson and the troupe refused to be dismayed or unprofessional, successfully fulfilling the engagement of seven performances. Afterwards the company appeared in Kansas City, Missouri, Topeka, St. Joseph, Cheyenne, Salt Lake City.

The artists then entrained for the part of the tour that since its inception had been eagerly anticipated: San Francisco. Patti led the way, leaving the company in Kansas City to spend a week socializing in the Golden Gate before the troupe arrived on Sunday, March 1.

As the caravan made its way to San Francisco, news from the auctioneer there sent the impresario into ecstasies: Joe Eldridge had sold, on February 23, all of the pit, dress circle, parquet, mezzanine, family circle, boxes for the two weeks' season, with the premiums on the tickets alone amounting to about $20,000. Gallery seats were to be offered later. The phenomenal sale already surpassed the past season's, in part, no doubt, owing to this man's expert salesmanship.

Mapleson later learned that Eldridge, profusely perspiring at the auction, had worked himself to such a lather that he caught pneumonia and in a matter of days died. Mapleson subsequently elegized him in his own inimitable fashion: "Poor Joe Eldridge . . . I suppose they say I killed him, but he could not have died more gloriously." [1]

Not all the telegrams, however, bore financial tidings; a number concerned Patti and her reentry into San Francisco. Petulant, she absolutely refused to appear first in *Semiramide,* the opera Mapleson had advertised for opening night. Unwilling to share the limelight with Scalchi, Patti determined the evening would be hers alone, at first suggesting Rosina in place of the Assyrian queen. Then told Nevada proposed to sing "Home, Sweet Home" at her San Francisco debut, Patti, who considered the air her personal property, decreed the opera must be *Linda di Chamounix,* into which she regularly interpolated the song.

Angered and annoyed, Mapleson at first refused Patti but finally wisely accepted the inevitable, agreeing to *Linda* as the opening-night vehicle, on March 2. In it Scalchi would also appear, but in a smaller, less showy role than that in *Semiramide.*

During January and February matters had remained unsettled between the Academy and the Metropolitan Opera, with, once again, recurrent rumors of an amalgamation. It was said various Metropolitan stockholders were informally meeting with their Academy counterparts, proposing advantageous financial terms in a settlement and promising the old guard boxes at the new house. In press interviews, on January 18, a spokesman for each interest, though not denying a merger possibility, revealed that no official action had yet been taken. Both sides admitted, however, that "there was not room for two rival establishments devoted to grand opera, and that the law of the 'survival of the fittest' must eventually determine the fate of one of them." [2]

Financially, the future now promised much to the new house. Mapleson's departure at the end of December had contributed to its present prosperity, a fact readily admitted by E. C. Stanton, Secretary of the Metropolitan: "Naturally we have done better since the other house closed. . . ." [3] The Academy's Herman R. Le Roy, having in mind prices for opera tickets at the two places, riposted: "It is not so difficult after all . . . to fill a house. People are very glad to listen to good music when it costs them nothing." [4] By the end of the Metropolitan season the loss was approximately $40,000, quite a contrast to that of the year before.

Socially, the new house was also doing well, with Society attending in great numbers. By the middle of January the *American Queen* reported that the Metropolitan was "crowded every night, with all the boxes on the three tiers filled." [5] Ever joining the box-holders were Academy aristocrats, gradually acknowledging and accepting the new house, finding the unfamiliar surroundings neither unpleasant nor uncongenial to their patrician tastes, though the audience response to their manners was somewhat disquieting, a number demonstrating "disapproval of conversations in the boxes while the curtain is up. . . ." [6] Individuals who would not tolerate disrespect to the Bayreuth master, or to opera itself, were a new experience for the elite.

Musically and artistically, German opera under the inspired direction of Dr. Damrosch continued to generate critical and public acclaim. The debut of Amalia Materna as Elisabeth in *Tannhäuser*, on January 5, created a sensation with her "powerful and ringing voice," [7] consummate artistry, dramatic involvement. Later that month she impressed as Valentine in *Les Huguenots* and Rachel in

La Juive; but it was her assumption of the role of Brünnhilde in the production of *Die Walküre* on January 30 that seemed to make the deepest impression on critics, she overwhelming in scenes with Siegmund and Wotan, always singing with deep feeling, creating an indelible impression with her portrayal.

In the remaining weeks of the season this stellar performer and a number of others gave much pleasure, and when the series ended on February 21, Krehbiel in the *Tribune* marveled that the promises of the prospectus had been fulfilled (a shaft aimed at Mapleson?) and that the enterprise, seemingly "the most venturesome ever undertaken with opera"[8] in New York, had triumphed. *Harper's* concurred: "A more satisfactory series of opera presentations has not been known in New York, and for the first time 'German opera' has not been an occasional and curious experiment on off evenings and with a chance-medley company, but it has been approved and accepted by 'fashion' and 'the town.' "[9]

Despite reviews that were cause for rejoicing, recent tragedies first at the Academy and then at the Metropolitan precluded any complete celebration. Death had cut down a major figure in each house. The Academy lost Augustus L. Brown, President of the Board of Directors, who, after several days' illness, died on January 28. A few weeks later the new house was reeling from the loss of Leopold Damrosch, who after a short illness died on February 15. His son Walter and John Lund, the company's chorus master, directed performances the remainder of the season and on tour.

To succeed Brown, the Academy stockholders elected Herman R. Le Roy, while the Metropolitan powers finally chose Edmund C. Stanton to manage the business side of the enterprise and Anton Seidl, the eminent conductor who had worked with Wagner himself, to supervise the musical portion for the 1885–1886 season.

How these changes would affect Mapleson remained to be seen. At the moment he was beginning his second Golden Gate season.

CHAPTER 12

Return to
El Dorado

༄

A ROYAL WELCOME awaited the troupe in San Francisco,
where for days opera had monopolized the concerns of many
citizens. The press had been touting the company in a series of
articles, while the sale of tickets was creating a sensation. Commenting on it, Mapleson quipped: "Well . . . one isn't apt to get
dyspepsia under such circumstances."[1] As in the previous season,
so once more San Francisco was going berserk.

In virtually all ways opening night on Monday, March 2, with
Linda di Chamounix duplicated the frenzied scenes of Patti's appearances the past season, with enormous crowds outside the
house, excited shouts of hackmen and scalpers, the gathering of
sightseers gawking at social topliners, police everywhere trying to
keep order, the clatter of carriages forcing their way through mul-
titudes rending the air with "the intensity of a maelstrom,"[2] all
available space inside occupied with many standing and Society
out in force. What made the difference between this occasion and
past Patti galas was the fact that the police and opera house staff
maintained better order.

The performance itself inspired rapture from beginning to end.
Upon Patti's entrance applause and cheers mounted; then the diva,
"that arch autocrat of the world,"[3] came to the footlights all smiles,
glorying in her overwhelming reception, in seconds dissipating any

possible disappointment over the choice of opera with the enchantment of her voice. She carried all before her. Appearing with Patti were Vicini (Charles), De Pasqualis (Antonio), Cherubini (Prefect), and Scalchi (Pierotto). Though the vis-à-vis acquitted themselves creditably, only Patti drew superlatives, still "preeminently the great operatic artist of this generation."[4]

For the second performance Mapleson selected *Trovatore* with Fursch-Madi as Leonora, Scalchi as Azucena, Cardinali as Manrico, and De Anna as Di Luna. Playing to a huge house, the artists outdid themselves, roundly cheered and applauded for their efforts. Of these principals, the *Chronicle* considered Scalchi the greatest, praising her highly. As for Cardinali, critics generally reviewed the tenor's singing favorably; but one expressed disappointment in his having transposed "Di quella pira," so that the highest note was B, not C, commenting that "a genuine high C from the chest is like the rattle of a rattle-snake, unmistakable even to those who have never heard it before; it carries a moral conviction with it to one's ears and you know it is a high C almost by instinct."[5] Several critics devoted as much if not more space to Cardinali's appearance than to his voice, with the *Argonaut* outdoing the others in this respect: "Cardinali is as beautiful as Narcissus—a comparison which easily suggests itself, because, like that beautiful antique, he would be perfectly content to gaze at his own image in a fountain all day long."[6]

Apparently the tenor enjoyed gazing at other images, since he shared love letters with individuals who could read them to him, as he himself, according to Mapleson, did not possess this skill, nor could he write. In San Francisco he became engaged to a young lady who several years later burst upon the opera world as the protégée of Massenet: Sybil Sanderson, the soprano for whom the composer wrote *Esclarmonde*, *Le Mage*, and *Thaïs*. Although engaged to the young singer, Cardinali did not fulfill his pledge, soon pursuing other American beauties, always Don Juan incarnate, hither and thither hearkening to the call of libido.

Though Mapleson had originally scheduled Nevada's San Francisco debut for the third night of the season, informed of another indisposition he brought out *La Favorita;* and while cherishing the hope of soon presenting the soprano to her fellow Californians, Mapleson found her in such poor health that he delayed the debut until the final week of a supplementary season that extended from March 16 to March 28.

Meanwhile Friday's performance, on March 6, eclipsed all that had preceded, for it was *Semiramide* with Patti and Scalchi, overshadowing in the mob scene outside and excitement inside all the diva's earlier appearances in San Francisco. Patti apparently reveled in the performance. Interviewed after the second act with Scalchi at her side, she fairly cooed: "They say operatic singers are jealous of their rivals . . . but it is not so. Why, here is Scalchi, who fairly divided the honors with me to-night, and yet I love her like a sister. Don't I, Sofia?" [7] Oscar Wilde once observed that women address each other as sisters only after having exhausted other names first.

In reviewing the first week's series of performances, the *Chronicle* enumerated the company's weaknesses and strengths. Though admiring and praising many of the artists, the critic maintained that they generally did not work together as an ensemble, except in the Patti operas, too often laws unto themselves; that at times the performances needed more rehearsal; and that aside from the diva and the phenomenal contralto of Scalchi the voices were not impossible to duplicate. Regretted, of course, was the absence of Nevada, whose appearances might possibly provide the attraction San Francisco had celebrated last season in Gerster.

Mapleson was aware of the fact that had it not been for Patti, the season thus far would undoubtedly have been unsuccessful. It was hoped Nevada would at last appear with the company and create a box-office sensation; but once again such hope remained unrealized.

Since Nevada's health did not sufficiently improve in the next two weeks, beginning with March 8, Mapleson repeatedly presented Patti, Scalchi, Fursch-Madi. The diva appeared on six occasions, Scalchi seven, and Fursch-Madi three. At first Patti refused to sing in more than two performances in each of these two weeks; but fortunately for the impresario his politesse remained so effective that she consented to two extra performances.

Nevada had meanwhile been recuperating, and Mapleson continued to cast her in various presentations but on each occasion to no avail. All the while, her father, her manager, Mapleson himself were issuing virtually daily bulletins, and the quoted verbal exchanges became increasingly heated. By March 18 the situation reached a boiling point.

Mapleson charged that Dr. Palmer, the agent, had habitually issued statements on the singer's health before informing him of her physical state: "All my news from her is received at second hand. The public knows all about her before I do. . . . I read with surprise and alarm in a paper this morning . . . that Miss Nevada will not be able to use her voice during the season; also the statement that Dr. Palmer had two of her teeth extracted in Salt Lake and was carrying them around in his pocket exhibiting them to people. I repeat I was alarmed, because I thought if they were going to take her to pieces, bit by bit, there would be nothing left of her. The reason why I have advertised Miss Nevada from time to time here was because I honestly felt she would be able to make her appearance." [8]

An armistice was finally reached on March 20, when the subject of the crossfire issued a statement she would positively appear three days hence.

Nevada in her San Francisco debut as Amina in *La Sonnambula*, on Monday, March 23, scored a complete triumph. Pride in a native Californian's having achieved star status played its part; thousands appeared to honor "the first artist on the opera stage California has turned out." [9] Officers of the law had all they could do to contain the crowd, further swollen by some who gained admittance through a ventilator hole. The following day police and Mapleson discovered that a person in an adjacent lodging house had devised a swing that conveyed people to the opening on the roof of the opera house, and that apparently it had been in use for some time.[10] The ingenious device no doubt contributed considerable numbers to the long-awaited debut.

At the end of the first act Nevada, having taken the house by storm, responded to what it demanded: "Home, Sweet Home." Women cried, while "even strong men covered their faces with their hands."[11] Then the audience went wild again and in one of the recalls thereafter Nevada presented Arditi with a laurel wreath containing a diamond ring and a note thanking him for what he had meant to her career. The veteran conductor so treasured the message he later quoted it in his memoirs. At the end of the opera enthusiasm passed all bounds, the house a mad scene.

Four evenings later Nevada bade farewell to her fellow Californians in *Mireille* on Friday, March 27, attracting a huge and enthusiastic house. During the performance the *Chronicle* interviewed Mapleson, who, while ecstatic about the evening and the season, nonetheless felt the series had been a costly pleasure for him: "No one has any idea of the expense I am under with this company. I have paid Mme. Patti over $50,000 since she has been here; the railway fares amount to $16,000 and I have had to pay $20 a day for each of the four special cars lying idle at Oakland. That alone is an expense of $2400. Then there are the orchestra, chorus and the salaries of the leading artists. It is something enormous—astonishing—over $20,000 a week. . . ."[12] Despite Mapleson's protestations the earnings in San Francisco, according to local estimates, amounted to $175,000.

In the first of two farewell galas Patti appeared as Aida, on Tuesday, March 24, with Nicolini (Radames), Scalchi (Amneris), De Anna (Amonasro), and Cherubini (Ramfis). According to the *Chronicle,* no other performance of the opera in San Francisco had ever approached the high level of this presentation.

For the final performance Patti repeated one of her greatest successes of the season, Gounod's Marguerite, presented at the Saturday matinee, March 28, with Giannini as Faust, Cherubini as Méphistophélès, De Anna as Valentin, Scalchi as Siébel. In cer-

"A Winning Hand," cartoon in The Wasp. *The queens are,
left to right: Scalchi, Patti, Nevada, Fursch-Madi.*
COURTESY SAN FRANCISCO PUBLIC LIBRARY.

tain ways this offering eclipsed all that had preceded. The size,
enthusiasm, social brilliance of the audience; the rapport between
performers and audience; the fervor marking the performers' work;
the myriad curtain calls; the floral tributes; Patti's glorious singing
together with her affecting portrayal of the hapless Marguerite—
for many the occasion was a cornucopia of musical joy which glorified the experience of grand opera. It reached its climax when a
local dignitary came on stage, praised Patti in a prepared speech,
and placed upon her brow a laurel wreath with leaves of solid gold
and blossoms of solid silver. In the front blazed a star brilliant
with diamonds.

Hours later Mapleson and virtually all members of the company departed for final engagements on tour, looking forward to them as well as to the subsequent return to New York, where as on a similar occasion the year before they determined to enter the city in victorious array, undaunted by the Metropolitan.

CHAPTER 13

Season's Endings

෨

$\mathcal{M}$APLESON ARRANGED for one performance in Burlington, Iowa, on Thursday, April 2: *Faust* with Fursch-Madi as Marguerite, Giannini as Faust, Cherubini as Méphistophélès, Scalchi as Siébel, De Anna as Valentin. Knowing the city possessed a large hall, he intended to use it for a rehearsal of *L'Africaine*, a work not in the company's repertoire for a considerable time but one in the series of performances he intended to present at a great festival in Chicago. He dared not rehearse it in the Loop, as word might get out to the press that it was not ready for a public hearing.

For months Chicago had been awaiting the opening of the great festival. Though it had had its genesis in February 1882, several years had passed before a committee of public-spirited individuals made the first definite arrangements; but since then, despite all obstacles the dream had been materializing, inspiring those who had participated, unique in its objective of democratizing grand opera as presented by a company of the first magnitude with admission prices of $1, $2, $2.50 a seat.

The erection of a temporary opera house, seating more than 6,000, at the north end of the huge Exposition Building began on February 12, 1885, and before the end of six weeks the structure was complete. The Chicago *Indicator* marveled at this miracle: "March 28 the vast hall was ready for the final touches of drapery and gas chandeliers. The taste and plans of the architects are so beautifully expressed in the great hall itself that no further praise is needed. It is but just to add that the acoustics of the place are all that could have been wished. . . ."[1] The dimensions of the stage, 80 by 100 feet,[2] the scenery especially constructed for this space, the stage accessories, the auditorium with its elegant decorations, tiers of proscenium boxes, dress circle, balconies, the promenades—all impressed the thousands subsequently attending.

It opened on Monday, April 6, with one of the most potent of Mapleson's attractions: Patti and Scalchi in *Semiramide*. Other performances duly followed, with the public's response astounding. A review of the first week revealed that some 50,000 people had paid approximately $100,000 to attend the seven presentations, deemed critical and popular successes. The second week generated a like response, and by its end, on April 18, between 112,000 and 115,000 people had attended. In all, the receipts approximated $200,000.

Mapleson may have long remembered other features of this festival. One concerns the spectacular elements of several productions. For *Semiramide* the stage band and chorus had numbered approximately 450 individuals, while in the triumphal scene of *Aida*, on April 14, Mapleson employed 600 state militia as supernumeraries, a military band on stage, and 350 extra choristers.[3] He may also have cherished the critics' reception of his production of *Der Freischütz*. Given at the conclusion of the first week, it attracted a large house while giving local critics the first opportunity to compare a presentation of the same opera by Mapleson and the Metropolitan, which had presented a series in Chicago from February 23 to March 14. The comparison favored Mapleson. A possible lingering memory may have concerned Patti, whose contract demanded her name on printed announcements to be a third larger than that of any other artist. Viewing operatic wall posters in Chicago, Nicolini saw the diva's and Nevada's printed names too alike in size, even using a ruler to prove the horror. Mapleson subsequently ordered Nevada's name altered on all offending advertisements.[4]

Mapleson's American season of 1884–1885 closed with a week in New York (April 20–25) and one in Boston (April 27–May 2). In each city he presented six performances, with Nevada starring in *Sonnambula, Mireille, Lucia* and Patti in *Semiramide* and *Marta*. The sixth opera he brought forward in New York, on April 22, was *Rigoletto*, and in Boston, on April 29, he introduced *La Favorita*.

Once again the impresario returned to the East a conquering hero. Now a national figure, Mapleson, interviewed at the Academy during the opening night's *Semiramide* on April 20, expressed pleasure in the tour. Maintaining he had been royally treated throughout his absence, Mapleson indulged in some persiflage concerning New York and the Academy.

Elsewhere he had enjoyed clear stages for rehearsals, and in Chicago not only had the mayor awarded him the freedom of the city but the festival board of directors, in contrast with his own at the Academy, had actually given him a vote of thanks. As for plans involving New York next season, Mapleson, with his Academy contract ending in days, refused to commit himself but maintained Italian opera would outlast all competition: "The sauerkraut opera cannot last. Italian opera is the only opera that can depend upon fashionable support."[5]

Whatever his future plans, the New York press celebrated his return. "Colonel Mapleson has come back from the wars," the *Herald* wrote. "The Academy was ablaze last night to greet him. . . . It was the return of a conqueror, and the town turned out in his honor."[6] It continued to do so with the largest crowd at Patti's Gotham farewell in *Marta* on Friday, April 24.

Then, like New York, Boston honored Mapleson with enormous crowds. In many ways the six presentations there duplicated those in New York, with one extraordinary exception: Patti's ostensibly final farewell to the American stage, on Thursday, April 30, at which time she appeared in *Marta* with the usual cast. It was an intensely emotional evening.

At the close of the opera Mapleson appeared hand in hand with

Patti to express gratitude. Of all his remarks, one seemed to epit-
omize the diva, timeless in its resonance: Patti, said Mapleson,
was an artist who, above all, had never with her brilliant voice and
artistry disappointed the public. The audience roared in unani-
mous agreement.

The company now completed arrangements to embark for Europe. Of the principals Patti was among the first to depart, leaving
New York early in May. To representatives of the press she bade
her farewell to the United States:

> I felt that America should have only my best, and that the country
> where I first was received with open arms when a mite of a child should
> not remember me as a worn-out singer. I shall not sing much longer
> anywhere. I have all my old friends in Europe to say good-bye to, and
> when my adieus are all made I shall live, I hope, happy and contented
> in my dear home among the people who have learned to love me for
> myself, and not for my voice alone.[7]

The diva did change her mind, subsequently returning to the
United States for a number of "farewell" tours, repeatedly singing
there as well as elsewhere until a final appearance in October 1914.
Appropriately enough, it was at London's Albert Hall, the scene
of past triumphs, and in the presence of King George V and Queen
Mary.

According to the Royal Library at Windsor Castle, the King
later recalled the occasion in his diary: "At 3.0. we all went to a
Patriotic concert at the Albert Hall in aid of the Order of the
Hospital of St. John of Jerusalem, there were 10,000 people present. Patti sang, wonderfully still. . . ."[8] Queen Mary expressed
an analogous sentiment in her diary: "Mme. Patti sang really remarkably well . . . she had a wonderful reception."[9]

Patti thus closed her extraordinary career in glory. Few of the
world's musical greats have experienced the like.

In the time following Patti's departure, on May 2, Mapleson attended to business arrangements in New York. One of these concerned Nicolini, who Mapleson said had not fulfilled his contract,
failing to sing the specified number of times. Setting the damages

at $10,000, Mapleson ruefully attributed the breach of agreement to an obsession: "You know billiards have turned poor Nic's head. He's playing all the time, and I have been paying him for learning how to make ninety-three caroms a day. I don't want to get anything out of him. I only want him to treat me properly and not calmly refuse to sing, as his contract calls for." [10] He maintained the diva understood: "I am sure . . . that Patti understands the matter fully. She has often told me that she would stop Nicolini's billiard playing and lock up his cue if necessary." [11] Apparently there was no ill will between Mapleson and the tenor, nor was there a subsequent break in their relationship. No doubt at a later date the matter was amicably settled. Other important business affairs related to the Academy, where the board of directors elected Herman R. LeRoy president and unanimously agreed to alter and decorate the building during the summer months. It was also said there would be another series of Italian operas with the impresario no doubt providing the entertainment, but action upon his offer to lease the Academy next season was tabled for later consideration.

Regardless of the directors' lack of action on the lease, Mapleson expressed confidence in his plans for the fall in New York, asserting he would return with all means to devastate the Metropolitan in the next rencontre with it and its rumored new principal conductor, Hans Richter.

Even up to final minutes before his departure for Europe, on Thursday, May 7, he spoke in this vein: "With a good company, good and sufficiently novel operas, and new scenery and dresses, I think there ought to be no trouble in giving Mr. Richter all he bargains for. . . ." [12]

CHAPTER 14

Optimism Reigns— Briefly

∽

*D*URING THE summer of 1885 Mapleson's musical activities primarily related to two major projects: a season at London's Covent Garden and preparations for the new American campaign.

According to his own account, he returned to England with a profit of $150,000, but as he often exaggerated figures, the total probably was less.[1] Perhaps he overstated to frustrate the Gyes, whose contract with him—before its cancellation—had guaranteed them half his American profits. By this time Fortune no longer favored the Gyes, their operatic interests having collapsed. Still, whatever the amount in Mapleson's possession, it gave him the means to plan for a series of performances at Covent Garden from June 20 to July 25 with Patti, Giannini, De Anna, Scalchi, Del Puente among the principals. Of course the short season revolved around Patti, who at this time assumed a new part: the role of Carmen. Unfortunately it was a virtual fiasco, for Patti was no Carmen, she more the kitten than the cat; but as always she triumphed with her war-horses, the *Illustrated London News* celebrating her reentry as Violetta: "Indeed, whether as to vocal charm and refinement, or intense dramatic power, Madame Patti has never been heard and seen to greater advantage. . . ."[2] After the final performance of the series, on July 25, which marked the diva's twenty-fifth consecutive season at Covent Garden, Mapleson reenacted the New York torchlight procession with hundreds and a band escorting Patti from the opera house to her hotel. Like its American counterpart, the spectacle reflected more form than worthy substance or good taste. To finalize plans concerning the forthcoming American season, Mapleson journeyed about Europe in search of new talent. Among the leading artists he signed to appear in the United States for the first time were the tenor Serafino de Falco, the sopranos Félia Litvinne, Marie Engle, and Alma Fohström. He reengaged some outstanding singers absent from his company for several seasons: the tenor Luigi Ravelli, the baritone Giuseppe del Puente, the soprano Mathilde Bauermeister, the mezzo-soprano Emily Lablache, and, above all, the gifted American soprano Minnie Hauk. Later he added Lillian Nordica to this list. Then, too, Mapleson again secured, among others, Dotti, Giannini, De Anna, Cherubini, De Vaschetti, Caracciolo. As for the repertoire, he said he intended to vary the traditional bill of fare, promising new productions of *Maritana, Fra Diavolo, Mignon*, and a work not yet heard in the United States: Massenet's *Manon*.

Such preparations seemed to provide the requisite variety and scope. The Metropolitan would again tremble—yes, indeed! Arrangements with the Academy directors having been successfully completed for his renting of the facilities, Mapleson would once more direct his campaign from its battlements.

As in the past, so again Charles Mapleson preceded his father to New York, arriving there in the early fall to direct preliminary arrangements and publicity, which acclaimed the artists and the planned productions in a more modest fashion. A portion of a letter from Mapleson in London to Charles struck this moderate note: "I have had to give in to the press, and it is clear I must abolish the old system and give good performances equally balanced and at prices suitable to all."[3]

After arriving in New York on October 23, the impresario reiterated his determination to pay more attention to ensemble per-

formances: "At last I have determined to do what I have for long
ardently desired. I have abolished the star system! If I am successful, I think I ought to have a monument erected to me by a
grateful public. . . . Meanwhile, our old friends are rather out in
the cold. . . . It is not the high salary alone that I object to. It is
the airs they had got into the habit of assuming. How could we
give good opera when the principals would not come to rehearsal?
Galassi came down one day with a cigar in his mouth, and refused
to rehearse because the stage manager would not let him sing and
smoke at the same time. Scalchi got so high and mighty that she
would not come in at the stage door, and a special side door had
to be opened for her."[4] Mapleson had another grievance against
the stars: "Then they insist on cutting the music all to pieces. If
it is a little too high they cut it out—eight bars out here, four
there, and this or that must be made two notes lower. So it goes.
Why, you should see the orchestra score. It is so dissected that it
is all patches. They won't stand that in most places, you know.
The government interferes, and if you cut the music off you go to
prison."[5]

Mapleson now intended Italian opera, according to an announcement in the 1885 Academy programs, to be *"truly the music
for the people"* and "an educational institution." Thus he announced the series would begin with a work he had presented in
its American premiere his first season at the Academy: Bizet's
Carmen, with two of the principals from the 1878 cast: Giuseppe
del Puente and the illustrious Minnie Hauk.

Like Patti, Hauk, one of America's great singing actresses,
gained her first prominence in New York, where in the 1860s while
in her teens she made a number of sensational appearances in such
works as *Sonnambula* and *L'Etoile du Nord.* Ralph G. Martin, in
Jennie, maintains that she was the illegitimate daughter of Win-
ston Churchill's American grandfather, Leonard Jerome, and that
both Jerome and August Belmont had sponsored her musical education.[6] At the age of fourteen Hauk made her operatic debut at
the old Brooklyn Academy of Music, on October 13, 1866, as
Amina in *Sonnambula.* One day short of her sixteenth birthday,

she created the role of Gounod's Juliette in its American premiere, on November 15, 1867, at New York's Academy of Music, bowling over critics and the public with her superior acting ability as well as her vocalism. After triumphing in other cities in the United States, Hauk made successful appearances with a wide, varied repertoire in Paris, London, St. Petersburg, Moscow, Vienna, Budapest, Berlin, Brussels.

One of the most celebrated of her roles was Carmen, which under Mapleson's aegis she introduced to London, on June 22, 1878, and New York, on October 23, 1878. For many Hauk and Carmen became indissoluble, one of the reasons her reentry was awaited with anticipation.

The previous season's redecoration of the Metropolitan may have partly inspired like efforts at the Academy, where for weeks the house had undergone a rejuvenation in the Italian Renaissance style at a cost of some $80,000. The results gratified.[7] When the season opened with *Carmen* on Monday, November 2, freshly painted corridors, a magnificent new center chandelier with 250 burners beaming through brilliant crystals, colorful medallions of musical and literary figures adorning the gilded proscenium and ceiling, warm, bright colors throughout the hall, new crimson rugs, new chairs, garnet satin upholstery in the golden boxes—all elicited commendation from public and press. The house's superb acoustics were recelebrated: "Its very walls and floors seem saturated and permeated with sound, and every atom of its structure to be ready to vibrate in sympathy with music!"[8] Past seasons had seasoned it to true perfection.

The social element, though without some of the brightest names, nonetheless appeared in large numbers to form a "showy and amiable audience."[9] The *World*, for one, insisted that "the general atmosphere of enjoyment and promise . . . and the well-filled house . . . made the absence of many well known faces less noticeable than might have been expected."[10]

The performance was pleasurable, though it did not efface from memory earlier presentations of *Carmen* at the Academy. The *Times* critic thought the four leads—Hauk as Carmen, Ravelli as Don José, Del Puente as Escamillo, and Dotti as Micaela—great artists, but rued the condition of their voices, not, he said, so lovely nor so vibrant as of old: "Experience, observed a French wit, is a comb that one gets after losing one's hair."[11] The *Herald* and *Sun* disagreed, maintaining that Hauk's voice was now richer and more mellow and that Ravelli was "a lovely singer."[12] Of Hauk's interpretation, the *Sun* said: "So completely has she made the part her own that prima donnas have seemed to be shy of undertaking the role and of putting themselves into a position where comparison must be almost sure to result in disaster to them."[13] Under Arditi's inspired direction the performance augured well for the season.

Mapleson, conversing with Academy regulars and "looking as fresh as the red and white roses of his boutonniere,"[14] expressed pleasure in the first night: "I don't think Italian opera is dead yet . . . or, at any rate, it's a pretty lively sort of corpse."[15]

Mapleson had originally planned to introduce the Finnish soprano Alma Fohström as Lucia the second night, November 4, but illness forced a rescheduling: *Trovatore* with Giannini as Manrico, De Anna as Di Luna, Emily Lablache as Azucena, and Félia Litvinne, making her New York debut, as Leonora. A large house except for many empty proscenium boxes greeted the artists, who gave pleasure, with Giannini and De Anna's performances especially memorable. Lablache impressed with her delineation. Litvinne received mixed reviews, none overwhelmingly favorable. Krehbiel said her voice was of "commonplace quality"[16] used "according to the vocal conventions that offend much oftener than they please."[17] Mapleson presented this opera with the same cast the third evening, Friday, November 6, once more substituting it for *Lucia*, Fohström still indisposed. At the next day's matinee he again brought forward *Carmen* with the same cast as on opening night. Critics generally thought it a better performance than Monday's.

The second week began with Fohström's debut as Lucia on

Monday, November 9, in a cast including Giannini (Edgardo) and De Anna (Ashton). No doubt hoping to find the young soprano another Gerster or Nevada, Mapleson had secured her for his past season at Covent Garden, where she had made her first appearance replacing an indisposed Patti, coming through that baptism with aplomb, though it was patent she had more promise than artistry. Earlier she had appeared in such operatic centers as St. Petersburg, Moscow, Vienna, Milan, Rome. At her Academy debut, while making a favorable impression, Fohström did not eclipse Gerster or Nevada, the first appearance "effected without great enthusiasm, but with much satisfaction."[18] Critics agreed her singing was lovely, often brilliant, but lacked that "finesse and perfection of execution that might be desired."[19] After her second appearance, on Friday, November 13, as Amina in *Sonnambula*, Fohström received like notices. Still, Krehbiel maintained she was one of the most interesting debutantes Mapleson had introduced to New York, while the *Herald* thought her "sure to attract."[20] The week also featured two presentations of *L'Africaine*, on November 11 and 14, with Hauk as Selika, Dotti as Inez, Giannini as Vasco da Gama, De Anna as Nelusko. Giannini and De Anna sang beautifully, while Hauk's voice was "especially round, full, and resonant, and showing that clear ringing bell-like quality of tone that . . . made her famous the world over."[21] It did much to obliterate the not altogether favorable impression of the opening night's *Carmen*. The scenery, marches, and ballet at the beginning of the fourth act impressed, though an elephant did not; the creature "seemed rather tipsy and soon shambled off."[22]

After the November 14 matinee of *L'Africaine*, marking the end of the first two weeks, Mapleson announced that prices for tickets were to be lowered, beginning November 16, one of the first public indications all was not well. Subscription sales before the season's opening disappointed; the public thus far had not sufficiently responded; the stockholders were increasingly absent. To make current experiences even more bitter, Mapleson on the very day of the announcement of reduction in prices may have read that advance sales at the Metropolitan already totaled over $32,000, not including boxes, and that there had been "no lack of competition among those anxious to secure desirable boxes for the season."[23] Without the magic presence of Patti, Mapleson may have realized that what critics had repeatedly been saying was true: Italian opera per se no longer attracted.

Apparently at this time he was experiencing other difficulties. He complained that rehearsals on the stage were becoming nearly impossible, citing problems in preparing *L'Africaine.* Rehearsal for the opera's fourth act, a spectacle critics highly praised, had taken place under platforms some thirty feet high placed there for a chorus and orchestra under the direction of Theodore Thomas. Then, too, Mapleson was facing competition at the Academy, where a newly founded company, the American Opera, was preparing for its opening early in the new year. Under Thomas' artistic direction, the organization planned to present music dramas in English, appealing to those advocating opera in the vernacular. Members of this company were increasingly making their presence known at the Academy, either rehearsing or carrying out business affairs while, according to Mapleson, intriguing against him and his interests.

Mapleson began the third week with another *Carmen* on Monday, November 16, with the same cast and to a full house except for the proscenium boxes, the lower prices having contributed to the larger assemblage. *Town Topics* sneered that the audiences had now become "operatic enthusiasts of the bill board class."[24] On Wednesday, November 18, he brought forward *La Favorita,* with two artists making their New York debuts: De Falco as Fernando and Virginia Pervini as Leonora. The cast also included De Anna (Alfonso) and Cherubini (Balthazar). Of these, the *Times* critic praised De Anna, the lavish applause for whom "was but a deserved tribute to a well-nigh flawless performance."[25] De Falco, a good musician, failed to impress with his light tenor voice; at times there was nonetheless "abundant evidence of intelligence and technical ability and of an artistic temperament."[26] As for Pervini, the same critic dismissed her rather cruelly: "a powerful metallic voice, but her appearance and style would counteract the good influence of Mme. Patti's tones, even, if these had been vouch-safed her."[27] The highlight of the third week was the beautifully sung and excellently portrayed *Fra Diavolo*, first presented on Friday, November 20, with Ravelli (Fra Diavolo), Fohström (Zerline), Del Puente (Beppo), Cherubini (Giacomo), Caracciolo (Milord), Lablache (Pamela), and Rinaldini (Lorenzo). Hightly praised, the performance, said the *Times*, was "uncommonly spirited and effective"[28] while the *Herald* ranked it "a most brilliant success,"[29] an evaluation also endorsed by the *Tribune*. Ravelli sang with superb phrasing and ringing tones; Fohström charmed by her delightful singing and acting; Del Puente and Cherubini amused in their well-thought-out delineations, their comic efforts provoking much laughter. The week concluded the following day with a matinee *Lucia* and an evening presentation of *Don Giovanni*, a benefit for Del Puente, who had suffered financial losses. Mapleson arranged for this special performance while ruefully commenting on his own situation: "He ought to have put his money in an Italian opera company if he yearned to lose it. . . . Then it would have melted away by degrees, and he would hardly have known he had lost it until it was gone. I could have given him some valuable points on 'How to lose money cheaply and expeditiously.' "[30]

At the benefit Del Puente as the Don dominated the proceedings, generally capably assisted by Litvinne (Donna Anna), Bauermeister (Donna Elvira), Hauk (Zerlina), Ravelli (Don Ottavio), and Cherubini (Leporello). Hauk was in unusually good form; to Ravelli's rendition of "Il mio tesoro" the house responded with "an unusual pitch of excitement,"[31] while Del Puente was "often recalled by an audience eager to applaud him. . . ."[32]

Still hampered in rehearsal time and not receiving sufficient public support, Mapleson announced at the beginning of the fourth week, which also inaugurated the Metropolitan's third season, that he intended to conclude his series on Saturday, November 28. Frustrated in his attempts to bring forward the novelties *Maritana* and *Manon*, a result, he claimed, of conditions at the Academy, Mapleson determined to close the New York season before the originally announced time, presenting *Fra Diavolo* on November 23 and 27, *Don Giovanni* on November 25, and *Faust* at the concluding Saturday matinee, November 28, with Hauk (Marguerite), Giannini (Faust), De Anna (Valentin), Cherubini (Méphistophélès). In a *World* interview he explained: "I simply could not fight a battle with all Wall Street, which is bent on supporting German opera now."[33]

A cursory review of the concluded series indicates heavy reliance on the traditional, which the past two seasons had made money for him. With Patti in the company such a repertoire was attractive, her presence alone a powerful magnet. Without her, Mapleson must at last have realized, his list of works held little interest; but as in the past two years, he again counted on the tour to fill the treasury and furnish the ammunition to continue the war. By now his was something of a national company, whereas the Metropolitan was not. Convinced that German opera could not last, Mapleson needed, so it seemed, only to outlast his adversary; and when New York tired of the new experience, as he maintained it inevitably would, he would then resume his former place in the cultural life of the city.

In December the company held a number of rehearsals of operas scheduled for the tour, presented three performances in Brooklyn as well as several Sunday concerts at New York's Academy, and finally brought forward the novelties *Maritana*, at the December 19 matinee, and Massenet's *Manon*, on December 23, both at the Academy. These two operas made quite a stir.

First presented in Brooklyn on December 17, *Maritana* met with an enthusiastic reception, Ravelli as Don Caesar especially evoking wild demonstrations for his magnificent singing. The cast included Del Puente (King), De Anna (Don José), Fohström (Maritana). Repeated two days later in New York with the same cast, according to the *Times* it "progressed amid demonstrations of enthusiastic delight the like of which had not been known at the Academy for many a day,"[34] while the *Herald* pronounced it an "unqualified success."[35] During the performance the artists favored the audience with a number of encores.

Then on Wednesday, December 23, Massenet's *Manon* was introduced to the United States in a cast featuring Hauk as Manon, Giannini as Des Grieux, Del Puente as Lescaut, Cherubini as Count des Grieux, Bauermeister as Poussette, Lablache as Javotte, De Vigne as Rosette. Its world premiere had occurred almost two years before, on January 19, 1884, at the Paris Opéra-Comique. At one time Mapleson's production had seemed impossible, but the impresario, desirous above all of impressing the directors and his public, succeeded in overcoming all possible obstacles, determined to leave the city with flags flying.

He was also determined to leave with Hauk as his leading prima donna. In her memoirs she maintained that had he not prepared *Manon* for production she would have left the company.

"The War of the Operas—A Harmonious Battle," cartoon in Puck.
Arditi is to the right and Anton Seidl to the left.
COURTESY NEW YORK PUBLIC LIBRARY.

The American premiere of *Manon*, on December 23, a benefit for Mapleson, generated considerable interest among critics and in the audience, which was fairly large. No doubt Christmas season activities and perhaps some uncertainty as to whether the opera would be presented precluded a full house. The *Sun* maintained that had *Manon* been produced during the regular season, it would have proved good box office, calling it a "charming opera." [36] The critic continued: "There are many changes of mood as well as of scenery, and interest is admirably sustained throughout. . . . Much of its charm lies in the orchestral portion of the opera, Massenet knowing cleverly how to make attractive his instrumental forces, though his means are often affectedly meagre." [37] The *Herald* and the *Times* said the opera needed more rehearsals, the former maintaining the production was "deficient in smoothness and spirit" [38] while the latter complained of "imperfect rehearsals, that neither invited nor repaid attention. . . ." [39]

Critics tended to agree that though no genius, Massenet had composed passages of surprising loveliness and marked originality. The *Herald* said the composer's taste was "elegant, though not always refined"; [40] the *Sun* preferred the St. Sulpice scene to all else in the score, "a strikingly fine one"; [41] the *Times* critic, detecting Wagnerian influences in the composer's use of leitmotifs and in the "unduly heavy" orchestration, [42] admired portions of the work, assessing Massenet as "a writer of talent, ingenious and somewhat imitative, and a master of the science of instrumentation." [43]

Though they generally agreed Hauk's dramatic interpretation of Manon was well thought out and convincing, critics did not unanimously acclaim her singing. As Des Grieux, Giannini triumphed in his singing but failed to interest from a dramatic standpoint. The others in the large cast, especially Del Puente and Lablache, shared in the generally favorable reception. Arditi, as usual, conducted.

Fulfilling his promise to produce novelties somewhat restored Mapleson's reputation in New York, which he now was ready to quit.

"Col. Mapleson's Masterly Inactivity: 'I will let the German and American Operas fight it out, and then I will come and vanquish the victor,' " cartoon in Puck.

Departing, he fired a broadside at his inimical rival: "I am willing to bide my time, for the American women have ears, and it will not take them very long to find out the difference between the substitutes and the genuine thing. When the millionaires get tired of this sort of thing, if they will give me 1 per cent on what they will have lost in trying to make substitutes for opera popular, I will give opera here as well as it is given anywhere."[44]

Ever defiant, Mapleson was withdrawing but for a time, stating to a representative of the press: "We are not dead yet, nor do we propose to die. We will let the German and American operas fight it out, and then we will come and vanquish the victor."[45]

For a considerable time the press had been heralding the Metropolitan's forthcoming season, whetting the operatic appetite with some choice items. New artists, new productions, several Wagner premieres, the anticipated New York debut of the conductor and Wagner protégé Anton Seidl created tremendous interest and a large advance sale.

One of the proposed innovations, double casts, evoked comment from Mapleson: "It reminds me of old E. T. Smith, a well-known London manager. . . . He came to me one day and said, 'Mapleson, my boy, things are getting very bad and something must be done. Here the Duchess of Kent is on her death bed and people won't come to the opera. Now I have a great idea. You know I was the first man to play a pantomime with two clowns and two pantaloons, and so on. Well, look at this model.' And he showed me a model of his stage divided into two tiers by a horizontal platform. 'I am going . . . to electrify the public. I'm going to do the *Trovatore* with two complete casts at the same time. On top I shall have Mario and Grisi on one floor and Tietjens and Trebelli on the other. One orchestra will be for both and we can divide the chorus.' "[46] As for the Metropolitan artists, he commented: "A famous cook tried once to make soup without meat, and gave it up at last. They are trying to give opera without voices, and the attempt is bound to fail."[47]

Nonetheless, a large brilliant audience applauded the Metropolitan's opening-night *Lohengrin*, on Monday, November 23, 1885, with Auguste Kraus as Elsa, Marianne Brandt as Ortrud, Adolf Robinson as Telramund, and Albert Stritt as Lohengrin. Seidl in his American debut was ranked as an exceptional conductor, though he was criticized for overdoing some effects and being too physical in his directing. Socially, *Town Topics* rhapsodized over the affair as "distinctively fashionable."[48]

The next two performances also impressed, featuring the American debuts of several artists, the first one more important to the history of the Metropolitan. On Wednesday, November 25, Lilli Lehmann as Carmen made a deep impression in her first appearance with the company, immediately establishing herself as an artist of uncommon distinction. Another American debut on this occasion was that of Max Alvary (Don José), a heroic tenor admired for a voice of great power, imposing mien, artistic sincerity. Two evenings later Eloi Sylva as John of Leyden in *Le Prophète* aroused enthusiasm with his singing, which had "all the smoothness and finish characterizing the best work of tenori di grazia."[49] Also lauded were Kraus as Bertha and Brandt as Fidès. The week closed with another *Carmen* with the same cast as on Wednesday.

In December the Metropolitan created a sensation with its magnificent production of Karl Goldmark's *Die Königin von Saba* with Lehmann as Sulamith. First presented on December 2, it triumphed with its rich, full music, solo artists, lavish mise-en-scène, ensemble playing, superb chorus, faultless orchestra, Seidl's inspired leadership. The next day the *Times* said no opera had "ever been placed upon the stage with anything approaching the gorgeousness and historical accuracy of last night's production; the scenes, the costumes, and the pageants—the latter involving the services of an efficient corps de ballet, and of a personnel aggregating 600 persons—offer to the eye a succession of pictures that for dazzling color, correctness, and life-like realism have had no equals within the recollection of the present generation of theatregoers."[50] This opera became the season's hit, presented fifteen times in all, with seven of these in December before the company interrupted its New York series after the Saturday, December 19 matinee to play a fortnight's engagement in Philadelphia. By then Lehmann had become an increasingly important factor in New York's opera world, having impressed also as Brünnhilde in *Die Walküre* and Bertha in *Le Prophète*.

The month ended with many in New York looking forward to two New Year's operas: the American premiere of Wagner's *Die Meistersinger*, on January 4, 1886, and a new production of the master's *Rienzi* on February 5, 1886.

CHAPTER 15

On the Road

ᗡ

*I*N NEW YORK, while critics generally praised the singing of
Mapleson's two leading tenors, Giannini and Ravelli, his two
outstanding baritones, Del Puente and De Anna, the basses
Cherubini and Caracciolo, they had not always expressed unre-
served admiration for Hauk and Fohström. To strengthen his
forces, Mapleson reengaged Nordica, who since her last appearance with the company in 1884 had experienced tragedy in her
marriage. In July 1885 her husband, having extended his interest
in science to the field of aeronautics, disappeared in a balloon as-
cension from Cherbourg, not heard of since. Free of him, the soprano resumed her operatic career, which he had always resented.
In securing Nordica, Mapleson added luster to his progresses.

The tour opened, on January 4, in Boston, where in two weeks
the company appeared on twelve occasions, presenting operas earlier performed in New York while adding for the first time this
season *La Traviata* on January 8, *Rigoletto* on the fourteenth, and
Marta at the final January 16 Saturday matinee.

Nordica made her reentry as Violetta, the first time she had
appeared in this role in Boston. The soprano with Giannini (Alfredo) and De Anna (Germont) created a sensation, singing with
"brilliancy and facile execution,"[1] heartily cheered and applauded
by the largest house of the first week. Though scheduled to appear
as Donna Elvira in *Don Giovanni* on the twelfth, the soprano did
not sing, Bauermeister replacing her. Of Nordica's final perfor-

mance as Gilda, with Giannini as the Duke and De Anna as Rigoletto, the *Herald* said that hers was "one of the most evenly satisfying interpretations of this role seen here in many years"[2] and that she "displayed a dramatic intelligence that surprised those familiar with her earlier efforts upon the operatic stage."[3] On this occasion the immense house witnessed a most brilliant performance, with all the principals outdoing themselves. In an extended review of the series, the *Herald* made this appraisal: "The organization as a whole compares favorably with any that Manager Mapleson has ever brought to this country. . . ."[4]

From Boston the troupe journeyed to Philadelphia, where from January 18 to 27 it presented eleven performances. Although critics found much pleasure in the performers and performances, the public did not swarm to the theater in sufficient numbers, with the result that by the twenty-fourth Mapleson lowered prices and reduced the size of the orchestra.[5] A letter in the archives of the Library of Congress reveals his financial plight. Writing the final day of the series, he asked a creditor for forbearance: "I had paid up everything feeling sure there would be sufficient surplus from the two performances, to take up cheque—and also to pay the R.R. to Baltimore, but it leaves me unable to do either. Kindly allow it to remain over until I reach Chicago on *Monday week*— 8th Feb."[6] The morning of the day Mapleson wrote this letter the *North American* said it regretted the imminent departure of the troupe with "so much good material in its composition."[7]

After favoring Baltimore with four presentations (January 28– 30), Mapleson brought forward three performances in the national capital from February 1 to 3. Here the critic of the *Washington Post*, though admiring the principals, censured the company, calling it "incapable of interpreting an opera of the higher order to the satisfaction of an experienced audience."[8] Of the three performances, *Carmen* attracted the largest house. From the national capital the company entrained for Pittsburgh, presenting four performances. Like Washington, Pittsburgh, according to the local *Dispatch*, noted the troupe did not measure up to its past.[9]

Mapleson now prepared for an engagement from February 8 to

20 in Chicago, where the successes of the festival there the past April were still remembered.

On opening night, Monday, February 8, during the third act of *Carmen* Ravelli as Don José was about to take an electrifying high note. Just then the dramatic Hauk, according to Mapleson, rushed forward, holding on to the tenor's waistcoat until the buttons gave way one after another. Outraged, Ravelli charged to the footlights with so much fury that the house, thrilled by the drama, broke into thunderous applause. The *Inter Ocean* said the next day: "Few can forget his passionate reproach to the coquette. . . ."[10]

After the curtain fell on this act there was a horrendous scene, punctuated with such threats that the soprano feared for her life, hardly able to finish the performance. The next day her husband, Baron Ernst von Hesse-Wartegg, wrote Mapleson a letter in which he stated his wife would be unable to sing with the company for a considerable time. On February 10 the baron's lawyer followed up his client's letter with one of his own, threatening to issue a warrant against Ravelli unless Mapleson was willing to guarantee a $2,000 bond for the tenor's future behavior as regarded Hauk. The lawyer assured Mapleson the soprano wished, above all, to avoid notoriety. Mapleson of course gave the bond, no doubt hoping this would end the affair, but soon found it public knowledge, with disastrous consequences for the tour.

Unfortunately for Mapleson, the Hauk-Ravelli imbroglio was only the beginning of a number of adversities in Chicago. Arditi caught a cold which later developed into pneumonia; an assistant conductor also became ill, as did other artists, including Hauk and Nordica. So ill was Arditi, however, that Mapleson thought he would soon die, the conductor's doctor having advised him of this imminent possibility. Before leaving Chicago, Mapleson prepared a cable to the maestro's wife in which he inquired what he should do with the remains.

Despite such problems the season proceeded, with the assistant conductor Oreste Bimboni replacing Arditi at all performances for a considerable time. The local *Tribune* appraised the company as a good one, though not so large as formerly; still, "tried by any American standard but his own or that of the extravagant and unfortunate Abbey, it is perhaps sufficient. . . ." [11]

The week following the Chicago engagement Mapleson brought forward seven productions, with three in Minneapolis and four in St. Paul. Bimboni conducted all seven. Then, although he had planned and advertised a week's series of scope and variety for St. Louis, the impresario changed the program as the result of illnesses. The first occurred with the opening night presentation, on Monday, March 1.

Originally announced as *Carmen*, it was replaced by *Maritana* with the usual cast. Two evenings later Mapleson substituted *Faust* for *Manon*, Hauk being unable to perform. Of the seven performances, Fohström assumed the principal soprano roles in three, Dotti in two, Nordica in one. Hauk finally appeared at the Saturday matinee, February 6, as Carmen, with De Falco as Don José. Earlier Mapleson had protested the press reaction to the changes: "Some of the papers intimate that I am responsible. . . . Now, how utterly absurd that is! As if I made it a business to go and make singers sick in order to disappoint the public! I am disappointed myself. I am distinctly vexed by the whole business. . . . One-half of the company is ill, and the other half is quarreling like . . . Hades." [12] Criticism mounted, as the *Globe-Democrat* clearly demonstrated: "It is not owing to the fact that the company is an inferior one, because it is not, but alone because of the insincerity of the management in making announcements and statements." [13] Mapleson protested such comments, particularly angered by an editorial in the *Missouri Republican* accusing him of occasionally substituting "artisans for artists." [14] Furious, he wrote a letter to the editor defending his action in replacing, for example, *Carmen* with *Maritana* "with a most perfect cast of artists, (not artisans)," [15] reminding St. Louis that an "opera singer must not be confounded with a brazen-throated comedian or opera bouffe vocalist, who can sing at all hours and under any circumstances." [16]

Still, despite changes, the short season had not disappointed.

The leading artists were praised as well as Signor Bimboni, who during Arditi's sickness had "shown himself an able substitute for the king of all orchestral leaders. . . ."[17]

The monarch referred to in the review rejoined the company in St. Louis. Upon arrival Arditi had fully recovered—apparently much to Mapleson's surprise. From March 8 to 18 the troupe played in six other Western cities: Kansas City, Missouri, Topeka, St. Joseph, Denver, Cheyenne, and Salt Lake City, the noteworthy feature of this series being Arditi's return to the podium in Cheyenne.

Then at long last it was time for what to many was the highlight of the year: the return to San Francisco.

Back in New York the Metropolitan continued to give many superb performances, from the new year to the final performance on March 6. Among the best received were the American premiere of *Die Meistersinger,* on January 4, with Emil Fischer as a definitive Hans Sachs, Kraus as Eva, and Brandt as Magdalene; the lavish presentation of *Faust,* on January 20, with Lehmann (Marguerite), Stritt (Faust), Fischer (Méphistophélès); and the new production of *Rienzi,* on February 5, with Lehmann as Irene, Brandt as Adriano, and Sylva as Rienzi. These impressed for their ensemble performances, the superb chorus and orchestra, mise-en-scène, costuming, and the musical intelligence commanding the productions. As for *Die Meistersinger,* Krehbiel heaped praise on the rich fulfillment of a most difficult work to produce, maintaining that never before had the artists appeared to greater advantage. In *Faust,* according to the *Times,* the company "acquitted itself with honor,"[18] a judgment also made of the brilliant presentation of *Rienzi,* which at its first performance received "such demonstrations of delight as are seldom beheld. . . ."[19]

These and other productions, the dedication and artistry of many of the principals, but, above all, the masterful conducting of Seidl had a profound influence on operagoers and critics. By the time the Metropolitan ended its third New York season, there were no doubts as to its artistic worth to the city's music life. In contrast, the American Opera at the Academy made no lasting impact. For the moment the Metropolitan seemed peerless.

New York marveled at the triumph of German opera. Though formerly stars attracted, now the ensemble drew. The Metropolitan determined to extend German opera for at least three more years, going ahead with plans for the 1886–1887 season. For the one just concluded the deficit was $25,000, not much when divided among the wealthy stockholders.

New York also marveled at the esprit de corps of the company, with the artists and management working together as one, reveling in their grand reception and accomplishments as they served the cause of German opera with an almost holy zeal. In a letter dated January 1, 1886, Lehmann wrote: "It is a wonder how all the operas get along so well, although the institute is so young and one does not find one's self where opera is 200 years old, as in Europe." [20] Of the management, all acknowledged the genius of Seidl, who inspired the artists, kindling them to oustanding performances; but another, Stanton, had won their confidence, a fact evident in the same letter from Lehmann: "Mr. Stanton, our director, is a gentleman all over. Every individual member, from the soloist down to the last workman, loves and respects him." [21] After the final performance, a matinee of *Die Königin von Saba* on March 6, a number of distinguished individuals gathered at a dinner in this gentleman's honor. Perhaps on this occasion various members in the assemblage proposed toasts to the culmination of a most successful series.

Apparently, though, not all associated with the new house would have joined in such toasts. Some of the boxholders and guests had not at all times displayed enthusiasm for the operas, unwilling to concentrate on them or to extend common courtesy. George William Curtis in the April 1886 edition of *Harper's* commented: "On behalf of the excellent people who chatter and giggle in the boxes . . . and who are wholly ignorant of good-breeding, it must be said that they behave after their kind, and furnish a spectacle and entertainment which were not promised in the bills." [22] Despite such seeming indifference the boxholders continued to support

German opera. They did so, Irving Kolodin in *The Metropolitan Opera* maintains, for three reasons: "because it was economical, because the public responded in sizable numbers, and because the enthusiastic reception of the press for the unfamiliar masterpieces of Wagner gave them a flattering status as art patrons." [23]

Thus by the end of its third season the Metropolitan loomed as an extraordinary force, its artistic powers as well as the support of fashionables and the public making it seem unassailable.

Mapleson, at the moment about to begin the San Francisco season, knew his survival on the American scene depended upon the unfolding events of the next few weeks. The Golden Gate had not failed him before; he hoped it would not now.

CHAPTER 16

Hope Springs Eternal

SOME TEN hours behind schedule, a tired company arrived in San Francisco late on Saturday, March 20. A number were suffering from various maladies, Mapleson himself somewhat testy either because of gout or from news of poor subscription sales. At any rate, always mindful of the value of publicity, he assured the press that his forthcoming season would again be spectacular, with such productions as *William Tell, Masaniello, L'Africaine,* and that his artists would surpass themselves in the entire series. By now accustomed to Maplesonian ballyhoo, the papers adopted a moderate tone in describing the coming attractions.

When the season opened on Monday, March 22, with Hauk, Ravelli, Dotti, and Del Puente in *Carmen,* a large audience applauded the presentation, with the most enthusiasm reserved for Hauk and Del Puente. According to the *Chronicle,* the performance impressed as a good all-around one. The same publication commented, however, that the troupe seemed dispirited and that Hauk and Ravelli were not in good voice, the tenor cutting some of his part. Still, Hauk's Carmen remained the ideal; Ravelli's acting was mediocre but much of his singing had "magnetism and clearness and considerable power";[1] Dotti surprised by her vocal improvement; Del Puente used his splendid baritone "with excellent effect."[2] Arditi, greeted by roars of welcome at the opera's beginning, reaffirmed the good impression he had made in the past two seasons, still demonstrating his wonted authority.

For the second performance Mapleson introduced Fohström as Lucia, on Tuesday, March 23, with Giannini as Edgardo and De Anna as Ashton. Although small, the audience enthusiastically applauded a more spirited performance than that of the previous evening. Fohström impressed in her debut; Giannini sang gloriously, it being "worth the admission to hear him almost alone";[3] De Anna captivated dramatically and vocally, his voice "always used with an artist's judgment."[4] The following day the *Chronicle*, appreciative of the first two presentations and aware of public apathy, commented on the fairness of Mapleson's price scale and the merits of his troupe.

On the third evening the impresario brought forward *Manon* with the usual cast. Hauk and Giannini triumphed in their roles, the soprano's acting and singing more favorably received than before, while the tenor sang so well that critics declared he had surpassed all his past efforts on this occasion. They also commented on the beautiful orchestration and a vocal score "full of melody from the beginning to the end."[5]

Thus far Mapleson presented what had been advertised, but on Thursday, March 25, he had to substitute *Lucia* for the scheduled *Marta*, Ravelli being ill, with the same cast as on Tuesday except that Del Puente assumed the role of Ashton. De Anna's nonappearance created rumors that subsequently proved to have substance. It was said he was leaving the company, furious with Mapleson over past and present grievances concerning salary. Before long his antipathy toward Mapleson and departure from the company became public knowledge.

Nordica, as Violetta, made her San Francisco debut on Friday, March 26, with Giannini (Alfredo) and Del Puente (Germont), before a house only fair in numbers. Again, what it lacked in size it made up for in interest and approving demonstrations. Considered a success, the soprano charmed with her "delightful voice, a sympathetic quality and an enthusiastic musical instinct,"[6] but compared with former Violettas, she gave, according to the *Morn-*

"The King of the Scalpers," cartoon in The Wasp.
COURTESY SAN FRANCISCO PUBLIC LIBRARY.

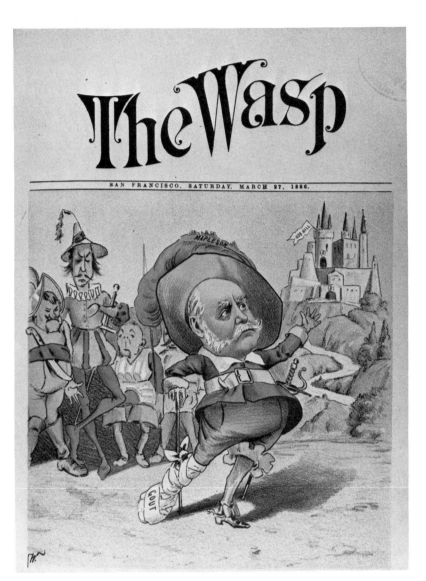

"The 'Ero of the 'Tower-Hamlets'—A Forlorn Hope,"
cartoon in The Wasp.

ing Call, "but a rough-cast idea of the sentimental and sinning Camille."[7]

The next day the first week concluded with a matinee of *Carmen* featuring the same cast as Monday's except for De Falco as Don José. By now Mapleson was no doubt realizing he would be fortunate if he made expenses or, at best, a slight profit. Despite generally favorable reviews, attendance for the preceding six performances had remained only fair. Without Patti, Her Majesty's Company seemed neither better nor worse than others. The following series, however, might make the difference.

The second week began well, on Monday, March 29, with Fohström's assumption of the role of Amina in *La Sonnambula,* she being highly praised; but many expressed disappointment in Ravelli's nonappearance. His role of Elvino was assumed by De Falco, who was as deficient in notes of current value as a broken bank. Next evening's offering, *L'Africaine,* evoked tremendous interest,[8] the house filled "with as fashionable an audience as ever gathered inside the four walls of the building,"[9] all reminiscent of Patti nights. Hauk's magnificent singing and acting, Giannini's powerful voice, and Del Puente as Nelusko, replacing the departed De Anna and learning his role in four days, scored a triumph with the public and most of the press. The performance, compact of action, vivid, and spectacular, aroused the huge audience like nothing else in the series. Apparently its grandeur was what pleased, for according to the *Argonaut* it was this that San Francisco required: "Grandeur . . . we must have."[10] *L'Africaine* was the week's highlight.

Supplementary performances followed, the chief interest in these being the return of Ravelli and his assumption of the principal tenor parts in *Marta,* on April 6, *Maritana,* on April 8, and *Don Giovanni* on April 9. It was said his singing of "Il mio tesoro" warranted "the most enthusiastic encore given to anything during the season."[11]

Mapleson then made known there would be still another week, obviously a desperate move to accumulate as much money as possible; but before it got underway pent-up emotions exploded.

Probably for a considerable time members of the troupe had looked forward to the legendary financial rewards of the Golden Gate; and no doubt earlier Mapleson had urged his artists to patience over their salaries. San Francisco surely would again furnish ammunition for the campaign and allow him to settle all pecuniary claims. It was but a short while, though, before it became clear such was no longer the situation. De Anna's earlier break had indicated all was not well; now the public heard of another revolt by the artist who had recently covered himself with glory.

On Saturday, April 10, Ravelli sued Mapleson for salary past due, claiming that between February 4 and April 4 he had not received the contractual amount of $2,400 a month. Cherubini and De Vigne later joined him. Mapleson forthwith had to fight these and soon others of his company. The war had evolved into a revolution. Mapleson now prepared a countersuit: a cross-complaint against Ravelli of $5,000 in damages for the tenor's breach of contract. Interviewed on April 14 by the *Chronicle*, Mapleson said: "I am struggling to save the fortunes of the season. . . . Three or four members of the company have been kicking up the very Old Knick. The last is Ravelli, who admits to my lawyer that he hasn't the slightest real grievance. . . . And he has been in bed three weeks at a time, simply to revenge himself because I would not pay him when he did not sing. I was in the right, and acting strictly under my contract."[12]

Ravelli received word of Mapleson's countersuit on the afternoon of Friday, April 16, and fumed: "He claims to have fined me for not being at rehearsals, and different other things, which are a total lie, but of course the Colonel has all the people there who will swear to what he says, or he will leave them on the ground, as none of them have any money, and of course they are all working in the interest of the Colonel and going against me, anyway, as I am not any longer a member of the company."[13] The tenor then denied having assaulted Hauk in Chicago, and stated he had never refused to sing when able. Several days later the irate artist informed the press his lawyers had seized the company's music and would take further action on Monday, April 19;

but they could not get their hands on the costumes or scenery, since these were serving as a guarantee of payment of railroad fares.

On Sunday, April 18, Mapleson himself met with Ravelli, trying to effect a reconciliation while also attempting to persuade the tenor to remain with the company. Apparently the meeting had a positive effect, for later in the day Ravelli confided to a reporter his decision to release the music his lawyers had seized as well as a $4,800 attachment, but on the morrow he changed his mind.

By Tuesday other troubles conspired against Mapleson. The chorus and orchestra, in miserable circumstances, were camping outside the opera house, having left their hotels for want of sufficient funds; and since Ravelli's embargo extended to the troupe's baggage, no one was allowed access to the trunks, presently stored in a hall of the opera house and guarded by a deputy sheriff with a gun who kept off the owners. Unsure whether Mapleson would be able to settle his financial claims and fearful over the chances of returning home, some of the troupe had apparently begun ruminating as to employment in San Francisco, considering such possibilities as sales, restaurant work, domestic service.

Then, too, Ravelli, Cherubini, De Falco in their public remarks had more and more disparaged the impresario, portraying him as a pasteboard Colonel while ever clamoring for their back pay. As if this were not enough, competing railway companies added to Mapleson's problems when they suddenly settled their differences in a railroad war, with the unhappy consequence that fares from San Francisco were raised.

All seemed ominous until a meeting held the following day, when Mapleson's and Ravelli's lawyers met to draw up the terms of settlement. It was finally agreed Mapleson would pay the sheriff's and the tenor's lawyer's fees while providing endorsed notes for $1,000. The remaining $3,800 Ravelli claimed was to be settled at a subsequent time. Once the attachment was released, Mapleson satisfied the claims of his other creditors, paid the hotel bills, and settled with the railroad company for the fares.

Rumors soon circulated as to the source of the money, but the prevailing impression was that Mapleson had possessed the funds all the time. Some said, however, that a wealthy newspaper owner, possibly De Young, had rescued Mapleson from his perilous straits, while others maintained Dotti had pawned her diamonds. According to the *Daily Examiner*, Mapleson at three in the afternoon left his hotel carrying three jewelry boxes and, returning at four, immediately gave orders for the troupe to be at the Oakland ferry at six. To a representative of the *Morning Call* he said: "I have at last succeeded in unravelling the Ravelli skein of tangled trouble and brushing away all the other bothersome cobwebs of my present bad luck."[14]

The news of departure galvanized the company, with the scene around the opera house now intensely lively.[15] By about eight that evening the opera caravan of some 160 persons again was on the road, the special train having left Oakland with all aboard except Ravelli, Cherubini, De Vigne and Fohström, who, though now ill, said she would rejoin the company in Cincinnati in May. Mapleson was presently widely advertising her and others to alert remaining cities on the tour that Her Majesty's Opera Company was still a vital force. Characteristically, he refused to dip his standard to adversity.

CHAPTER 17

Finis

∽

IN THE evacuation from the Pacific Mapleson devised a strategy
to sustain the operation in its retreat, arranging for performances en route, sending Hauk ahead for publicity purposes.
Then, wiring to the scheduled site before arrival, he generally received advance funds to enable progress to the East Coast while
also satisfying financial claims. Mapleson, however, subsequently
changed the original design, proceeding via detours to Louisville, Kentucky, arriving there nearly at midnight on Monday,
April 26.

The impresario began the engagement the following evening with
the disadvantage of bad publicity from the coast and with the onus
of not having opened, as advertised, the night before. Here and
elsewhere Mapleson and the troupe felt victimized. In this city
and in those that followed—Indianapolis, Cincinnati, Detroit,
Milwaukee—the public's response disappointed, finances at low
ebb. The Detroit *Evening News*, one of many, empathized: "The
operation of lifting the principal signors and signori out of the
leading hotel at each place is almost as great an agony as the fabled
anguish of the mandrake when pulled up by the roots." [1]

Mapleson's 1885–1886 American season ended in Chicago,
where, beginning with a Sunday concert on May 16 and ending
with one a week later, he repeated six of the most popular operas
in his repertoire. Here seemingly all went well as far as the general

public was concerned, but in the company itself there still was disaffection, Giannini being one example.

On Wednesday, May 19, the tenor refused to participate in *Faust* that evening unless Mapleson paid him some $2,000 owed for past performances. By the time the curtain went up Mapleson had apparently met his demands, for Giannini did appear. The next day the orchestra struck. Interviewed by the *Daily News*, a member said: "We have had no salaries for three weeks, and most of us have no money to pay our hotel bills. We are sorry for Mr. Mapleson's bad luck, but we are poor men with families to support. . . ." [2] Pleas ultimately having no effect, Arditi implored Bimboni to play the piano for the evening's performance of *Carmen;* but he, too, was on strike. The stage manager, apparently a firm believer in the tradition the show must go on, was so angered that he struck Bimboni and started a fist fight.

Somehow Mapleson was able to get together enough players from the local musical societies for the performance as scheduled. By the next evening's *Traviata* a number of the regulars had returned to their places.

The manager of the opera house, David Henderson, interviewed in the *Inter Ocean* on the twenty-second, commented that the Musical Union in Chicago disapproved of the orchestra's strike, maintaining the players should have performed, and that thus far Mapleson himself had not used any of the box-office receipts. Henderson added: "I have distributed the money as equitably as I could, giving to each artist, on present and past salaries, as much as the receipts would permit. I have learned that the Colonel is not as much in arrears to his company as newspaper reports led the public to believe. . . . The best proof of the belief on the part of his company that the Colonel intends doing what is right by its members is the willingness with which every one of them . . . consented to appear at his benefit Saturday evening, without compensation." [3]

All the while, the turmoil inside the opera house mirrored like catastrophes outside. Chicago, it would be Mapleson's fate, was in a state of siege, with labor-management unrest, riots, strikes, conspiracies, bomb explosions, lockouts. The mayor had called in troops. Under these circumstances interest in opera was somewhat muted.

Despite the tribulations Mapleson never disappointed, bringing forward the performances originally advertised; in a speech to the audience at his benefit, he seemed his usual self, ostensibly unperturbed, the urbane gentleman thanking public and press for their support. The following day the *Inter Ocean* hailed him as the greatest contemporary opera impresario, lauding him for persevering "against the very elements and almost insurmountable difficulties and discouragements." [4]

The discouragements had in fact become increasingly insurmountable. In Mapleson's final days in the city, bolts of outrageous fortune had thundered in crescendos of Wagnerian proportions, a horrific ending to his American career given his aversion to anything remotely connected with Bayreuth. Creditors from as far away as San Francisco howled; the chorus, orchestra, dancers, stagehands, supernumeraries, and others rent the air with cries of *money, money, money!* Further claims in the form of attachments, writs, summonses swelled the volume. The loudest demands of all, however, emanated from the company controlling the opera house. Having advanced Mapleson $4,100, the firm now roared for repayment. Providentially, directors of last year's opera festival, led by President Peck, came forth with the necessary amount to settle the claim.

Finally Mapleson issued the entraining order and the troupe began the journey home. Arriving in Jersey City early on Tuesday, May 25, the company immediately boarded the ship, which was to leave in the afternoon.

Mapleson meanwhile hastened to New York, where at the Inman Steamship Office he secured passage for the troupe by leaving his belongings as collateral. Having successfully concluded this business, Mapleson next met with his lawyer, who had serendipitous tidings. Legal proceedings against the U.S. government protesting the past years' payment of duty on the company's costumes, scenery, and properties had finally been settled in

Mapleson's favor, whereupon Customs House authorities re-
funded the duties paid over the years, as well as 6 percent interest.

Now at last ready to depart, Mapleson, warned that process
servers might lie in wait, determined to leave from New York, not
Jersey City, where a plant had actually been arranged. Joining the
troupe somewhere in New York harbor, he may not have realized
he would again see the city only after a long time.

The debacle so devastated Mapleson that he was never again an
operatic force of the first rank in the United States. For a number
of years after his return to Europe, he produced opera in London,
toured the British Isles, managed artists; but he waited a decade
before returning to the American scene of past triumphs, New
York's Academy, in the fall of 1896 to present a brief season.
There he offered no serious competition to the Metropolitan, by
this time the preeminent opera company in the republic. This was
his final American tour. Five years later, on November 14, 1901,
the old warrior died in London in his seventy-first year.

Mapleson in his siege of the Metropolitan was no longer the
man of the hour, too Italianate in operatic tastes, too conservative
in management. Still, the war he fought created a tremendous interest in opera and no doubt made many Americans opera-con-
scious. This is no mean accomplishment.

Then, too, the concurrent rise of the Metropolitan and fall of
the Academy of Music symbolized a rivalry at times less musical
than social. Mutual interests drew the social elements together,
and they ultimately fused in the rulership of the new house. Caught
up in the transition, Mapleson, as he said, could not fight all of
Wall Street.

What in retrospect especially emerges, however, is that the
competition contributed to some of the most fascinating episodes
in American operatic history, memorable in leading artists who
served art well, whether in Italian or in German opera; rich in
repertoires that provided variety and scope as well as several historic American premieres; brilliant in the possibilities for a new

musical order, the earlier one too exclusive in its taste, no longer sufficient for operatic progress.

Above all, what remains ever is a formidable legacy: the Metropolitan seized its time, determined to overcome obstacles, then and thereafter a vital force in the cause of opera in the United States.

A Gesture to the Social Invaders

∽

*T*HESE MATERIALS now in the Museum of the City of New York Archives—a letter to Mapleson from the Board of Directors of New York's Academy of Music and a supplement to his April 7, 1880, contract with the Academy—reveal plans for adding boxes at the Academy to the existing ones, long held by members of the Knickerbocker gentry.

Exhibit A

Colonel
     James H. Mapleson,
       Her Majesty's Opera,
         Haymarket,
           London.

Dear Sir:

The annual meeting of the Stockholders of the New York Academy of Music was held last Monday evening and the gentlemen named in the enclosed slip were elected as Directors for the ensuing year.

After the election some two hours were spent in discussing the most practicable plan for insuring the permanent welfare of the

Academy. As a result we were appointed a Committee to confer with you in reference thereto and hence we address you this letter with its enclosure.

As you are aware a Company has been formed for the erection of a new Opera House and it is stated that Sixty subscriptions of $10,000 each have been provisionally made. There are repeated rumors that one after another of these subscribers has withdrawn his subscription so that we do not regard the new organization as so far an accomplished fact as to ensure, beyond all possibility, the erection of the new building.

The chief reason assigned for the erection of a new Opera House is the deficiency in the number of Boxes in the present one and several suggestions have been made that, if such deficiency could be remedied, there would be no necessity for the new building.

It is, in view of these suggestions and for other reasons of joint benefit, that, acting under the instructions of the Board of Directors newly chosen, we, as a sub-Committee, now address you:

There is reason to believe that, if a number of new Boxes properly placed are constructed and offered for sale with the privilege of free admission, they can be sold with profit to the Academy and with, perhaps, satisfaction to some of those who now favor the new movement. We would like, if possible, to construct such boxes and to dispose of them to those who, on purchasing the same, will withdraw from the new movement and become permanent friends of the Academy or else let them to persons whose patronage would aid and strengthen the Academy and our joint interests.

The Architect reports that it is feasible to construct six new Proscenium Boxes—three adjoining Mr. Belmont's Box and three upon the opposite side—and that such new Boxes when constructed will be capable of holding conveniently six persons each or in all Thirty-six persons. The practical result of this would be as if the occupants of twelve of the present Proscenium Boxes should at every representation of Opera invite three persons each as their guests. The Architect further reports that in order to construct the six new Boxes it will be necessary to take twenty balcony seats or thereabout on each side. Before you left we discussed the plan which is now expected shall be carried out—among other things—of erecting six additional Artists' Boxes on the Grand Tier, and of moving back the Stage so as to give you two new rows of Parquette seats in front of those now existing. The Architect further says that he can, in addition to these two new rows of seats, by a re-arrangement of the chairs and the division between the Balcony and Parquette and by otherwise economizing space gain a considerable number of more chairs and we hope and expect to be able to return you a greater amount of seats than will be taken away for the erection of the Boxes. Of course you must leave this to us; we shall endeavor in good faith to do everything in our power to assist you and to bring to a favorable result your Operatic enterprise and result to our joint benefit. In that hope we enclose you an addition to the Contract, which we would like you to sign and acknowledge before the United States Consul or his Deputy and return to Mr. Belmont who, on receiving it, will return to you a Duplicate executed by the Academy.

We are, dear sir,

Yours very truly

P.S. Mr. Belmont to whom this note and accompanying consent has been shown, writes you a note which we also enclose; and he requests us also to ask you in returning the consent to him to write and say whether you adhere to your view expressed to him shortly before leaving for Europe that the Orchestra, on being moved back should be restored to the dimensions existing before the change made at the opening of last Fall season whereby you will gain several seats at each end of the Orchestra, or whether you desire the Orchestra to extend from Proscenium to Proscenium as last season. 2nd: He desires especially that, on signing the consent, you *immediately* cable the following: "Belmont, New York. Supplement signed. Mapleson." This so that we can proceed with our estimates and work at once before the Summer is upon us and especially as several of our Executive Committee having the work in charge will soon be leaving the City for Europe and elsewhere.

Exhibit B

Whereas, by a contract entered into between the New York Academy of Music and James H. Mapleson on the 7th day of April 1880, to which reference is hereby made, it was provided that the two hundred seats in the said Academy belonging to the stockholders were reserved to them, with the right of free admission and ingress on every evening and day representation of Italian Opera to be given therein by the said Mapleson; and

Whereas, since the making of the said contract, it has been contemplated to erect six new Proscenium Boxes—three on each side and adjoining the present lower Proscenium Boxes in said Academy—with a capacity for seating six persons in each Box; and

Whereas, in order to construct said six Boxes, it will be necessary to take up twenty seats on each side of the Balcony as at present arranged in said Academy, or forty seats in all; and

Whereas, it is contemplated, in order to restore an equal number of seats to the said Mapleson for the said forty Balcony seats so taken for said Boxes, to place forty new chairs in the Parquette in said Academy; and

Whereas, it is also contemplated to place eighteen further new and additional chairs in said Parquette. . . .

It is agreed by and between the said New York Academy of Music and the said James H. Mapleson, and by way of supplement to said contract of the 7th of April 1880, that, if the said Boxes are so constructed with the capacity aforesaid, and if the said eighteen additional chairs are placed in the Parquette for the use of the said Mapleson during his said contract—the said Mapleson will accept the revenue arising to him from the sale to the public of said eighteen chairs at each evening or day representation of Italian Opera in full satisfaction and discharge of any and all entrance fees or moneys which might otherwise be due to him from the sale of thirty-six entrance fees to said Boxes at such representation of opera; and that the New York Academy of Music may sell or rent the said Boxes, with consideration, free from any obligation on its part, or on the part of any or all of the purchasers or lessees thereof, to pay any entrance fee thereto, either for evening or day representations of Italian Opera to be given in said Academy under the direction of the said Mapleson—the said Mapleson hereby accepting the revenue arising from the sale of said eighteen seats as aforesaid in full satisfaction and discharge of said thirty-six entrance fees as aforesaid.

The said contract of the said 7th of April 1880 between the parties hereto is, in all respects, hereby ratified and confirmed.

Witness the hands and seals of the parties this   day of May 1880.

Mapleson's Casts
and Performances

∽

*J*HE MATERIAL in appendix 2 was compiled from official programs of Mapleson's company in New York (1883–1885) and on
tour (1883–1886), newspaper advertisements, and reviews. Where
there was a doubt as to whether an artist appeared in a given performance or when it was impossible to verify a cast, a question
mark has been inserted. The notation (*c*) indicates the conductor,
which is given only when Luigi Arditi did not conduct. Finally,
with the exception of the Patti concerts in San Francisco and Salt
Lake City in 1884, only opera presentations are listed; other occasional concerts arranged by Mapleson in New York and on tour
during the preceding American seasons are thus excluded.

New York's Academy of Music, 1883–1885
1883–1884 Season
PERSONNEL

Male Artists

Anton, Andres
Bellati, Sgr.
Bello, Sgr.
Bertini, Tobia
Bieletto, Sgr.
Caracciolo, Ernesto

Cherubini, Enrico
De Vaschetti, Antonio
Falletti, Ernesto
Galassi, Antonio
Lombardelli, Luciano
Nicolini, Ernest
Perugini, Giovanni

Pruetti, Sgr.
Rinaldini, Sgr.
Sivori, Ernesto
Vicini, Eugenio

Scalchi, Sofia
Tiozzo, Gemma
Valerga, Ida
Vianelli, Emilia
Yorke, Josephine

Female Artists

Bartlett-Davis, Jessie
Bianchi-Fiorio, Maria
Dotti, Louise
Gerster, Etelka
Nordica, Lillian
Pappenheim, Eugenie
Patti, Adelina
Pattini, Raphéla
Prioria, Mlle

Ballet

Brambilla, Fiorina
De Gillert, Theodora
De Sortis, Bettina

Conductor

Arditi, Luigi

NEW YORK SCHEDULE

October 22
La Sonnambula
Amina: Gerster
Elvino: Vicini
Rodolfo: Cherubini
Alessio: Rinaldini
Notary: Bieletto
Lisa: Valerga
Teresa: Prioria

Adalgisa: Dotti
Clotilde: Valerga
Oroveso: Cherubini
Flavio: Bieletto

October 27 (mat.)
La Sonnambula
Same as October 22

October 24
Rigoletto
Duke: Bertini
Rigoletto: Galassi
Gilda: Gerster
Sparafucile: Lombardelli
Maddalena: Vianelli
Giovanna: Valerga
Monterone: Cherubini
Marullo: De Vaschetti
Borsa: Rinaldini
Ceprano: Bieletto
Countess: ?

October 29
Lucia di Lammermoor
Lucia: Gerster
Alisa: Valerga
Edgardo: Vicini
Ashton: Galassi
Raimondo: Lombardelli
Arturo: Rinaldini
Normanno: De Vaschetti

October 31
Il Trovatore
Leonora: Pappenheim
Manrico: Vicini
Count di Luna: Galassi
Azucena: Tiozzo
Inez: ?
Ferrando: Lombardelli
Ruiz: Rinaldini

October 26
Norma
Norma: Pappenheim
Pollione: Falletti

November 2
Faust
Faust: Perugini
Marguerite: Pattini
Méphistophélès: Cherubini
Valentin: Sivori
Siébel: Yorke
Marthe: Valerga
Wagner: De Vaschetti

November 3 (mat.)
Norma
Same as October 26

November 5
Linda di Chamounix
Linda: Gerster
Pierotto: Yorke
Maddalena: Valerga
Charles: Vicini
Antonio: Galassi
Prefect: Lombardelli
Marquis de Boisfleury: Caracciolo
Intendant: Rinaldini

November 7
Rigoletto
Same as October 24 except:
Duke: Falletti
Rigoletto: Bellati
Maddalena: Yorke

November 9
La Gazza Ladra
Giannetto: Vicini
Fernando: Galassi
Isacco: Rinaldini
Podestà: Cherubini
Fabrizio: Lombardelli
Pippo: Vianelli
Ninetta: Patti

November 10 (mat.)
Lucia di Lammermoor
Same as October 29

November 12
Il Trovatore
Same as October 31 except:
Manrico: Bello

November 14
Marta
Harriet: Gerster
Nancy: Yorke
Lionel: Vicini
Plunkett: Cherubini
Tristan: Lombardelli
Sheriff: ?

November 16
La Traviata
Violetta: Patti
Alfredo: Vicini
Germont: Galassi
Flora: ?
Annina: Valerga
Gastone: Rinaldini
Baron Douphol: Caracciolo
Marquis d'Obigny: Bieletto
Dr. Grenvil: Lombardelli

November 17 (mat.)
Marta
Same as November 14

November 19
Lucia di Lammermoor
Same as October 29 except:
Lucia: Patti
Arturo: ?
Normanno: ?

November 21
La Sonnambula
Same as October 22

November 23
Ernani
Elvira: Patti
Giovanna: Valerga
Ernani: Bello

Don Carlo: Galassi
Don Ruy Gomez: Cherubini
Iago: ?
Don Riccardo: ?

November 24 (mat.)
Linda di Chamounix
Same as November 5

November 26
Faust
Same as November 2 except:
Faust: Vicini
Marguerite: Nordica
Valentin: Galassi
Marthe: ?

November 28
Aida
King: Lombardelli
Amneris: Tiozzo
Aida: Patti
Radames: Nicolini
Amonasro: Galassi
Ramfis: Cherubini
Messenger: ?
Priestess: ?

November 30
I Puritani
Lord Walton: De Vaschetti
Sir George: Cherubini
Elvira: Gerster
Henrietta: Valerga
Lord Arthur: Vicini
Sir Richard: Galassi
Sir Bruno: Bieletto

December 1 (mat.)
La Traviata
Same as November 16

December 3
Faust
Same as November 2 except:
Faust: Bello

Marguerite: Nordica
Valentin: Bellati
Siébel: ?
Marthe: ?
Wagner: ?

December 5
Ernani
Same as November 23

December 7
L'Elisir d'Amore
Adina: Gerster
Giannetta: Valerga
Nemorino: Vicini
Belcore: Lombardelli
Dulcamara: Caracciolo

December 8 (mat.)
Aida
Same as November 28

December 31
Aida
Same as November 28

January 2
L'Elisir d'Amore
Same as December 7 except:
Giannetta: ?

January 4
Crispino e la Comare
Crispino: Caracciolo
Annetta: Patti
Dr. Fabrizio: Bellati
Mirabolano: Lombardelli
Count del Fiore: Bello
Don Asdrubale: De Vaschetti
Comare: Valerga
Bartolo: Bieletto

January 5 (mat.)
Faust
Same as November 2 except:
Faust: Vicini

Marguerite: Gerster
Valentin: Galassi
Marthe: ?

January 7
Semiramide
Semiramide: Patti
Arsace: Tiozzo
Idreno: Bello
Oroe: Lombardelli
Ghost of Ninus: De Vaschetti
Assur: Cherubini

January 9
L'Elisir d'Amore
Same as December 7 except:
Giannetta: ?

January 11
Les Huguenots
Marguerite: Gerster
St. Bris: Galassi
Valentine: Patti
Nevers: Sivori
Cossé: ?
Tavannes: ?
Retz: ?
Raoul: Nicolini
Marcel: Cherubini
Urbain: Yorke
Maurevert: ?
Bois Rosé: ?
Lady of Honor: ?
Soldier: ?
Thoret: ?
Meru: ?

January 12 (mat.)
Marta
Same as November 14

January 14
Crispino e la Comare
Same as January 4

January 16
I Puritani
Same as November 30

January 18
Les Huguenots
Same as January 11

January 19 (mat.)
L'Elisir d'Amore
Same as December 7

April 14
Linda di Chamounix
Same as November 5 except:
Linda: Patti
Pierotto: Tiozzo
Maddalena: ?
Prefect: Cherubini

April 16
L'Elisir d'Amore
Same as December 7 except:
Giannetta: ?
Belcore: Bellati

April 18
Roméo et Juliette
Juliette: Patti
Stephano: Tiozzo
Gertrude: Valerga
Friar Laurence: Cherubini
Capulet: Galassi
Tybalt: Bello
Mercutio: Bellati
Duke of Verona: Pruetti
Gregorio: Caracciolo
Benvolio: De Vaschetti
Roméo: Nicolini

April 19 (mat.)
Lucia di Lammermoor
Same as October 29 except:
Raimondo: Cherubini

April 21
La Favorita
Leonora: Bianchi-Fiorio
Inez: Valerga
Balthazar: Cherubini
Alfonso: Galassi
Don Gaspar: ?
Fernando: Anton

April 22
Crispino e la Comare
Same as January 4 except:
Mirabolano: Cherubini

April 23
La Sonnambula
Same as October 22

April 25
Semiramide
Same as January 7 except:
Arsace: Scalchi
Idreno: Rinaldini
Oroe: Caracciolo

April 26 (mat.)
Faust
Same as November 2 except:
Marguerite: Gerster
Valentin: Galassi
Siébel: Bianchi-Fiorio

1884–1885 Season

PERSONNEL

Male Artists

Bassetti, Carlo
Bieletto, Sgr.
Caracciolo, Ernesto
Cardinali, Franco
Cherubini, Enrico
De Anna, Innocente
De Pasqualis, Sgr.
De Vaschetti, Antonio
Giannini, Francesco
Manni, Sgr.
Nicolini, Ernest
Pruetti, Sgr.
Rinaldini, Sgr.
Serbolini, Enrico
Vicini, Eugenio

Female Artists

Calvelli, Maria
Dotti, Louise

Fiorio, Mlle
Fursch-Madi, Emmy
Nevada, Emma
Pappenheim, Eugenie
Patti, Adelina
Riccetti, Ida
Saruggia, Mlle
Scalchi, Sofia
Steinbach, Emma
Valerga, Ida

Ballet

Cavalazzi, Malvina

Conductors

Arditi, Luigi
Bimboni, Oreste

NEW YORK SCHEDULE

November 10
Il Barbiere di Siviglia
Almaviva: Vicini
Dr. Bartolo: Caracciolo
Rosina: Patti
Figaro: De Pasqualis
Don Basilio: Cherubini
Berta: Saruggia
Fiorello: Rinaldini
Sergeant: Bieletto

November 12
Il Trovatore
Leonora: Riccetti
Manrico: Cardinali
Count di Luna: De Pasqualis
Azucena: Scalchi
Inez: ?
Ferrando: Manni
Ruiz: Rinaldini

November 14
La Traviata
Violetta: Patti
Alfredo: Vicini
Germont: De Anna
Flora: ?
Annina: Saruggia
Gastone: Rinaldini
Baron Douphol: Caracciolo
Marquis d'Obigny: Bieletto
Dr. Grenvil: Manni

November 15 (mat.)
Il Trovatore
Same as November 12

November 17
La Favorita
Leonora: Steinbach
Inez: Saruggia
Balthazar: Cherubini
Alfonso: De Anna
Don Gaspar: Rinaldini
Fernando: Vicini

November 19
Semiramide
Semiramide: Patti
Arsace: Scalchi
Idreno: Bassetti
Oroe: Cherubini
Ghost of Ninus: De Vaschetti
Assur: De Pasqualis

November 21
Ernani
Elvira: Riccetti
Giovanna: Saruggia
Ernani: Cardinali
Don Carlo: De Anna
Don Ruy Gomez: Cherubini
Iago: De Vaschetti
Don Riccardo: Rinaldini

November 22 (mat.)
La Traviata
Same as November 14

November 24
La Sonnambula
Amina: Nevada
Elvino: Vicini
Rodolfo: Cherubini
Alessio: Rinaldini
Notary: Bieletto
Lisa: Saruggia
Teresa: ?

November 26
Marta
Harriet: Patti
Nancy: Scalchi
Lionel: Vicini
Plunkett: Cherubini
Tristan: Caracciolo
Sheriff: ?

November 28
La Sonnambula
Same as November 24

November 29 (mat.)
Semiramide
Same as November 19

December 1
Linda di Chamounix
Linda: Patti
Pierotto: Scalchi
Maddalena: Saruggia
Charles: Vicini
Antonio: De Pasqualis
Prefect: Cherubini
Marquis de Boisfleury: Caracciolo
Intendant: ?

December 3
Rigoletto
Duke: Cardinali
Rigoletto: De Anna
Gilda: Dotti
Sparafucile: Cherubini
Maddalena: Scalchi
Giovanna: Saruggia
Monterone: ?
Marullo: ?
Borsa: ?
Ceprano: ?
Countess: ?

December 5
La Traviata
Same as November 14

December 6 (mat.)
Lucia di Lammermoor
Lucia: Nevada
Alisa: Saruggia
Edgardo: Cardinali
Ashton: De Anna
Raimondo: Manni
Arturo: Rinaldini
Normanno: De Vaschetti

December 8
Semiramide
Same (?) as November 19

December 10
Il Trovatore
Same as November 12 except:
Leonora: Pappenheim

December 12
Aida
King: Manni
Amneris: Scalchi
Aida: Patti
Radames: Nicolini
Amonasro: De Anna
Ramfis: Cherubini
Messenger: ?
Priestess: ?

December 13 (mat.)
La Sonnambula
Same (?) as November 24

December 15
Faust
Faust: Vicini
Marguerite: Patti
Méphistophélès: Cherubini
Valentin: De Anna
Siébel: Scalchi
Marthe: ?
Wagner: ?

December 17
La Favorita
Same as November 17

December 19
Crispino e la Comare
Crispino: Caracciolo
Annetta: Patti
Dr. Fabrizio: De Pasqualis
Mirabolano: Cherubini
Count del Fiore: Bassetti
Don Asdrubale: De Vaschetti
Comare: Saruggia
Bartolo: Bieletto

December 20 (mat.)
Mireille
Mireille: Nevada
Taven: Scalchi
Clemence: Steinbach
Vincent: Vicini
Ourrias: De Anna
Ramon: Cherubini
Ambroise: Manni
Young Shepherd: Calvelli

December 22
Aida
Same as December 12 except:
Aida: Fursch-Madi
Radames: Cardinali
Priestess: Calvelli

December 23
Semiramide
Same as November 19

December 26
Lucia di Lammermoor
Same as December 6 (mat.) except:
Edgardo: Giannini

December 27 (mat.)
Les Huguenots
Marguerite: Dotti
St. Bris: De Pasqualis
Valentine: Fursch-Madi
Nevers: De Anna
Cossé: ?
Tavannes: ?
Retz: ?
Raoul: Cardinali

Marcel: Cherubini
Urbain: Scalchi
Maurevert: ?
Bois Rosé: ?
Lady of Honor: ?
Soldier: ?
Thoret: ?
Meru: ?

April 20
Semiramide
Same as November 19 except:
Idreno: Rinaldini

April 21
La Sonnambula
Same as November 24

April 22
Rigoletto
Same as December 3 except:
Duke: Giannini

April 23
Mireille
Same as December 20 (mat.) except:
Ambroise: ?
Young Shepherd: ?

April 24
Marta
Same as November 26

April 25 (mat.)
Lucia di Lammermoor
Same as December 6 (mat.) except:
Edgardo: Giannini

1885–1886 Season

PERSONNEL

Male Artists

Baldanza, Ernesto
Bieletto, Sgr.
Campobello, Enrico

Caracciolo, Ernesto
Cherubini, Enrico
De Anna, Innocente
De Falco, Serafino

De Vaschetti, Antonio
Del Puente, Giuseppe
Foscani, Sgr.
Giannini, Francesco
Perrario, Sgr.
Ravelli, Luigi
Rinaldini, Sgr.
Vetta (Wetter), Franz

Dotti, Louise
Engle, Marie
Fohström, Alma
Hauk, Minnie
Lablache, Emily
Litvinne (Litvinoff), Félia
Nordica, Lillian
Pervini, Virginia

Female Artists

Bauermeister, Mathilde
Biache, Mlle
Carrington, Abbie
De Meric, Mlle
De Vigne, Jane
De Vivo, Mlle

Ballet

Cavalazzi, Malvina

Conductors

Arditi, Luigi
Bimboni, Oreste

NEW YORK SCHEDULE

November 2
Carmen
Carmen: Hauk
Don José: Ravelli
Micaela: Dotti
Escamillo: Del Puente
Zuniga: Cherubini
Morales: Bieletto
Frasquita: Bauermeister
Mercedes: Lablache
Dancaíre: Caracciolo
Remendado: Rinaldini

November 4
Il Trovatore
Leonora: Litvinne
Manrico: Giannini
Count di Luna: De Anna
Azucena: Lablache
Inez: Bauermeister
Ferrando: Cherubini
Ruiz: Rinaldini

November 6
Il Trovatore
Same as November 4

November 7 (mat.)
Carmen
Same as November 2

November 9
Lucia di Lammermoor
Lucia: Fohström
Alisa: Bauermeister
Edgardo: Giannini
Ashton: De Anna
Raimondo: Cherubini
Arturo: Bieletto
Normanno: De Vaschetti

November 11
L'Africaine
Selika: Hauk
Anna: Bauermeister
Inez: Dotti
Nelusko: De Anna
Don Pedro: Cherubini
Grand Inquisitor: Vetta
Grand Brahmin: ?
Don Diego: Caracciolo
Don Alvar: Rinaldini
Usher: ?

Vasco da Gama: Giannini
Inquisitors: Bieletto
          Perrario
Officer: ?

November 13
La Sonnambula
Amina: Fohström
Elvino: Ravelli
Rodolfo: Del Puente
Alessio: Rinaldini
Notary: Bieletto
Lisa: Bauermeister
Teresa: Lablache

November 14 (mat.)
L'Africaine
Same as November 11

November 16
Carmen
Same as November 2

November 18
La Favorita
Leonora: Pervini
Inez: Bauermeister
Balthazar: Cherubini
Alfonso: De Anna
Don Gaspar: Rinaldini
Fernando: De Falco

November 20
Fra Diavolo
Fra Diavolo: Ravelli
Milord: Caracciolo
Pamela: Lablache
Lorenzo: Rinaldini
Matteo: ?
Zerline: Fohström
Beppo: Del Puente
Giacomo: Cherubini

November 21 (mat.)
Lucia di Lammermoor
Same as November 9

November 21
Don Giovanni
Don Giovanni: Del Puente
Donna Anna: Litvinne
Donna Elvira: Bauermeister
Zerlina: Hauk
Commendatore: ?
Don Ottavio: Ravelli
Leporello: Cherubini
Masetto: Rinaldini

November 23
Fra Diavolo
Same as November 20 except:
Lorenzo: ?

November 25
Don Giovanni
Same as November 21 except:
Commendatore: Vetta

November 27
Fra Diavolo
Same as November 20 except:
Lorenzo: Bieletto

November 28 (mat.)
Faust
Faust: Giannini
Marguerite: Hauk
Méphistophélès: Cherubini
Valentin: De Anna
Siébel: De Vigne
Marthe: Lablache
Wagner: De Vaschetti

December 19 (mat.)
Maritana
Maritana: Fohström
Don Caesar de Bazan: Ravelli
Don José de Santarem: De Anna

Lazarillo: De Vigne
Marchioness of Montefiore: Lablache
Captain: ?
Marquis of Montefiore: Foscani
King: Del Puente
Alcade: ?

December 23
Manon
Manon: Hauk

Rosette: De Vigne
Poussette: Bauermeister
Javotte: Lablache
Lescaut: Del Puente
Count des Grieux: Cherubini
Guillot: Rinaldini
De Brétigny: Foscani
Des Grieux: Giannini
Innkeeper: De Vaschetti
Attendant: Bieletto

On Tour, 1883–1886

1883–1884 Season

BROOKLYN

November 1
Lucia di Lammermoor
Lucia: Gerster
Alisa: Valerga
Edgardo: Vicini
Ashton: Galassi
Raimondo: Lombardelli
Arturo: Bieletto
Normanno: De Vaschetti

November 8
Norma
Norma: Pappenheim
Pollione: Falletti
Adalgisa: Dotti
Clotilde: Valerga
Oroveso: Cherubini
Flavio: Bieletto

November 13
La Sonnambula
Amina: Gerster
Elvino: Vicini
Rodolfo: Cherubini
Alessio: Rinaldini
Notary: Bieletto
Lisa: Valerga
Teresa: ?

November 22
Il Trovatore
Leonora: Pappenheim
Manrico: Bello
Count di Luna: Bellati
Azucena: Yorke
Inez: ?
Ferrando: Lombardelli
Ruiz: ?

PHILADELPHIA

December 4
Lucia di Lammermoor
Same as November 1 except:
Arturo: Rinaldini

December 10
Ernani
Elvira: Patti
Giovanna: Valerga
Ernani: Bello
Don Carlo: Galassi
Don Ruy Gomez: Cherubini
Iago: ?
Don Riccardo: Rinaldini

December 11
Linda di Chamounix
Linda: Gerster

Pierotto: Yorke
Maddalena: Valerga
Charles: Vicini
Antonio: Galassi
Prefect: Lombardelli
Marquis de Boisfleury: Caracciolo
Intendant: Rinaldini

December 12
Norma
Same as November 8

December 13
Marta
Harriet: Gerster
Nancy: Yorke
Lionel: Vicini
Plunkett: Cherubini
Tristan: Lombardelli
Sheriff: Bieletto

December 14
Semiramide
Semiramide: Patti
Arsace: Tiozzo
Idreno: Rinaldini
Oroe: Lombardelli
Ghost of Ninus: De Vaschetti
Assur: Cherubini

December 15
La Sonnambula
Same as November 13

BOSTON

December 17
Linda di Chamounix
Same as December 11 except:
Pierotto: Tiozzo

December 18
La Traviata
Violetta: Patti
Alfredo: Vicini
Germont: Galassi
Flora: ?

Annina: Valerga
Gastone: Rinaldini
Baron Douphol: Caracciolo
Marquis d'Obigny: Bieletto
Dr. Grenvil: Lombardelli

December 19
Faust
Faust: Bello
Marguerite: Nordica
Méphistophélès: Cherubini
Valentin: Galassi
Siébel: Yorke
Marthe: Valerga
Wagner: De Vaschetti

December 20
L'Elisir d'Amore
Adina: Gerster
Giannetta: Valerga
Nemorino: Vicini
Belcore: Lombardelli
Dulcamara: Caracciolo

December 21
Semiramide
Same as December 14

December 22 (mat.)
Lucia di Lammermoor
Same as November 1 except:
Arturo: ?

December 22
Norma
Same as November 8

MONTREAL

December 24
La Sonnambula
Same as November 13

December 26
La Traviata
Same as December 18 except:
Alfredo: Nicolini

December 28
Lucia di Lammermoor
Same as November 1 except:
Arturo: ?

December 29
Il Trovatore
Same as November 22 except:
Count di Luna: Galassi
Azucena: Tiozzo
Ruiz: Rinaldini
Inez: Valerga

BROOKLYN

January 15
L'Elisir d'Amore
Same as December 20

PHILADELPHIA

January 21
Aida
King: Lombardelli
Amneris: Tiozzo
Aida: Patti
Radames: Nicolini
Amonasro: Galassi
Ramfis: Cherubini
Messenger: Rinaldini
Priestess: ?

January 22
L'Elisir d'Amore
Same as December 20

January 23
Crispino e la Comare
Crispino: Caracciolo
Annetta: Patti
Dr. Fabrizio: Bellati
Mirabolano: Lombardelli
Count del Fiore: Bello
Don Asdrubale: De Vaschetti
Comare: Valerga
Bartolo: Bieletto

BALTIMORE

January 24
Ernani
Same as December 10 except:
Elvira: Dotti

January 25
Lucia di Lammermoor
Same as November 1 except:
Lucia: Patti
Arturo: Rinaldini
Normanno: Bieletto

January 26 (mat.)
L'Elisir d'Amore
Same as December 20

January 26
Il Trovatore
Same as November 22 except:
Leonora: Dotti
Count di Luna: Galassi
Azucena: Tiozzo
Ruiz: Rinaldini

La Sonnambula (last scene)
Amina: Gerster
Elvino: Vicini
Rodolfo: Cherubini
Teresa: ?
Alessio: ?

CHICAGO

January 28
Crispino e la Comare
Same as January 23

January 29
L'Elisir d'Amore
Same as December 20

January 30
Les Huguenots
Marguerite: Gerster
St. Bris: Galassi

Valentine: Patti
Nevers: Bellati
Cossé: Bieletto
Tavannes: Caracciolo
Retz: Lombardelli
Raoul: Nicolini
Marcel: Cherubini
Urbain: Yorke
Maurevert: De Vaschetti
Bois Rosé: ?
Lady of Honor: Valerga
Soldier: Rinaldini
Thoret: ?
Meru: ?

January 31
La Favorita
Leonora: Bianchi-Fiorio
Inez: Valerga
Balthazar: Cherubini
Alfonso: Galassi
Don Gaspar: Rinaldini
Fernando: Anton

February 1
Linda di Chamounix
Same as December 11 except:
Pierotto: Tiozzo

February 2 (mat.)
Lucia di Lammermoor
Same as November 1 except:
Lucia: Patti
Edgardo: Nicolini
Arturo: Rinaldini
Normanno: Bieletto

February 4
I Puritani
Lord Walton: Lombardelli
Sir George: Cherubini
Elvira: Gerster
Henrietta: Valerga
Lord Arthur: Vicini
Sir Richard: Galassi
Sir Bruno: Bieletto

February 5
Roméo et Juliette
Juliette: Patti
Stephano: Tiozzo
Gertrude: Valerga
Friar Laurence: Cherubini
Capulet: Galassi
Tybalt: Bello
Mercutio: Bellati
Duke of Verona: Pruetti
Gregorio: Lombardelli
Benvolio: Rinaldini
Roméo: Nicolini

February 6
Rigoletto
Duke: Anton
Rigoletto: Galassi
Gilda: Nordica
Sparafucile: Lombardelli
Maddalena: Bianchi-Fiorio
Giovanna: Valerga
Monterone: Cherubini
Marullo: De Vaschetti
Borsa: Rinaldini
Ceprano: Bieletto
Countess: ?

February 7
Faust
Same as December 19 except:
Marguerite: Gerster
Valentin: Bellati
Siébel: Bartlett-Davis

February 8
La Traviata
Same as December 18 except:
  Marquis d'Obigny: ?

February 9 (mat.)
L'Elisir d'Amore
Same as December 20

February 9

Rigoletto
Same as February 6 except:
Marullo: ?
Borsa: ?
Ceprano: ?

February 13
Benefit for Cincinnati Flood Victims

La Sonnambula (Acts 1 and 3)
Same as November 13

Il Trovatore (Acts 2 and 3)
Same as November 22 except:
Leonora: Dotti
Count di Luna: Galassi
Azucena: Tiozzo
Inez: Valerga
Ruiz: Rinaldini

Lucia di Lammermoor (Mad Scene)
Lucia: Patti

MINNEAPOLIS

February 14
La Sonnambula
Same as November 13

February 15
Rigoletto
Same (?) as February 6 except:
Gilda: Dotti

February 16 (mat.)
Lucia di Lammermoor
Same as November 1

ST. LOUIS

February 18
La Sonnambula
Same as November 13

February 19
La Traviata
Same as December 18

February 20
L'Elisir d'Amore
Same as December 20

February 21
Rigoletto (Acts 1 and 2)
Same as February 6 except:
Duke: Vicini
Gilda: Gerster

Lucia di Lammermoor (Acts 2 and 3)
Same as November 1 except:
Lucia: Patti
Edgardo: Nicolini
Arturo: Rinaldini
Normanno: Bieletto

February 22
La Favorita
Same as January 31

February 23 (mat.)
Marta
Same as December 13 except:
Nancy: Tiozzo
Sheriff: ?

February 23
Ernani
Same (?) as December 10 except:
Elvira: Dotti

KANSAS CITY

February 25
La Sonnambula
Same as November 13 except:
Alessio: ?
Notary: ?

February 26
La Favorita
Same as January 31

ST. JOSEPH

February 27
Lucia di Lammermoor
Same as November 1

DENVER

February 29
La Sonnambula
Same as November 13

March 1 (mat.)
La Traviata
Same as December 18

March 1
La Favorita
Same (?) as January 31

March 3
Lucia di Lammermoor
Same as November 1

CHEYENNE

March 4
La Sonnambula
Same as November 13

SALT LAKE CITY

March 6
Lucia di Lammermoor
Same as November 1

SAN FRANCISCO

March 10
Lucia di Lammermoor
Same as November 1 except:
Edgardo: Anton

March 12
L'Elisir d'Amore
Same as December 20

March 13
La Traviata
Same as December 18 except:
Alfredo: Anton

March 14
Rigoletto
Same as February 6 except:
Gilda: Dotti
Giovanna: ?
Marullo: ?
Borsa: ?
Ceprano: ?

March 15 (mat.)
La Sonnambula
Same as November 13 except:
Alessio: ?
Notary: ?

March 17
I Puritani
Same as February 4 except:
Lord Walton: Bieletto
Henrietta: ?
Sir Bruno: ?

March 18
Il Trovatore
Same as November 22 except:
Leonora: Patti
Manrico: Nicolini
Count di Luna: Galassi
Azucena: Tiozzo
Ferrando: Cherubini

March 19
Marta
Same as December 13 except:
Nancy: Tiozzo
Tristan: Caracciolo

March 21
La Favorita
Same as January 31

March 22 (mat.)
Faust
Same as December 19 except:
Marguerite: Gerster
Siébel: Bianchi-Fiorio
Marthe: ?
Wagner: ?

March 22
Crispino e la Comare
Same as January 23 except:
Mirabolano: Cherubini

March 24
La Sonnambula
Same (?) as November 13

March 25
Linda di Chamounix
Same as December 11 except:
Linda: Patti
Pierotto: Tiozzo
Prefect: Cherubini

March 26
Lucia di Lammermoor
Same as November 1 except:
Edgardo: Anton
Raimondo: Cherubini

March 27
Patti Concert

"O Signore" (*I Lombardi*): Chorus and
  Orchestra
"Viravviso, O luaghi ameni" (*La Son-
  nambula*): Cherubini
"Bel raggio" (*Semiramide*): Patti
"Noël" (Fauré): Nicolini
Harp Fantasia: Mme Sacconi★
"Inflammatus" (Rossini's *Stabat Ma-
  ter*): Dotti
"O tu bel astro" (*Tannhäuser*): Galassi

" 'Twas Within a Mile of Edinboro
  Town": Patti
"Miei rampoili" (*La Cenerentola*): Car-
  acciolo
"L'ardita" (Arditi): Dotti
"Non piu andrai" (*Le Nozze di Fi-
  garo*): Galassi
"Il Bacio" (Arditi): Patti
"Turkish March": Mme. Sacconi
Neopolitan Song: Cherubini
"Home, Sweet Home" (Bishop): Patti
"Chi mi frena" (*Lucia di Lammermoor*):
  Dotti, Bello, Galassi, Cherubini

March 28
L'Elisir d' Amore
Same as December 20 except:
Belcore: Cherubini

March 29 (mat.)
Crispino e la Comare
Same as January 23 except:
Mirabolano: Cherubini

SALT LAKE CITY

April 1
Patti Concert
Same as March 27

OMAHA

April 4
Lucia di Lammermoor
Same as November 1 except:
Raimondo: Cherubini
Arturo: Rinaldini
Normanno: Bieletto

BROOKLYN

April 24
L'Elisir d'Amore
Same as December 20 except:
Belcore: Bellati

★Mme Sacconi was the orchestra's harpist.

Appendix 2

1884–1885 Season

BROOKLYN

November 20
Il Trovatore
Leonora: Riccetti
Manrico: Cardinali
Count di Luna: De Pasqualis
Azucena: Scalchi
Inez: Saruggia
Ferrando: Manni
Ruiz: ?

December 11
Rigoletto/Bimboni (c)
Duke: Cardinali
Rigoletto: De Anna
Gilda: Dotti
Sparafucile: Cherubini
Maddalena: Scalchi
Giovanna: Saruggia
Monterone: Manni
Marullo: De Vaschetti
Borsa: Rinaldini
Ceprano: Bieletto
Countess: ?

December 18
Mireille
Mireille: Nevada
Taven: Scalchi
Clemence: Saruggia
Vincent: Vicini
Ourrias: De Anna
Ramon: Cherubini
Ambroise: Manni
Young Shepherd: Calvelli

BOSTON

December 29
La Sonnambula
Amina: Nevada
Elvino: Vicini
Rodolfo: Cherubini

Alessio: Rinaldini
Notary: Bieletto
Lisa: Saruggia
Teresa: Fiorio

December 30
La Traviata
Violetta: Patti
Alfredo: Vicini
Germont: De Anna
Flora: ?
Annina: Saruggia
Gastone: Rinaldini
Baron Douphol: Caracciolo
Marquis d'Obigny: Bieletto
Dr. Grenvil: Manni

December 31
Il Trovatore
Same as November 20 except:
Leonora: Fursch-Madi

January 1
Mireille
Same as December 18

January 2
Semiramide
Semiramide: Patti
Arsace: Scalchi
Idreno: Rinaldini
Oroe: Cherubini
Ghost of Ninus: De Vaschetti
Assur: Serbolini

January 3 (mat.)
Lucia di Lammermoor
Lucia: Nevada
Alisa: Saruggia
Edgardo: Giannini
Ashton: De Pasqualis
Raimondo: Serbolini
Arturo: Rinaldini
Normanno: ?

January 3
Rigoletto/Bimboni (c)
Same (?) as December 11

January 5
Aida
King: Serbolini
Amneris: Steinbach
Aida: Fursch-Madi
Radames: Giannini
Amonasro: De Anna
Ramfis: Cherubini
Messenger: ?
Priestess: ?

January 6
Marta
Harriet: Patti
Nancy: Scalchi
Lionel: Vicini
Plunkett: Cherubini
Tristan: Caracciolo
Sheriff: ?

January 7
I Puritani
Lord Walton: Manni
Sir George: Cherubini
Elvira: Nevada
Henrietta: Saruggia
Lord Arthur: Vicini
Sir Richard: De Anna
Sir Bruno: Bieletto

January 8
Faust
Faust: Giannini
Marguerite: Fursch-Madi
Méphistophélès: Serbolini
Valentin: De Anna
Siébel: Scalchi
Marthe: ?
Wagner: De Vaschetti

January 9
Linda di Chamounix
Linda: Patti
Pierotto: Scalchi
Maddalena: Saruggia
Charles: Vicini
Antonio: De Pasqualis
Prefect: Cherubini
Marquis de Boisfleury: Caracciolo
Intendant: Rinaldini

January 10 (mat.)
Mireille
Same as December 18

PHILADELPHIA

January 12
Aida
Same as January 5 except:
King: Manni
Amneris: Scalchi
Messenger: Rinaldini

January 13
La Traviata
Same as December 30

January 14
La Sonnambula
Same as December 29 except:
Teresa: ?

January 15
Ernani
Elvira: Dotti
Giovanna: Saruggia
Ernani: Giannini
Don Carlo: De Anna
Don Ruy Gomez: Cherubini
Iago: De Vaschetti
Don Riccardo: Rinaldini

January 16
Semiramide
Same as January 2

January 17 (mat.)
Lucia di Lammermoor/Bimboni (c)
Same (?) as January 3 (mat.) except:
Ashton: De Anna

January 17
Lucrezia Borgia
Lucrezia Borgia: Fursch-Madi
Maffio: Scalchi
Gennaro: Cardinali
Don Alfonso: Cherubini
Rustighello: Rinaldini
Astolfo: Caracciolo
Liverotto: Manni
Gazella: ?
Gubetta: Serbolini
Vitellozzo: Bieletto
Petrucci: ?

January 19
Mireille
Same as December 18

January 20
Linda di Chamounix
Same as January 9

January 21
I Puritani
Same as January 7 except:
Lord Walton: Manni
Lord Arthur: Cardinali

NEW ORLEANS

January 26
La Sonnambula
Same as December 29 except:
Teresa: ?

January 27
La Traviata
Same (?) as December 30 except:
Alfredo: Giannini

January 28
Il Trovatore
Same as November 20 except:
Leonora: Fursch-Madi
Ruiz: Rinaldini

January 29
Mireille
Same as December 18

January 30
Semiramide
Same as January 2 except:
Idreno: ?

January 31 (mat.)
Lucia di Lammermoor
Same as January 3 (mat.) except:
Normanno: De Vaschetti

January 31
Ernani
Same as January 15 except:
Ernani: Cardinali

February 2
Linda di Chamounix
Same as January 9 except:
Maddalena: ?
Intendant: ?

February 3
Lucrezia Borgia
Same as January 17 except:
Liverotto: ?
Gazella: Manni
Vitellozzo: ?

February 4
Crispino e la Comare
Crispino: Caracciolo
Annetta: Patti
Dr. Fabrizio: De Pasqualis
Mirabolano: Cherubini
Count del Fiore: Rinaldini

Don Asdrubale: De Vaschetti
Comare: Saruggia
Bartolo: Bieletto

February 5
Faust
Same as January 8 except:
Marguerite: Nevada
Méphistophélès: Cherubini
Siébel: Steinbach
Marthe: ?
Wagner: ?

February 6
Marta
Same as January 6 except:
Tristan: ?
Sheriff: ?

February 7 (mat.)
La Favorita
Leonora: Steinbach/Scalchi (?)
Inez: Saruggia (?)
Balthazar: Cherubini (?)
Alfonso: De Anna (?)
Fernando: Giannini (?)
Don Gaspar: ?

February 7
Les Huguenots
Marguerite: Dotti
St. Bris: De Pasqualis
Valentine: Fursch-Madi
Nevers: De Anna
Cossé: ?
Tavannes: ?
Retz: ?
Raoul: Cardinali
Marcel: Cherubini
Urbain: Scalchi
Maurevert: ?
Bois Rosé: ?
Lady Of Honor: ?
Soldier: ?
Thoret: ?
Meru: ?

ST. LOUIS

February 9
La Sonnambula
Same as December 29

February 10
Semiramide
Same as January 2 except:
Assur: De Pasqualis

February 11
Aida
Same as January 5 except:
King: Manni

February 12
Rigoletto
Same as December 11 except:
Monterone: Manni

February 13
Linda di Chamounix
Same as January 9

February 14 (mat.)
Ernani
Same as January 15

February 14
Lucrezia Borgia
Same as January 17 except:
Rustighello: ?
Astolfo: ?
Gubetta: ?
Vitellozzo: ?

KANSAS CITY

February 16
Il Trovatore
Same as November 20 except:
Leonora: Fursch-Madi
Ruiz: Rinaldini

February 17
La Sonnambula
Same as December 29 except:
Alessio: ?
Notary: ?

TOPEKA

February 18
Il Trovatore
Same as November 20 except:
Leonora: Dotti

ST. JOSEPH

February 19
La Sonnambula
Same as December 29

CHEYENNE

February 24
Lucia di Lammermoor
Same as January 3 (mat.) except:
Ashton: De Anna
Raimondo: Cherubini
Normanno: Bieletto

SALT LAKE CITY

February 26
Il Trovatore
Same as November 20 except:
Leonora: Fursch-Madi
Count di Luna: De Anna
Ruiz: Rinaldini

SAN FRANCISCO

March 2
Linda di Chamounix
Same as January 9 except:
Maddalena: ?

March 3
Il Trovatore
Same as November 20 except:
Leonora: Fursch-Madi
Count di Luna: De Anna
Ruiz: Rinaldini

March 4
La Favorita
Leonora: Steinbach
Inez: Saruggia
Balthazar: Cherubini
Alfonso: De Anna
Don Gaspar: ?
Fernando: Giannini

March 5
Lucrezia Borgia
Same as January 17 except:
Rustighello: ?
Astolfo: ?
Gubetta: ?
Vitellozzo: ?

March 6
Semiramide
Same as January 2 except:
Assur: De Pasqualis

March 7 (mat.)
Aida
Same as January 5 except:
King: Manni

March 9
Ernani
Same as January 15 except:
Ernani: Cardinali
Iago: ?
Don Riccardo: ?

March 10
Il Barbiere di Siviglia
Almaviva: Vicini
Dr. Bartolo: Caracciolo
Rosina: Patti

Figaro: De Pasqualis
Don Basilio: Cherubini
Berta: Saruggia
Fiorello: Rinaldini
Sergeant: ?

March 11
Il Trovatore
Same as November 20 except:
Leonora: Fursch-Madi
Count di Luna: De Anna
Ruiz: Rinaldini

March 12
Faust
Same as January 8 except:
Marguerite: Patti
Méphistophélès: Cherubini
Marthe: Saruggia
Wagner: De Vaschetti

March 13
Les Huguenots
Same (?) as February 7

March 14 (mat.)
Crispino e la Comare
Same as February 4

March 16
Semiramide
Same as January 2 except:
Assur: De Pasqualis

March 17
Rigoletto/Bimboni (c)
Same as December 11 except:
Duke: Giannini

March 18
La Favorita
Same as March 4 except:
Leonora: Scalchi

March 19
La Traviata
Same as December 30

March 20
Norma
Norma: Fursch-Madi
Pollione: Giannini
Adalgisa: Dotti
Clotilde: Saruggia
Oroveso: Cherubini
Flavio: Bieletto

March 21 (mat.)
Marta
Same as January 6

March 23
La Sonnambula
Same as December 29

March 24
Aida
Same as January 5 except:
King: Manni
Amneris: Scalchi
Aida: Patti
Radames: Nicolini

March 25
Lucia di Lammermoor
Same as January 3 (mat.) except:
Edgardo: Cardinali
Raimondo: Cherubini
Normanno: Bieletto

March 26
Der Freischütz
Ottokar: Rinaldini
Agathe: Fursch-Madi
Aennchen: Dotti
Max: Giannini
Caspar: De Anna
Bridesmaid: Saruggia
Hermit: Manni

Kuno: Cherubini
Kiliano: Caracciolo

March 27

Mireille
Same as December 18 except:
Young Shepherd: Steinbach

March 28 (mat.)

Faust
Same as January 8 except:
Marguerite: Patti
Méphistophélès: Cherubini
Marthe: Saruggia
Wagner: De Vaschetti

BURLINGTON

April 2

Faust
Same as January 8 except:
Méphistophélès: Cherubini
Marthe: ?
Wagner: ?

CHICAGO

April 6

Semiramide
Same as January 2

APRIL 7

L'Africaine
Selika: Fursch-Madi
Anna: ?
Inez: Dotti
Nelusko: De Anna
Don Pedro: Cherubini
Grand Inquisitor: Manni
Grand Brahmin: De Vaschetti
Don Diego: Caracciolo
Don Alvar: ?
Usher: ?
Vasco da Gama: Cardinali
Officer: ?

April 8

Mireille
Same as December 18 except:
Young Shepherd: Steinbach

April 9

Linda di Chamounix
Same as January 9 except:
Maddalena: ?

April 10

Lucia di Lammermoor
Same as January 3 (mat.) except:
Ashton: De Anna
Raimondo: Manni
Normanno: De Vaschetti

April 11 (mat.)

Marta
Same as January 6

April 11

Der Freischütz
Same as March 26 except:
Hermit: De Vaschetti

April 13

La Sonnambula
Same as December 29

April 14

Aida
Same as January 5 except:
King: Manni
Amneris: Scalchi
Aida: Patti
Radames: Nicolini
Messenger: Rinaldini

April 15

Il Trovatore/Bimboni (c)
Same as November 20 except:
Leonora: Fursch-Madi
Count di Luna: De Anna
Ruiz: Rinaldini

April 16
Rigoletto
Same as December 11 except:
Duke: Giannini
Gilda: Nevada

April 17
Faust
Same as January 8 except:
Faust: Nicolini
Marguerite: Patti
Méphistophélès: Cherubini

April 18 (mat.)
Lucia di Lammermoor/Bimboni (c)
Same as January 3 (mat.) except:
Ashton: De Anna
Raimondo: Manni
Normanno: De Vaschetti

April 18
Lohengrin
Lohengrin: Cardinali
King Henry: Cherubini
Telramund: De Pasqualis
Elsa: Fursch-Madi
Herald: De Vaschetti
Ortrud: Steinbach

BOSTON

April 28
La Sonnambula
Same (?) as December 29

April 29
La Favorita
Same as March 4 except:
Leonora: Scalchi
Don Gaspar: Rinaldini

April 30
Marta
Same as January 6

May 1
Mireille
Same as December 18

May 2 (mat.)
Lucia di Lammermoor
Same as January 3 (mat.) except:
Alisa: ?
Ashton: De Anna
Raimondo: Cherubini
Arturo: ?
Normanno: De Vaschetti

1885–1886 Season

NEW HAVEN

November 5
Carmen
Carmen: Hauk
Don José: Ravelli
Micaela: Dotti
Escamillo: Del Puente
Zuniga: Cherubini
Morales: Bieletto
Frasquita: Bauermeister
Mercedes: Lablache
Dancaire: Caracciolo
Remendado: Rinaldini

BROOKLYN

November 19
Carmen
Same as November 5 except:
Mercedes: De Vigne

December 10
Fra Diavolo
Fra Diavolo: Ravelli
Milord: Caracciolo
Pamela: Lablache
Lorenzo: De Falco
Matteo: Bieletto

Zerline: Fohström
Beppo: Del Puente
Giacomo: Cherubini

Des Grieux: Giannini
Innkeeper: De Vaschetti
Attendant: Bieletto

December 17
Maritana
Don Caesar de Bazan: Ravelli
King: Del Puente
Don José: De Anna
Marchese: Caracciolo
Marchesa: Lablache
Lazarillo: De Vigne
Maritana: Fohström
Alcade: ?
Captain: ?

January 7
Maritana
Same as December 17 except:
Marchese: Foscani
Alcade: Vetta
Captain: De Vaschetti

December 22
Faust
Faust: Giannini
Marguerite: Fohström
Méphistophélès: Cherubini
Valentin: De Anna
Siébel: De Vigne
Marthe: Lablache
Wagner: De Vaschetti

January 8
La Traviata
Violetta: Nordica
Alfredo: Giannini
Germont: De Anna
Flora: Biache
Annina: Bauermeister
Gastone: Rinaldini
Baron Douphol: Caracciolo
Marquis d'Obigny: Bieletto
Dr. Grenvil: Cherubini

BOSTON

January 9 (mat.)
Carmen
Same as November 5 except:
Zuniga: De Vaschetti

January 4
Carmen
Same as November 5 except:
Zuniga: De Vaschetti

January 11
Faust
Same as December 22

January 5
Fra Diavolo
Same as December 10

January 12
Don Giovanni
Don Giovanni: Del Puente
Donna Anna: Dotti
Donna Elvira: Bauermeister
Zerlina: Hauk
Commendatore: Vetta
Don Ottavio: Ravelli
Leporello: Cherubini
Masetto: Rinaldini

January 6
Manon
Manon: Hauk
Rosette: De Vigne
Poussette: Bauermeister
Javotte: Lablache
Lescaut: Del Puente
Count des Grieux: Vetta
Guillot: Rinaldini
De Brétigny: Caracciolo

January 13
Fra Diavolo
Same as December 10

January 14
Rigoletto
Duke: Giannini
Rigoletto: De Anna
Gilda: Nordica
Sparafucile: Cherubini
Maddalena: Lablache
Giovanna: Bauermeister
Monterone: De Vaschetti
Marullo: Caracciolo
Borsa: Rinaldini
Ceprano: Bieletto
Countess: ?

January 15
Carmen
Same as November 5 except:
Zuniga: De Vaschetti

January 16 (mat.)
Marta
Harriet: Fohström
Nancy: Lablache
Lionel: Ravelli
Plunkett: Cherubini
Tristan: Caracciolo
Sheriff: ?

PHILADELPHIA

January 18
Carmen
Same as November 5 except:
Zuniga: De Vaschetti

January 19
Fra Diavolo
Same as December 10 except:
Matteo: De Vaschetti

January 20
Manon
Same as January 6 except:
Count des Grieux: Cherubini

January 21
Maritana
Same as December 17 except:
Alcade: Vetta
Captain: De Vaschetti

January 22
La Traviata/Bimboni (c)
Same as January 8 except:
Flora: Lablache

January 23 (mat.)
Carmen
Same as November 5

January 23
Lucia di Lammermoor
Lucia: Fohström
Alisa: Bauermeister
Edgardo: Giannini
Ashton: De Anna
Raimondo: Cherubini
Arturo: Rinaldini
Normanno: De Vaschetti

January 25
Don Giovanni/Bimboni (c)
Same as January 12

January 26
Faust/Bimboni (c)
Same as December 22 except:
Marguerite: Nordica

January 27 (mat.)
Marta
Same as January 16 except:
Sheriff: De Vaschetti

January 27
Rigoletto/Bimboni (c)
Same as January 14 except:
Marullo: ?

BALTIMORE

January 28
Fra Diavolo
Same as December 10 except:
Lorenzo: ?

January 29
Manon
Same as January 6 except:
Count des Grieux: Cherubini
Innkeeper: ?
Attendant: ?

January 30 (mat.)
Lucia di Lammermoor
Same as January 23 except:
Arturo: Bieletto

January 30
Carmen
Same as November 5 except:
Zuniga: De Vaschetti

WASHINGTON, D.C.

February 1
Fra Diavolo
Same as December 10 except:
Lorenzo: Bieletto
Matteo: ?

February 2
Carmen
Same as November 5 except:
Zuniga: De Vaschetti

February 3
La Traviata
Same as January 8 except:
Flora: Lablache
Gastone: ?
Marquis d'Obigny: ?
Dr. Grenvil: ?

PITTSBURGH

February 4
Carmen
Same as November 5 except:
Zuniga: De Vaschetti
Morales: ?

February 5
Lucia di Lammermoor
Same as January 23 except:
Arturo: Bieletto

February 6 (mat.)
La Traviata
Same as January 8 except:
Flora: Lablache
Gastone: ?
Marquis d'Obigny: ?
Dr. Grenvil: ?

February 6
Faust
Same as December 22 except:
Valentin: Del Puente
Wagner: ?

CHICAGO

February 8
Carmen
Same as November 5 except:
Zuniga: De Vaschetti

February 9
Lucia di Lammermoor/Bimboni (c)
Same as January 23 except:
Raimondo: Vetta
Arturo: Bieletto

February 10
Manon/Bimboni (c)
Same as January 6 except:
Count des Grieux: Cherubini
De Brétigny: Foscani

February 11
Fra Diavolo/Bimboni (c)
Same as December 10 except:
Fra Diavolo: De Falco
Lorenzo: Bieletto

February 12
La Traviata/Bimboni (c)
Same as January 8 except:
Flora: Lablache

February 13 (mat.)
Carmen/Bimboni (c)
Same as November 5 except:
Don José: De Falco
Zuniga: De Vaschetti

February 13
Faust/Bimboni (c)
Same as December 22

February 15
Il Trovatore/Bimboni (c)
Leonora: Dotti
Manrico: Ravelli
Count di Luna: De Anna
Azucena: Lablache
Inez: Bauermeister
Ferrando: Cherubini
Ruiz: Rinaldini

February 16
Manon/Bimboni (c)
Same as January 6 except:
Count des Grieux: Cherubini
De Brétigny: Foscani

February 17
La Traviata/Bimboni (c)
Same as January 8 except:
Alfredo: Ravelli
Flora: Lablache

February 18
Rigoletto/Bimboni (c)
Same as January 14

February 19
Mignon/Bimboni (c)
Mignon: Hauk
Philine: Carrington
Wilhelm: De Falco
Lothario: Del Puente
Laerte: Rinaldini
Jarno: Vetta
Frederic: De Vigne

February 20 (mat.)
I Puritani/Bimboni (c)
Lord Walton: De Vaschetti
Sir George: Cherubini
Elvira: Fohström
Henrietta: Bauermeister
Lord Arthur: Ravelli
Sir Richard: De Anna
Sir Bruno: Rinaldini

February 20
Carmen/Bimboni (c)
Same as November 5 except:
Zuniga: De Vaschetti

MINNEAPOLIS

February 22
Faust/Bimboni (c)
Same as December 22 except:
Marguerite: Nordica

February 23
Carmen/Bimboni (c)
Same as November 5 except:
Zuniga: De Vaschetti

February 24
Maritana/Bimboni (c)
Same as December 17 except:
King: Cherubini
Alcade: Vetta
Captain: De Vaschetti

ST. PAUL

February 25
La Traviata/Bimboni (c)
Same as January 8 except:
Flora: Lablache
Annina: ?
Dr. Grenvil: De Vaschetti

February 26
Don Giovanni/Bimboni (c)
Same as January 12 except:
Donna Elvira: Lablache

February 27 (mat.)
Marta/Bimboni (c)
Same as January 16 except:
Tristan: ?
Sheriff: ?

February 27
Il Trovatore/Bimboni (c)
Same as February 15 except:
Manrico: Giannini
Inez: ?
Ferrando: De Vaschetti

ST. LOUIS

March 1
Maritana/Bimboni (c)
Same as December 17

March 2
Lucia di Lammermoor/Bimboni (c)
Same as January 23 except:
Arturo: Bieletto

March 3
Faust/Bimboni (c)
Same as December 22 except:
Marguerite: Dotti

March 4
Marta/Bimboni (c)
Same as January 16

March 5
La Traviata/Bimboni (c)
Same as January 8 except:
Flora: Lablache

March 6 (mat.)
Carmen/Bimboni (c)
Same as November 5 except:
Don José: De Falco
Morales: ?
Remendado: ?

March 6
Il Trovatore/Bimboni (c)
Same as February 15 except:
Manrico: Giannini
Ferrando: Vetta
Ruiz: ?

KANSAS CITY

March 8
Carmen/Bimboni (c)
Same (?) as November 5

March 9
Faust/Bimboni (c)
Same as December 22 except:
Marguerite: Nordica

TOPEKA

March 10
Lucia di Lammermoor/Bimboni (c)
Same as January 23 except:
Arturo: Bieletto

ST. JOSEPH

March 11
Carmen/Bimboni (c)
Same as November 5 except:
Zuniga: De Vaschetti

DENVER

March 13
Carmen/Bimboni (c)
Same as November 5 except:
Zuniga: De Vaschetti
Morales: ?
Remendado: ?

March 15
Faust/Bimboni (c)
Same as December 22 except:
Marguerite: Nordica

CHEYENNE

March 16
*Carmen
Same as November 5 except:
Zuniga: ?
Morales: ?
Dancaire: ?
Remendado: ?

SALT LAKE CITY

March 18
Carmen
Same (?) as November 5 except:
Don José: De Falco
Zuniga: De Vaschetti

SAN FRANCISCO

March 22
Carmen
Same as November 5 except:
Zuniga: De Vaschetti
Morales: ?

March 23
†*Lucia di Lammermoor*
Same as January 23 except:
Arturo: Bieletto

March 24
Lucia di Lammermoor
Same (?) as January 23 except:
Ashton: Del Puente
Arturo: Bieletto

March 26
La Traviata
Same as January 8 except:
Germont: Del Puente
Flora: Lablache
Gastone: ?
Marquis d'Obigny: ?

March 27 (mat.)
Carmen
Same as November 5 except:
Don José: De Falco
Zuniga: De Vaschetti
Morales: ?

March 29
La Sonnambula/Bimboni (c)
Amina: Fohström
Elvino: De Falco
Rodolfo: Cherubini
Alessio: Rinaldini
Notary: Bieletto
Lisa: Bauermeister
Teresa: Lablache

March 30
L'Africaine
Selika: Hauk
Anna: Bauermeister
Inez: Dotti
Nelusko: Del Puente
Don Pedro: Cherubini
Grand Inquisitor: Vetta
Grand Brahmin: ?
Don Diego: Caracciolo
Don Alvar: Rinaldini
Usher: ?

*Arditi returned to the podium after a long, severe illness.
†De Vaschetti replaced Cherubini after Act 1.

Vasco da Gama: Giannini
Officer: ?

April 1
Faust
Same as December 22 except:
Marguerite: Nordica
Valentin: Del Puente

April 2
Mignon
Same as February 19 except:
Philine: Engle

April 3 (mat.)
La Traviata
Same (?) as January 8 except:
Germont: Del Puente
Flora: Lablache
Gastone: ?
Marquis d'Obigny: ?

April 5
L'Africaine
Same as March 30

April 6
Marta
Same as January 16

April 7
Rigoletto
Same (?) as January 14 except:
Sparafucile: Vetta

April 8
Maritana
Same as December 17 except:
King: Cherubini
Don José: Campobello
Alcade: Vetta
Captain: De Vaschetti

April 9
Don Giovanni
Same as January 12

April 12
Il Trovatore
Same (?) as February 15 except:
Count di Luna: Del Puente

April 13
Faust
Same as December 22 except:
Marguerite: Hauk
Valentin: Del Puente
Wagner: ?

April 15
L'Africaine
Same as March 30

April 16
Mapleson Benefit
Manon (Act III)
Same as January 6 except:
Count des Grieux: Cherubini

Dinorah (Act III)
Dinorah: Fohström
Goatherds:?
Harvester: ?
Huntsman: ?
Hoel: ?

Mignon (Act 3, Scene 2)
Mignon: ?
Philine: Engle
Wilhelm: ?
Lothario: Del Puente
Laerte: ?
Jarno: ?
Frederic: ?

Il Trovatore (Act IV)
Leonora: Dotti
Count di Luna: Del Puente
Manrico: Giannini
Azucena: Lablache
Ruiz: ?

April 17

Mignon
Same as February 19 except:
Philine: Engle
Laerte: ?

LOUISVILLE

April 27

Carmen
Same as November 5 except:
Don José: De Falco
Zuniga: De Vaschetti

April 28

Faust
Same as December 22 except:
Marguerite: Dotti
Méphistophélès: Vetta
Valentin: Del Puente
Siébel: Lablache
Marthe: Bauermeister

INDIANAPOLIS

April 29

Carmen
Same as November 5 except:
Don José: De Falco
Zuniga: ?
Morales: ?

April 30

La Traviata
Same as January 8 except:
Germont: Del Puente
Flora: Lablache
Dr. Grenvil: ?

May 1

Il Trovatore/Bimboni (c)
Same as February 15 except:
Manrico: Giannini
Count di Luna: Del Puente
Ferrando: De Vaschetti

CINCINNATI

May 3

Carmen
Same as November 5 except:
Don José: Baldanza
Zuniga: De Vaschetti

May 4

La Traviata
Same as January 8 except:
Germont: Del Puente
Flora: ?
Dr. Grenvil: De Vaschetti

May 5

Mignon
Same as February 19 except:
Philine: Engle
Frederic: Lablache

May 6

Lucia di Lammermoor
Same as January 23 except:
Edgardo: Baldanza
Ashton: Del Puente
Raimondo: Vetta
Arturo: Bieletto

May 7

Manon
Same as January 6 except:
Rosette: De Vivo

May 8 (mat.)

La Sonnambula
Same (?) as March 29

May 9

Il Trovatore
Same (?) as February 15 except:
Manrico: Giannini
Count di Luna: Del Puente
Ferrando: De Vaschetti

DETROIT

May 10
Carmen
Same as November 5 except:
Don José: De Falco
Micaela: Bauermeister
Zuniga: De Vaschetti
Frasquita: ?

May 11
La Traviata
Same as January 8 except:
Germont: Del Puente
Flora: Lablache
Dr. Grenvil: De Vaschetti

May 12
Manon
Same as January 6 except:
Rosette: Lablache
Javotte: De Meric
Innkeeper: ?

MILWAUKEE

May 13
Lucia di Lammermoor
Same as January 23 except:
Edgardo: Baldanza/De Falco (?)
Ashton: Del Puente
Raimondo: Vetta
Arturo: Bieletto

May 14
Carmen
Same as November 5 except:
Don José: Baldanza/De Falco (?)
Zungia: ?

May 15 (mat.)
La Sonnambula
Same as March 29 except:
Rodolfo: De Vaschetti
Notary: ?
Teresa: ?

May 16
La Traviata
Same (?) as January 8 except:
Germont: Del Puente
Flora: ?
Dr. Grenvil: De Vaschetti

CHICAGO

May 17
Lucia di Lammermoor
Same as January 23 except:
Ashton: Del Puente
Raimondo: Vetta
Arturo: Bieletto

May 18
Mignon
Same as February 19 except:
Philine: Engle
Frederic: Lablache

May 19
Faust
Same as December 22 except:
Marguerite: Nordica
Méphistophélès: Vetta
Valentin: Del Puente
Siébel: Lablache
Marthe: De Meric

May 20
Carmen
Same as November 5 except:
Don José: Baldanza
Zuniga: De Vaschetti

May 21
La Traviata
Same as January 8 except:
Alfredo: Baldanza
Germont: Del Puente
Flora: Lablache
Gastone: ?
Baron Douphol: ?
Marquis d'Obigny: ?
Dr. Grenvil: De Vaschetti

May 22 (mat.)
La Sonnambula/Bimboni (c)
Same as March 29 except:
Elvino: Giannini
Rodolfo: Vetta
Teresa: ?

May 22
Mapleson Benefit

Rigoletto (Act I)
Duke: Baldanza
Rigoletto: Del Puente
Gilda: Nordica
Sparafucile: Vetta
Giovanna: ?
Monterone: ?
Marullo: ?
Borsa: ?

Ceprano: ?
Countess: ?

Manon (Act III)
Same as January 6 except:
Count des Grieux: ?

Mignon—Polonaise
Philine: Engle

Il Trovatore (Act IV, Scene 1)
Lenora: Dotti
Manrico: Giannini
Ruiz: ?

Dinorah (Act III)
Same (?) as April 16

Ballet: Cavalazzi

Notes

∾

1. Alarums and Excursions

1. "The Opera House Lease," *Music and Drama* (January 6, 1883), 5:2.
2. *The* [New York] *World*, October 15, 1883.
3. Letter to Mapleson from August Belmont, June 17, 1878. August Belmont Sr. Papers.
4. *New-York Daily Tribune*, March 24, 1883.
5. *The New York Herald*, March 30, 1883.
6. *The New-York Times*, December 31, 1882.
7. *The New York Herald*, March 29, 1883.
8. Ibid., March 30, 1883.
9. *The New-York Times*, April 24, 1883.
10. *The New York Herald*, March 30, 1883.
11. *New-York Daily Tribune*, April 3, 1883.
12. Ibid.
13. Ibid., April 4, 1883.
14. Ibid., April 7, 1883.
15. Ibid., April 4, 1883.
16. Ibid., April 7, 1883.
17. Ibid., April 9, 1883.
18. *The New York Herald*, April 24, 1883.
19. Ibid., April 22, 1883.
20. Ibid., April 24, 1883.
21. *New-York Daily Tribune*, April 27, 1883.
22. Ibid., March 24, 1883.
23. Ibid., March 21, 1883.
24. *The New York Herald*, March 30, 1883.
25. *New-York Daily Tribune*, April 29, 1883.
26. *The New-York Times*, July 11, 1883.
27. Letter to Levi P. Morton from Mapleson, June 11, 1878. August Belmont Sr. Papers.

28. Letter to August Belmont from Mapleson, June 29, 1878. August Belmont Sr. Papers.

29. New York Academy of Music Prospectus for 1883–1884.

30. *The New-York Times,* July 11, 1883.

2. *The Gathering, Opening Night, Ensuing Events*

1. *New-York Daily Tribune,* October 15, 1883.
2. *The New York Herald,* October 15, 1883.
3. *The* [New York] *World,* October 23, 1883.
4. *New York Commercial Advertiser,* October 23, 1883.
5. *The* [New York] *World,* October 23, 1883.
6. *The New-York Times,* October 23, 1883.
7. *The New York Herald,* October 23, 1883.
8. Ibid.
9. Ibid.
10. *The* [New York] *World,* October 23, 1883.
11. Ibid.
12. *New-York Daily Tribune,* October 23, 1883.
13. Richard Grant White, "Opera in New York," p. 210.
14. *The New-York Times,* October 23, 1883.
15. *The New York Herald,* October 23, 1883.
16. *New-York Daily Tribune,* October 23, 1883.
17. *The* [New York] *Evening Telegram,* October 23, 1883.
18. *The* [New York] *Sun,* October 23, 1883.
19. *The New York Herald,* October 23, 1883.
20. *The American Queen* (October 27, 1883), 10:258.
21. *The* [New York] *World,* October 22, 1883.
22. *The* [New York] *Evening Telegram,* October 23, 1883.
23. *The American Queen* (October 27, 1883), 10:258.
24. *New-York Daily Tribune,* October 23, 1883.
25. *The American Queen* (November 3, 1883), 10:274.
26. *The* [New York] *Evening Post,* October 23, 1883.
27. *The* [New York] *World,* October 28, 1883.
28. *The* [New York] *Sun,* October 25, 1883.
29. *The* [New York] *World,* October 25, 1883.
30. *The* [New York] *Sun,* October 25, 1883.
31. *The* [New York] *Evening Post,* October 25, 1883.
32. *The* [New York] *World,* October 27, 1883.
33. *The* [New York] *Evening Post,* October 27, 1883.
34. *The* [New York] *Sun,* October 30, 1883.
35. Ibid.
36. *The* [New York] *World,* November 1, 1883.
37. *The* [New York] *Sun,* November 3, 1883.
38. *New-York Daily Tribune,* October 28, 1883.

39. "Gossip of the Stage," *Music and Drama* (November 17, 1883), 7:4.
40. *The* [New York] *Evening Post*, October 25, 1883.
41. *The* [New York] *World*, November 6, 1883.
42. *New-York Daily Tribune*, November 1, 1883.
43. *The New York Herald*, November 7, 1883.
44. *The* [New York] *World*, November 2, 1883.
45. *The New York Herald*, November 25, 1859.
46. *The Wasp* (March 14, 1885), 14:4.

3. The Queen and the Princess

1. *New-York Daily Tribune*, November 10, 1883.
2. *The* [New York] *Evening Post*, November 10, 1883.
3. *The* [New York] *Sun*, November 10, 1883.
4. *The New-York Times*, November 10, 1883.
5. *The New York Herald*, November 13, 1883.
6. *The* [New York] *Sun*, November 14, 1883.
7. *The New York Herald*, November 14, 1883.
8. *The* [New York] *Sun*, November 14, 1883.
9. *The* [New York] *Daily Graphic*, November 17, 1883.
10. *The* [New York] *Evening Post*, November 17, 1883.
11. Betsy B., "Drama," *The Argonaut* (March 15, 1884), 14:14.
12. *The* [New York] *Sun*, November 24, 1883.
13. *The* [New York] *World*, November 29, 1883.
14. *The* [New York] *Sun*, November 27, 1883.
15. *The* [New York] *Evening Post*, November 27, 1883.
16. *The* [New York] *Sun*, November 27, 1883.
17. Ibid.
18. *The New York Herald*, November 27, 1883.
19. Ibid., December 4, 1883.
20. Ibid.
21. Ibid., November 15, 1883.
22. *The Boston Daily Globe*, December 20, 1883.
23. *Boston Morning Journal*, December 20, 1883.
24. Harold Rosenthal, ed., *The Mapleson Memoirs*, pp. 182–83.
25. *The* [New York] *Sun*, January 12, 1884.
26. *The* [New York] *World*, January 12, 1884.
27. *The* [New York] *Sun*, January 19, 1884.
28. *The New-York Times*, January 21, 1884.
29. "The Fall Season of Italian Opera Reviewed," *The New-York Times*, January 20, 1884.
30. Ibid.
31. Ibid.
32. Ibid.
33. *The New-York Times*, December 31, 1883.
34. Ibid.

4. Grand Tour

1. *The* [Philadelphia] *North American,* January 22, 1884.
2. *Baltimore American,* January 24, 1884.
3. *The* [Baltimore] *Sun,* January 25, 1884.
4. Ibid., January 26, 1884.
5. *The Chicago Daily Tribune,* January 29, 1884.
6. Ibid., January 30, 1884.
7. Ibid., January 31, 1884.
8. Harold Rosenthal, ed., *The Mapleson Memoirs,* pp. 189–90.
9. Quaintance Eaton, *Opera Caravan,* p. 10.
10. *The Chicago Daily Tribune,* February 7, 1884.
11. Ira Glackens, *Yankee Diva,* p. 123.
12. *The New-York Times,* February 14, 1884.
13. *The* [St. Louis] *Missouri Republican,* February 22, 1884.
14. *St. Louis Post-Dispatch,* February 25, 1884.
15. *The* [San Francisco] *Morning Call,* March 30, 1884.
16. Harold Rosenthal, ed., *The Mapleson Memoirs,* p. 205.
17. *Cheyenne Daily Leader,* March 4, 1884.
18. Harold Rosenthal, ed., *The Mapleson Memoirs,* p. 193.
19. William Campton Bell, "The Theatrical Activities of Cheyenne," p. 152.
20. [Salt Lake City] *Deseret Evening News,* March 7, 1884.

5. Golconda

1. *The* [San Francisco] *Morning Call,* March 10, 1884.
2. [San Francisco] *Daily Alta California,* March 10, 1884.
3. *The* [San Francisco] *Morning Call,* March 10, 1884.
4. Ibid.
5. *San Francisco Chronicle,* March 11, 1884.
6. Ibid.
7. Ibid.
8. Ibid., March 12, 1884.
9. *The Wasp* (March 15, 1884), 12:3.
10. Betsy B., "Drama," *The Argonaut* (March 15, 1884), 14:14.
11. Harold Rosenthal, ed., *The Mapleson Memoirs,* p. 199.
12. Ibid., pp. 198–99.
13. Betsy B., "Drama," *The Argonaut* (March 15, 1884), 14:14.
14. *The Argonaut* (March 15, 1884), 14:6.
15. *San Francisco Chronicle,* March 14, 1884.
16. Ibid.
17. Betsy B., "Drama," *The Argonaut* (March 15, 1884), 14:14.
18. Ibid.
19. *The* [San Francisco] *Morning Call,* March 15, 1884.
20. *The Wasp* (April 12, 1884), 12:4.
21. *The Argonaut* (April 15, 1884), 14:1.

22. *San Francisco Chronicle*, March 19, 1884.
23. Ibid., March 23, 1884.
24. Ibid., March 19, 1884.
25. Ibid., March 23, 1884.
26. *The Argonaut* (March 22, 1884), 14:6.
27. Betsy B., "Drama," *The Argonaut* (March 29, 1884), 14:14.
28. *San Francisco Chronicle*, March 26, 1884.
29. Harold Rosenthal, ed., *The Mapleson Memoirs*, pp. 206–07.
30. [San Francisco] *Daily Alta California*, March 29, 1884.
31. *San Francisco Chronicle*, March 30, 1884.
32. Ibid.
33. [Salt Lake City] *Deseret Evening News*, April 2, 1884.
34. *The Omaha Daily Herald*, April 5, 1884.

6. Victories and Vicissitudes

1. *The* [New York] *World*, April 9, 1884.
2. *The New York Herald*, April 15, 1884.
3. *The New-York Times*, January 16, 1884.
4. *The* [New York] *World*, April 21, 1884.
5. *The New-York Times*, October 26, 1884.
6. Ibid., April 26, 1885.
7. Harold Rosenthal, ed., *The Mapleson Memoirs*, p. 240.
8. *New York Herald*, April 27, 1884.
9. *New-York Daily Tribune*, May 1, 1884.
10. *The* [New York] *World*, April 30, 1884.
11. *New-York Daily Tribune*, May 6, 1884.
12. Ibid., May 8, 1884.
13. Ibid., May 1, 1884.
14. Ibid., May 18, 1884.
15. Ibid.

7. A Long, Hot Summer

1. "Les Italiens en Amerique," *Freund's Music and Drama* (July 31, 1884), 2:1.
2. *The New-York Times*, August 14, 1884.
3. "Operatic," *Musical Review* (April 15, 1880), 2:7.
4. *Music and Drama* (November 18, 1882), 4:13.
5. *New-York Daily Tribune*, November 8, 1883.
6. Walter Damrosch, *My Musical Life*, p. 53.
7. *The New-York Times*, October 11, 1884.
8. Ibid., October 3, 1884.
9. Letter to Unidentified Individual from Adelina Patti, September 25, 1884. The Pierpont Morgan Library.

10. *The New-York Times,* October 26, 1884.
11. Ibid.
12. Ibid.
13. Ibid.

8. A New Campaign

1. *The* [New York] *Sun,* November 3, 1884.
2. Ibid.
3. *New-York Daily Tribune,* November 3, 1884.
4. *The New-York Times,* November 11, 1884.
5. Ibid.
6. *New-York Daily Tribune,* November 11, 1884.
7. *The New York Herald,* November 11, 1884.
8. *The* [New York] *Evening Post,* November 11, 1884.
9. *The New York Herald,* November 13, 1884.
10. *The* [New York] *Evening Post,* November 13, 1884.
11. *The New-York Times,* November 15, 1884.
12. Ibid., November 16, 1884.
13. *The* [New York] *World,* November 15, 1884.
14. *New-York Daily Tribune,* November 13, 1884.
15. *The* [New York] *World,* November 15, 1884.
16. Ibid., November 13, 1884.
17. Ibid.
18. *New-York Daily Tribune,* November 14, 1884.
19. *The New-York Times,* November 18, 1884.
20. Ibid.
21. *New-York Daily Tribune,* November 16, 1884.
22. *The New-York Times,* November 18, 1884.
23. *The* [New York] *World,* November 20, 1884.
24. *New-York Daily Tribune,* November 23, 1884.

9. A Banner Week

1. *New-York Daily Tribune,* November 18, 1884.
2. Mathilde Marchesi, *Marchesi and Music,* p. 209.
3. *The New-York Times,* November 25, 1884.
4. *The* [New York] *Evening Post,* November 25, 1884.
5. *The New York Herald,* November 25, 1884.
6. *The* [New York] *World,* November 25, 1884.
7. *The New-York Times,* November 25, 1884.
8. *New-York Daily Tribune,* November 27, 1884.
9. *The* [New York] *Sun,* November 27, 1884.
10. *New-York Daily Tribune,* November 27, 1884.
11. *The* [New York] *World,* November 27, 1884.
12. "Operatic Notes," *American Art Journal* (December 6, 1884), 42:517.

10. New Princess Problems, Among Others

1. *New-York Daily Tribune*, December 4, 1884.
2. Ibid.
3. *The* [New York] *World*, December 12, 1884.
4. *The New York Herald*, December 7, 1884.
5. *The* [New York] *World*, December 4, 1884.
6. *New-York Daily Tribune*, November 25, 1884.
7. *The New-York Times*, March 27, 1883.
8. Barbara Goldsmith, *Little Gloria . . . Happy at Last*, pp. 108–9.
9. Ibid.
10. *The New-York Times*, December 14, 1884.
11. Henry Edward Krehbiel, *Chapters of Opera*, p. 73.
12. *The New-York Times*, December 18, 1884.
13. Ibid., December 19, 1884.
14. Ibid.
15. *New-York Daily Tribune*, December 22, 1884.
16. *The New-York Times*, December 28, 1884.
17. *New-York Daily Tribune*, December 29, 1884.
18. Ibid.
19. Letter to August Belmont from Bernard Ullman, July 1, 1878. August Belmont Sr. Papers.
20. Ibid., September 6, 1878. August Belmont Sr. Papers.
21. Elizabeth Drexel Lehr, *"King Lehr" and the Gilded Age*, p. 21.

11. Transcontinental Journey

1. [San Francisco] *Daily Alta California*, March 2, 1885.
2. *New-York Daily Tribune*, January 19, 1885.
3. Ibid.
4. Ibid.
5. *The American Queen and Town Topics* (January 17, 1885), 13:6.
6. Ibid., (January 3, 1885), p. 3.
7. *New-York Daily Tribune*, January 6, 1885.
8. Ibid., February 23, 1885.
9. "German Opera in New York," *Harper's New Monthly Magazine* (April 1, 1885), 70:807.

12. Return to El Dorado

1. *The* [San Francisco] *Morning Call*, March 2, 1885.
2. *San Francisco Chronicle*, March 3, 1885.
3. Betsy B., "Drama," *The Argonaut* (March 7, 1885), 16:14.
4. [San Francisco] *Daily Alta California*, March 3, 1885.
5. Ibid., March 6, 1885.
6. Betsy B., "Drama," *The Argonaut* (March 7, 1885), 16:14.

7. [San Francisco] *Daily Alta California*, March 7, 1885.
8. *San Francisco Chronicle*, March 18, 1885.
9. Ibid., March 24, 1885.
10. Harold Rosenthal, ed., *The Mapleson Memoirs*, p. 228.
11. *San Francisco Chronicle*, March 24, 1885.
12. Ibid., March 28, 1885.

13. Season's Endings

1. "The Grand Opera Festival," *The* [Chicago] *Indicator* (April 18, 1885), 6:334.
2. A. T. Andreas, *History of Chicago*, p. 651.
3. Harold Rosenthal, ed., *The Mapleson Memoirs*, p. 232.
4. Ibid., p. 239.
5. *The New-York Times*, April 21, 1885.
6. *The New York Herald*, April 21, 1885.
7. *New-York Daily Tribune*, May 3, 1885.
8. King George V of England's Diary, October 1914. Windsor Castle Archives.
9. Queen Mary of England's Diary, October 1914. Windsor Castle Archives.
10. *New-York Daily Tribune*, May 4, 1885.
11. Ibid.
12. Ibid., May 7, 1885.

14. Optimism Reigns—Briefly

1. Harold Rosenthal, ed., *The Mapleson Memoirs*, p. 241.
2. "Royal Italian Opera," *The Illustrated London News* (June 27, 1885), 86:645.
3. *New-York Daily Tribune*, October 20, 1885.
4. Ibid., October 24, 1885.
5. *The New York Herald*, October 24, 1885.
6. Ralph G. Martin, *Jennie*, Vol. 1, p. 24.
7. *The* [New York] *Sun*, November 3, 1885.
8. Ibid.
9. Ibid.
10. *The* [New York] *World*, November 3, 1885.
11. *The New-York Times*, November 3, 1885.
12. *The* [New York] *Sun*, November 3, 1885.
13. Ibid.
14. Ibid.
15. *New-York Daily Tribune*, November 4, 1885.
16. Ibid., November 5, 1885.
17. Ibid.
18. *The* [New York] *World*, November 10, 1885.
19. *American Art Journal* (November 14, 1885), 44:53.
20. *The New York Herald*, November 14, 1885.
21. *American Art Journal* (November 14, 1885), 44:53.

22. *The New York Herald*, November 12, 1885.
23. *New-York Daily Tribune*, November 15, 1885.
24. *Town Topics* (November 20, 1885) 14:13.
25. *The New-York Times*, November 19, 1885.
26. Ibid.
27. Ibid.
28. Ibid., November 21, 1885.
29. *The New York Herald*, November 21, 1885.
30. *New-York Daily Tribune*, October 29, 1885.
31. Ibid., November 22, 1885.
32. Ibid.
33. *The* [New York] *World*, November 28, 1885.
34. *The New-York Times*, December 20, 1885.
35. *The New York Herald*, December 18, 1885.
36. *The* [New York] *Sun*, December 24, 1885.
37. Ibid.
38. *The New York Herald*, December 24, 1885.
39. *The New-York Times*, December 24, 1885.
40. *The New York Herald*, December 24, 1885.
41. *The* [New York] *Sun*, December 24, 1885.
42. *The New-York Times*, December 24, 1885.
43. Ibid.
44. Ibid., November 30, 1885.
45. Ibid., November 29, 1885.
46. *New-York Daily Tribune*, October 28, 1885.
47. Unidentified clipping.
48. *Town Topics* (November 27, 1885), 14:4.
49. *The New-York Times*, November 28, 1885.
50. Ibid., December 3, 1885.

15. On the Road

1. *The Boston Daily Globe*, January 9, 1886.
2. *The Boston Herald*, January 15, 1886.
3. Ibid.
4. Ibid., January 17, 1886.
5. *The Philadelphia Press*, January 26, 1886.
6. Letter to an individual by the name of Tretbar from Mapleson, January 27, 1886. The Library of Congress.
7. *The* [Philadelphia] *North American*, January 27, 1886.
8. *The Washington Post*, February 4, 1886.
9. *The Pittsburg Dispatch*, February 5, 1886.
10. *The* [Chicago] *Daily Inter Ocean*, February 9, 1886.
11. *The Chicago Daily Tribune*, February 9, 1886.
12. *The New-York Times*, March 4, 1886.
13. *St. Louis Globe-Democrat*, March 4, 1886.

14. *The* [St. Louis] *Missouri Republican,* March 3, 1886.
15. Ibid., March 4, 1886.
16. Ibid.
17. *St. Louis Globe-Democrat,* March 6, 1886.
18. *The New-York Times,* January 21, 1886.
19. Ibid., February 6, 1886.
20. Ibid., February 12, 1886.
21. Ibid.
22. "Good Manners at the Opera," *Harper's New Monthly Magazine* (April, 1886), 72:802.
23. Irving Kolodin, *The Metropolitan Opera,* p. 53.

16. Hope Springs Eternal

1. *San Francisco Chronicle,* March 23, 1886.
2. Ibid.
3. Ibid., March 24, 1886.
4. *The* [San Francisco] *Daily Examiner,* March 24, 1886.
5. *San Francisco Chronicle,* March 25, 1886.
6. Ibid., March 27, 1886.
7. *The* [San Francisco] *Morning Call,* March 28, 1886.
8. *San Francisco Chronicle,* March 31, 1886.
9. Ibid.
10. Betsy B., "Drama," *The Argonaut* (April 3, 1886), 18:14.
11. *San Francisco Chronicle,* April 11, 1886.
12. Ibid., April 15, 1886.
13. [San Francisco] *Daily Alta California,* April 17, 1886.
14. *The* [San Francisco] *Morning Call,* April 22, 1886.
15. [San Francisco] *Daily Alta California,* April 22, 1886.

17. Finis

1. *The* [Detroit] *Evening News,* May 13, 1886.
2. *The Chicago Daily News,* May 22, 1886.
3. *The* [Chicago] *Daily Inter Ocean,* May 22, 1886.
4. Ibid., May 23, 1886.

Bibliography

⟅⟆

Letters and Manuscripts

Bell, William Campton. "A History of the Theatrical Activities of Cheyenne, Wyoming, from 1867 to 1902." Unpublished Master's thesis, Northwestern University, 1935.

August Belmont, Sr. Papers. Rare Books and Manuscripts Division, New York Public Library. Astor, Lenox and Tilden Foundations.

Curtis, John. "One Hundred Years of Grand Opera in Philadelphia." 7 vols. Unpublished MS, the Historical Society of Pennsylvania, Philadelphia [n.d.].

Estavan, Lawrence, ed. "The History of Opera in San Francisco." 2 vols. Monograph 17 from Theatre Research, W.P.A. Project 8386, San Francisco, 1938.

King George V of England's Diary for October 1914. Windsor Castle Archives.

Linscome, Sanford Abel. "A History of Musical Development in Denver, Colorado, 1859–1908." Ph.D. dissertation, the University of Texas, Austin, 1970.

Mapleson, James Henry. Letter to an individual by the name of Tretbar, January 27, 1886. Music Division, Library of Congress.

Queen Mary of England's Diary for October 1914. Windsor Castle Archives.

New York Academy of Music Papers. Theatre Collection, Museum of the City of New York.

Patti, Adelina. Letter to an unidentified individual, September 25, 1884. Mary Flagler Cary Music Collection. The Pierpont Morgan Library.

Newspapers and Magazines

American Art Journal, 1884–1886.

American Queen, October 1883–December 1885.

American Queen and Town Topics, January–February 1885.

Baltimore American, January 1884; January 1886.

Baltimore *Sun*, January 1884; January 1886.

Boston Daily Advertiser, December 1883; December 1884; January–May 1885; January 1886.

Boston Daily Globe, December 1883; December 1884; January–May 1885; January 1886.
Boston Herald, January 1886.
Boston Morning Journal, December 1883.
Boston Post, December 1883; December 1884; January–May 1885; January 1886.
Brooklyn Daily Eagle, November 1883; January–April 1884; November–December 1884; November–December 1885.
Cheyenne Daily Leader, March 1884; February 1885.
Cheyenne *Democratic Leader*, March 1884; February 1885; March 1886.
Chicago *Daily Inter Ocean*, January–February 1884; April 1885; February–May 1886.
Chicago Daily News, May 1886.
Chicago Daily Tribune, January–February 1884; April 1885; February–May 1886.
Cincinnati Commercial-Gazette, May 1886.
Cincinnati Enquirer, May 1886.
Cincinnati *Freie Presse*, May 1886.
Cincinnati *Sun*, May 1886.
Cincinnati *Times-Star*, May 1886.
Cincinnati *Volksfreund*, May 1886.
Critic, October–December 1883.
Denver Republican, February–March 1884; March 1886.
Denver *Rocky Mountain Daily News*, February–March 1884; March 1886.
Detroit *Evening News*, May 1886.
Detroit Free Press, May 1886.
Freund's Music and Drama, October 1883–July 1886.
Gazette: Burlington, Iowa, April 1885.
Harper's New Monthly Magazine, December 1883–April 1886.
Illustrated London News, January 1883–June 1886.
Indianapolis Sentinel, April–May 1886.
Kansas City *Evening Star*, February 1884; February 1885; March 1886.
Kansas City Journal, February 1884; February 1885; March 1886.
Kansas City Times, February 1884; February 1885; March 1886.
Keynote, January 1883–June 1886.
L'Abeille de la Nouvelle-Orléans, January–February 1885.
London *Times*, January 1883–June 1886.
Louisville *Courier-Journal*, April 1886.
Milwaukee Sentinel, May 1886.
Minneapolis *Daily Minnesota Tribune*, February 1884; February 1886.
Minneapolis Tribune, February 1884; February 1886.
Montreal *Gazette*, December 1883.
Montreal *La Minerve*, December 1883–January 1884.
Montreal *Le Monde*, December 1883–January 1884.
Music and Drama, January 1882–December 1883.
New Haven Evening Register, November 1885.
New Orleans *Daily Picayune*, January–February 1885.
New Orleans *Times-Democrat*, January–February 1885.

New York Clipper, January 1883–June 1886.
New York Commercial Advertiser, October–December 1883.
New York *Daily Graphic*, January 1883–June 1886.
New-York Daily Tribune, January 1883–June 1886.
New York *Evening Post*, January 1883–June 1886.
New York *Evening Telegram*, October 1883.
New York Herald, November 1859–June 1886.
New York *Sun*, January 1883–June 1886.
New-York Times, September 1878–June 1886.
New York *World*, December 1882–June 1886.
Omaha Daily Herald, April 1884.
Omaha Daily Republican, April 1884.
Philadelphia *North American*, December 1883; January 1884; January 1885; January 1886.
Philadelphia Press, December 1883; January 1884; January 1885; January 1886.
Philadelphia *Public Ledger*, December 1883; January 1884; January 1885; January 1886.
Pittsburg Dispatch, February 1886.
Puck, December 1878–June 1886.
Salt Lake City *Deseret Evening News*, March–April 1884; February 1885; March 1886.
San Francisco *Argonaut*, March 1884; March 1885; March–April 1886.
San Francisco Chronicle, March 1884; March 1885; March–April 1886.
San Francisco *Daily Alta California*, March 1884; March 1885; March–April 1886.
San Francisco *Daily Examiner*, March 1884; March 1885; March–April 1886.
San Francisco *Morning Call*, March 1884; March 1885; March–April 1886.
San Francisco *Wasp*, January 1884–June 1886.
St. Joseph Daily Herald, February 1884; February 1885; March 1886.
St. Joseph Evening News, February 1884; February 1885; March 1886.
St. Louis Globe-Democrat, February 1884; February 1885; March 1886.
St. Louis Missouri Republican, February 1884; March 1886.
St. Louis Post Dispatch, February 1884; February 1885; March 1886.
St. Paul *Daily Pioneer Press*, February 1886.
Topeka *Daily Commonwealth*, March 1886.
Topeka *Kansas Daily State Journal*, February 1885; March 1886.
Topeka Sunday Capital, February 1885.
Town Topics, March 1885–June 1886.
Washington *Evening Star*, February 1886.
Washington Post, February 1886.

Books and Articles

Albani, Emma. *Forty Years of Song*. London: Mills & Boon [1911].
Alda, Frances. *Men, Women, and Tenors*. Boston: Houghton Mifflin, 1937.
Aldrich, Richard. *Musical Discourse*. Freeport: Books for Libraries Press [1967].

Altrocchi, Julia Cooley. *The Spectacular San Franciscans.* New York: Dutton, 1949.

Andreas, A. T. *History of Chicago from the Earliest Period to the Present Time.* Chicago: privately published, 1886.

Andrews, Wayne. *The Vanderbilt Legend.* New York: Harcourt Brace, 1941.

Apel, Willi. *Harvard Dictionary of Music.* Cambridge: Harvard University Press, 1944.

Arditi, Luigi. *My Reminiscences.* New York: Dodd, Mead, 1896.

Armstrong, W. G. A. *A Record of the Opera in Philadelphia.* Philadelphia: Porter & Coates, 1884.

Armstrong, William. *The Romantic World of Music.* New York: Dutton, 1922.

Aronson, Rudolph. *Theatrical and Musical Memoirs.* New York: McBride, Nast, 1913.

Balsan, Consuelo Vanderbilt. *The Glitter and the Gold.* New York: Harper's, 1952.

Beebe, Lucius. *Mansions on Rails.* Berkeley: Howell-North, 1959.

Beebe, Lucius and Charles Clegg. *San Francisco's Golden Era.* Berkeley: Howell-North, 1960.

Belmont, Eleanor. *The Fabric of Memory.* New York: Farrar, Straus and Cudahy [1957].

Bennett, Joseph. *Forty Years of Music, 1865–1905.* London: Methuen [1908].

Bispham, David. *A Quaker Singer's Recollections.* New York: Macmillan, 1920.

Black, David. *King of Fifth Avenue: The Fortunes of August Belmont.* New York: Dial, 1981.

Blom, Eric, ed. *Grove's Dictionary of Music and Musicians.* 5th ed. 9 vols. London: Macmillan, 1954.

Brockway, Wallace and Herbert Weinstock. *The Opera.* New York: Simon and Schuster, 1941.

Bülow, Hans von. *Briefe und Schriften.* 8 vols. Leipzig: Breitkopf und Härtel, 1899.

Burgess, Harry. *My Musical Pilgrimage.* London: Simpkin, 1911.

Calvé, Emma. *My Life.* Translated by Rosamond Gilder. New York: Appleton, 1922.

Cox, John Edmund. *Musical Reflections of the Last Half-Century.* 2 vols. London: Tinsley, 1872.

Dalmazzo, G. M. *Adelina Patti's Life.* London: Cooper Bros. and Atwood, 1877.

Damrosch, Walter. *My Musical Life.* New York: Scribner's, 1923.

Davis, Ronald L. *A History of Opera in the American West.* Englewood Cliffs, N.J.: Prentice-Hall, 1965.

—— *Opera in Chicago.* New York: Appleton-Century, 1966.

Eames, Emma. *Some Memories and Reflections.* New York: Appleton, 1927.

Eaton, Quaintance. *The Miracle of the Met.* New York: Meredith, 1968.

—— *Opera Caravan.* New York: Farrar, Straus and Cudahy, 1957.

Edwards, H. Sutherland. *The Prima Donna.* London: Remington, 1888.

Engel, Louis. *From Mozart to Mario.* London: Bentley, 1886.

Finck, Henry T. "Collapse of Italian Opera." *The Nation* (August 14, 1884), 39:129–130.

—— *My Adventures in the Golden Age of Music*. New York: Funk & Wagnalls, 1926.

—— *Success in Music and How It Is Won*. New York: Scribner's, 1913.

Gagey, Edmond M. *The San Francisco Stage*. New York: Columbia University Press, 1950.

Gaisberg, F. W. *The Music Goes Round*. New York: Macmillan, 1942.

Ganz, Wilhelm. *Memories of a Musician*. London: John Murray, 1913.

Gerson, Robert A. *Music in Philadelphia*. Philadelphia: Presser, 1940.

Gipson, Richard McCandless. *The Life of Emma Thursby*. New York: New-York Historical Society, 1940.

Glackens, Ira. *Yankee Diva*. New York: Coleridge Press, 1963.

Goldsmith, Barbara. *Little Gloria . . . Happy at Last*. New York: Dell, 1980.

"Grand Opera Festival." *The* [Chicago] *Indicator* (April 18, 1885), 6:334.

Grave, Théodore de. *Biographie d'Adelina Patti*. Paris: Librairie de Castel, 1865.

Grout, Donald Jay. *A Short History of Opera*. 2 vols. New York: Columbia University Press, 1947.

Hanslick, Eduard. *Vienna's Golden Years of Music: 1850–1900*. Selected, translated and edited by Henry Pleasants. New York: Simon and Schuster, 1950.

Harewood, Earl of, ed. *Kobbé's Complete Opera Book*. New York: Putnam, 1954.

Hauk, Minnie. *Memories of a Singer*. London: Philpot, 1925.

Hegermann-Lindencrone, Lillie de. *In the Courts of Memory*. New York: Harper, 1912.

Henderson, W. J. *The Art of Singing*. New York: Dial, 1938.

Hernendez Girbal, F. *Adelina Patti*. Madrid: Lira, 1979.

Huneker, James Gibbons. *Steeplejack*. 2 vols. New York: Scribner's, 1920.

Hurst, P. G. *The Golden Age Recorded*. [Lingfield, Surrey]: Oakwood Press, 1963.

Kellogg, Clara Louise. *Memoirs of an American Prima Donna*. New York: Putnam, 1913.

Klein, Herman. *Great Women-Singers of My Time*. New York: Dutton, 1931.

—— *The Reign of Patti*. New York: Century, 1920.

—— *Thirty Years of Musical Life in London: 1870–1900*. New York: Century, 1903.

Kobbé, Gustav. *Opera Singers*. Boston: Ditson, 1904.

Kolodin,Irving. *The Metropolitan Opera: 1883–1935*. New York: Oxford University Press, 1936.

—— *The Metropolitan Opera: 1883–1966*. New York: Knopf, 1967.

—— *The Story of the Metropolitan Opera: 1883–1950*. New York: Knopf, 1953.

Krehbiel, Henry Edward. *Chapters of Opera*. New York: Holt, 1908.

Lahee, Henry C. *Famous Singers of To-day and Yesterday*. Boston: Page, 1898.

—— *Grand Opera in America*. Boston: Page, 1902.

—— *The Grand Opera Singers of To-day*. Boston: Page, 1912.

Lauw, Louise. *Fourteen Years with Adelina Patti*. Translated by Clare Brune. London: Remington, 1884.

Lehmann, Lilli. *How to Sing*. New York: Macmillan, 1904.

—— *My Path Through Life*. Translated by Alice Benedict Seligman. New York: Putnam, 1914.

Lehr, Elizabeth Drexel. *"King Lehr" and the Gilded Age*. Philadelphia: Lippincott, 1935.

Leiser, Clara. *Jean de Reszke and the Great Days of Opera*. London: Gerald Howe, 1933.

Loewenberg, Alfred. *Annals of Opera, 1597–1940*. 2d ed. 2 vols. Geneva: Societas Bibliographica, 1955.

Loggins, Vernon. *Where the Word Ends*. Baton Rouge: Louisiana State University Press, 1958.

Lumley, Benjamin. *Reminiscences of the Opera*. London: Hurst & Blackett, 1864.

Mapleson, James Henry. *The Mapleson Memoirs, 1848–1888*. 2 vols. London: Remington, 1888.

Marchesi, Mathilde. *Marchesi and Music*. New York: Harper, 1898.

Maretzek, Max. *Revelations of an Opera Manager in Nineteenth-Century America*. New York: Dover, 1968.

Martin, Ralph D. *Jennie*. 2 vols. New York: New American Library, 1970.

Martin, Sadie E. *The Life and Professional Career of Emma Abbott*. Minneapolis: Kimba, 1891.

McCabe, James D., Jr. *Lights and Shadows of New York Life*. New York: Farrar, Straus & Giroux, 1970.

Melba, Nellie. *Melodies and Memories*. London: Butterworth, 1925.

Merkling, Frank, et al. *The Golden Horseshoe*. London: Secker & Warburg, 1965.

Moore, Edward C. *Forty Years of Opera in Chicago*. New York: Liveright, 1930.

Nelville, Amelia Ransome. *The Fantastic City*. New York: Houghton Mifflin, 1932.

Newman, Ernest. *The Life of Richard Wagner*. 4 vols. New York: Knopf, 1933–46.

O'Connor, Harvey. *The Astors*. New York: Knopf, 1941.

Odell, George C. D. *Annals of the New York Stage*. 15 vols. New York: Columbia University Press, 1927–49.

"Operatic." *Musical Review* (April 18, 1880), 2:7.

Patti, Adelina. "My Reminiscences." *The Strand Magazine* (December 1908), 36:706–15.

Pleasants, Henry. *The Great Singers*. New York: Simon & Schuster, 1966.

Rosenthal, Harold. *Two Centuries of Opera at Covent Garden*. London: Putnam, 1958.

——, ed. *The Mapleson Memoirs*. New York: Appleton-Century, 1966.

Ryan, Thomas. *Recollections of an Old Musician*. New York: Dutton, 1899.

Santley, Charles. *Student and Singer*. London: Edward Arnold, 1892.

Satterlee, Herbert L. *J. Pierpont Morgan*. New York: Macmillan, 1940.

Scholes, Percy A. *The Oxford Companion to Music*. 9th ed. London: Oxford University Press, 1955.

Schriftgiesser, Karl. *The Amazing Roosevelt Family*. New York: Wilford Funk, 1942.

Seltsam, William H. *Metropolitan Opera Annals*. New York: Wilson, 1947.

Shaw, George Bernard. *London Music in 1888–1889*. London: Constable, 1950.

—— *Music in London, 1890–1894*. London: Constable, 1949.

Stoullig, Edmond. *Les Annales du Théâtre et de la Musique.* 41 vols. Paris: Charpentier, 1876–1896 and Ollendorff, 1897–1918.

Strakosch, Maurice. *Souvenirs d'un Impresario.* Paris: Ollendorff, 1887.

Thompson, Oscar. *The American Singer.* New York: Dial Press, 1937.

——, ed. *The International Cyclopedia of Music and Musicians.* 7th ed. New York: Dodd, Mead, 1956.

Tully, Andrew. *Era of Elegance.* New York: Funk & Wagnalls, 1947.

Upton, George P. *Musical Memories.* Chicago: McClurg, 1908.

Wagnalls, Mabel. *Stars of the Opera.* New York: Funk & Wagnalls, 1907.

White, Richard Grant. "Opera in New York." *The Century Magazine* (June 1882), 24:193–210.

Index

∽